Changing Central-Local Relations in China

Changing Central-Local Relations in China

Reform and State Capacity

EDITED BY

Jia Hao
and Lin Zhimin

Routledge
Taylor & Francis Group
LONDON AND NEW YORK

First published 1994 by Westview Press, Inc.

Published 2018 by Routledge
52 Vanderbilt Avenue, New York, NY 10017
2 Park Square, Milton Park, Abingdon, Oxon OX14 4RN

Routledge is an imprint of the Taylor & Francis Group, an informa business

Library of Congress Cataloging-in-Publication Data
Changing central-local relations in China : reform and state capacity
/ edited by Jia Hao and Lin Zhimin.
p. cm.
Includes bibliographical references and index.
ISBN 0-8133-1898-X
1. Central-local government relations—China. 2. China—Politics and government—1976– . I. Jia, Hao. II. Lin, Zhimin.
JQ1506.S8C43 1994
354.5108'098—dc20
93-24882
CIP

ISBN 13: 978-0-367-00890-1 (hbk)

ISBN 13: 978-0-367-15877-4 (pbk)

Contents

PART THREE
Regional Differentiation and Case Studies

Tables and Figures

Tables

Figures

Preface

In late 1990, at the initiative of the association of Chinese Scholars of Political Science and International Studies, Inc. (CSPSIS), a group of Chinese scholars decided to work together to find a research topic that could best capture the changing nature of the Chinese polity in the wake of its decade-long reform process. The participants were either directly involved in or had followed China's reform process for years while lately engaged in studying, teaching, and research in the United States. Before long we came to the conclusion that no single subject would serve our purpose better than the enormous changes taking place in the nation's central-local relations. A research project was thus launched by CSPSIS and for almost three years it has involved a transcontinental collaboration. This volume represents the outcome of our collective endeavor.

While awaiting both academic critique and further testing of China's evolving situation, as well as reiterating "the usual disclaimer" that the editors and contributors alone are responsible for the views, interpretations, and of course errors in the work, several acknowledgments are in order.

This study would not have been possible without the overall support of the Rockefeller Foundation to CSPSIS in general, and a 1991-1992 research grant by the Chiang Ching-Kuo Foundation for International Scholarly Exchanges (USA) in particular. I especially wish to thank the Rockefeller Foundation's Senior Vice President Kenneth Prewitt, who over the years has provided us with enormous support and personal understanding. His assistant, Carol J. Tyler, had made the grant administration a most enjoyable experience. Special thanks also go to Dr. Hungdah Chiu and Dr. Hsing-wei Lee of the Chiang Ching-Kuo Foundation for their valuable support and consistent cooperation during the process.

I also wish to acknowledge three members of the CSPSIS Advisory Board: Professor Arend Lijphart at UC San Diego and Professors Andrew G. Walder and Ezra F. Vogel at Harvard, both for their scholarship on the subject and their specific advice on our research. Among my personal best memories of serving as the CSPSIS president between 1990 and 1992 was the chance to work with each of them.

We were extremely fortunate to get strong editing assistance from Madelyn C. Ross, whose experience as the former editor of the *China Business Review*, commitment to the work, and knowledge of China and the Chinese language considerably eased the process. Our gratitude also goes to Xiangdong Ma, a fellow Chinese scholar and my apartment neighbor in a suburb of Washington, D.C., who provided us with technical support in typesetting the whole volume.

We are grateful to Westview Press as well, which has made this publication possible. Special thanks go to Alison Auch for her support and cooperation. Julie Seko's assistance helped us typeset the volume.

Finally, this volume should most appropriately be dedicated to our organization, the association of Chinese Scholars of Political Science and International Studies, Inc. Established in 1986, it has for many years actively served Chinese scholars studying political science and international relations in the United States. The society's accomplishments contribute both to the disciplinary development and the organization of overseas Chinese scholars in the social sciences. It is thus worth mentioning the consistent support given to the project by CSPSIS and especially by James Chung. Serving as the vice president of CSPSIS and taking advantage of his proximity at Denver University, James worked for months with Westview Press and helped pave the way for the publication of this volume.

Jia Hao
Washington, D.C.

Introduction

Changing Central-Local Relations in China: Reform and State Capacity[1]

Jia Hao and Lin Zhimin

Since the late 1970s, China has witnessed dramatic changes in its central-local relations. While substantial disagreements may exist among students of the Chinese political economy over interpreting the meaning and implications of these changes, few will deny they are one of the most profound results of China's decade-long reform process. The purpose of this study is to provide a comprehensive examination of these changes--changes that may well determine China's future.

Centralization-Decentralization Dilemma and the Reform

Due to its vast territory, huge population, and social-economic complexity, the handling of China's central-local relationship has historically gone to the very heart of Chinese politics. As early as the *Qin* (B.C. 221-207) and *Han* (B.C. 206-A.D. 24) Dynasties, there were heated debates and power struggles over *junxianzhi* (a unified and centralized political system with local administrative prefectures and counties) versus *fengjianzhi* (a decentralized enfeoffment system).[2] Later, the rise and fall of numerous dynasties were also closely related to their handling of the central-local relationship. Since the mid-19th century, a constant theme in Chinese politics had been the decay of the supposedly centralized imperial system on the one hand and the rise of regionalism on the other. Despite the efforts of the late Qing Dynasty to restore central power by building new railroads and training the New Army, the trend toward greater local control--especially in the form of warlordism--continued. In the end, growing centrifugal forces had become such an "insoluble systemic problem"[3] that it not only helped end China's last imperial system but also precluded the birth of a strong post-Qing national consensus and leadership, the lack of which has been seen by many as a crucial element in China's abortive efforts at modernization.

The founding of the People's Republic in 1949 introduced a new twist into this long-running dilemma. On the one hand, the new regime managed to realize a level of centralization few of its predecessors could rival. Leninist principles such as "democratic centralism" were used to justify the effort of unifying both the action and thinking of the whole populace. A network of hierarchically organized institutions, centered on the Chinese Communist Party, made it possible for a few at the top to rule with virtually unchallenged legitimacy and little deviation in policy implementation. Moreover, the Chinese leadership's overall commitment to a state socialist path of development dictated the nation's prevailing system of central planning and command economy, with the center taking the lion's share of the nation's resources and the local control of resources and freedom of movement strictly limited. Finally, comprehensive social control was achieved through what Andrew Walder calls "institutional dependence,"[4] a network of party-client relations supported by a combination of coercion and conditional incentives. Through a set of institutions and public policies enforced from the top, such as the system of work units, personnel management, employment, housing, household registration, food-rationing, health care, etc., the state conditioned individuals' well-being on their loyalty and made central control both effective and inescapable.

On the other hand, the costs of maintaining such a high level of centralization were so stiff that it sometimes ran against Mao Zedong's own vision of "socialism." Mao did not trust the Soviet style of central planning and bureaucratic control. Accompanied by fierce internal power struggles, Mao had made his sometimes frantic search for an alternative "third road." He found his solution in what Carl Riskin calls "administrative decentralization."[5] It relied on neither the Soviet style of central planning nor a market mechanism. Instead, it tried to "substitute locally initiated mass economic activity for the detailed blueprints worked out by professional planners" and "gave greater economic and political authority to local and regional units."[6] Mao hoped that it would enable him to launch continued revolution with mass participation while still maintaining ultimate control in his own hands. That proved to be a gross miscalculation as the Great Leap Forward and the Cultural Revolution attested, resulting in great undermining of the centralized system and its authority.

Moreover, the centralized system itself also showed inherent deficiencies that in many ways precipitated the post-Mao reform process. Centralization suffocated local enthusiasm. It caused low efficiency or sheer waste in resource allocation, not to mention the heavy burden of administration it imposed on a giant country. But more importantly, the highly centralized control (not to be equated with strong state capacity and central authority) over both economic and political operation is fundamentally contradictory to the play of market mechanisms, which have time and again been verified as the most effective driving force behind the development of nations.[7]

It is against the backdrop of the above dilemma that decentralization became the breaking point of China's economic reform. Moreover, for the better part of the 1980s, "*fenquan rangli*" (administrative decentralization and allowing interests to be shared by provincial and local entities) served as the backbone of reform. It was not until recently that the focus of reform shifted to a more explicit call for marketization.[8] However, to introduce economic decentralization in a politically-centralized state has its own risks. In the first place, decentralization was limited to the role of helping "*diaodong difang jijixing*" (mobilize local enthusiasm) rather than embracing a new central-local relationship based on federal principles. On the other hand, the actual process of decentralization has gone far beyond its original intent. Once the process began and proceeded with some degree of consistency there was no guarantee that the essence of the nation's original system would remain untouched. To the contrary, all indications are that such a change has already occurred, and occurred in a fundamental way. Still in progress, changes have shattered China's traditional image of a party/state, in which the center wields unlimited power over different localities and effectively controls all aspects of social life. What we have witnessed in China during the last decade are: (1) significant shifts of control over national resources from the center to local governments and non-governmental entities; (2) declining central authority and effectiveness in rule-making and enforcing, demonstrated in the decay of policy discipline and chains of command; and (3) increasing boldness on the part of sub-national actors in initiating and pursuing policies or actions from their own interests, often in defiance of the will of the center. In short, by the late 1980s, the gap between what decentralization was supposed to accomplish and what had happened under its name had widened to such an extent that it was just a matter of time before the decision of whether or not to proceed with the very process had to be made.

New Developments Since 1989

The issue of decentralization became central in 1988 and 1989. Fearful of the runaway inflation that signifies loss of control at the macroeconomic level and worried about potential social disorder, the central government decided to launch a three-year economic retrenchment program in late 1988. It became clear that one of the casualties was various decentralization programs. The Chinese conservative leaders attempted to revoke almost all of the important economic reform policies, including the local fiscal responsibility system, the rural household responsibility system (HRS), the contractual management responsibility system for state enterprises, the decentralized foreign trade arrangements, and the dual pricing regime.

The crackdown on the 1989 Tiananmen event and its aftermath created an even more adverse environment for decentralization. As the political emphasis shifted from development to stability, opponents of the reform process began to link consequences of decentralization--such as decay of the economic order and decline of government share in national resources --to what they believed to be the sources of the social unrest.

However, as if to show how deeply decentralization had taken root, under the pressure both of unprecedentedly strong resistance from the local forces and the economic situation, these countermoves proved to be rather short-lived. By late 1990, the call for further reform (including more decentralization) could be heard again. After Deng's well-publicized southern China tour in early 1992, the localities soon changed from calls to action, with economic reform and decentralization taking on new momentum that became stronger than ever. By comparison, in the early 1960s and the 1970s, movements against decentralization served as a prelude to sustained periods of recentralization.

By early 1993, the decentralization process was once again in full swing, along with its even more profound repercussions. First, its scope went far beyond what had become known as the four core decentralization programs of the 1980s--fiscal and foreign trade contract systems (both between the center and provinces), the rural household responsibility system, and various forms of contract systems conducted by state-owned enterprises. It now extended to areas like finance, special development zones, real estate, land purchases, and all kinds of factor markets. By 1992, central planning accounted for less than 10 percent of industrial production, down from 30 percent just four years ago. The 1993 proportion could be as low as 6 percent.[9] As the scope of decentralization expanded, the amount of resources involved also rose sharply. In 1992, total investment by state-owned entities reached 510.6 billion yuan. Of that amount, more than 320 billion, or 63 percent came from local governments and enterprises themselves[10]--without even including the surging investment made by non-state entities. With that amount of funds controlled by localities, no wonder the growth of national investment surpassed the original central targets by more than 40 percent. Nor was the shift in resources from the central to local governments or enterprises limited to traditional channels such as the alteration of revenue-sharing ratios. For example, in 1992 Shanghai alone raised more than 20 billion yuan of funds through issuing stocks and bonds for local projects, far more than Shanghai's revenue income of 16.5 billion in the same year.[11]

Second, it is now the localities that often take the lead in providing new directions for economic reform. Areas like Guangdong and Shanghai are not only poles of development, but also provide much inspiration as a reference point for the reforms.[12] Accordingly, Chinese provinces have become increasingly bold in either ignoring central directives they do not like or introducing their own new policies and programs not formally approved by the center. In late 1992, the nation's central government--again alarmed that the national economy could become overheated--called for moderation in economic development in 1993. Several provinces (such as Guangdong, Hainan, and Guangxi) responded by openly declaring that overheating was not a problem in their respective regions and therefore they would not abide by the central call. By mid-1993, facing mounting economic problems, Beijing once again turned on the localities and resorted to strict measures to cooling the country's overheated economy.

Finally, even in the political arena where the decentralization process seems to have made the least impact, there are important signs of change as well. For instance, the current positions of both the governor and party secretary of Guangdong Province and the mayor and party secretary of Shanghai Municipality are filled by the native officials from each region respectively. Moreover, in several recent provincial elections such as those in Zhejiang and Hubei Provinces, candidates picked by the central government were unprecedentedly voted down while locally emerged candidates were elected.[13] All of these constitute the opposite to the post-1949 convention, which favored centrally-assigned, non-native local bosses for the sake of central control. These new developments indicate that, with growing economic muscle, many Chinese localities are increasingly assertive even in their political relations with the center.

State Capacity as a Key Variable

Given the changes already taking place, it is appropriate to ask some fundamental questions. What exactly has happened in China's central-local relations? Why did these changes occur and how have they proceeded? Are the changes profound enough to fundamentally alter the traditional patterns of central control, and finally, how much will they dictate the future of China?

There are a number of ways to study the process and effects of China's recent decentralization. Indeed, multiple approaches are a feature of this book, in that each author has decided how he/she will tackle a specific aspect of the economic reform in general and the decentralization in particular. Nevertheless, there is a rallying point of this book: explicitly or implicitly, most authors tend to focus their attention on the changes related to the capacity of the Chinese state. They seek to understand how this capacity is affected by reform on the one hand, and how the changes in that capacity affect the direction of reform on the other.

To begin with, this book is influenced by the recent resurgence of interest and literature on the role and function of states.[14] The starting point of scholars who associate themselves with the movement is that--whether in industrial societies or in developing countries--it is the state that serves as an autonomous, leading force behind social transformation, economic development, political evolution, and international interactions. They are particularly concerned about the issue of state capacity, which is defined by Joel Migdal as the ability of a state to "penetrate society, regulate social relationships, extract resources, and appropriate or use resources in determined ways."[15] State capacity thus is increasingly seen as the key variable in differentiating the variations in national experiences and the outcomes of various state-sponsored programs. For instance, the relative strength of state versus traditional society was at the center of a number of recent studies of Third World countries, especially in regard to their differentiated abilities to promote social changes.[16] Less state-centric but nevertheless holding the state as the key institution whose configuration is believed to have significant effects on policy outcomes, varying state capacity is also seen as crucial to the uneven economic performances among industrial societies.[17] There are also an increasing number of publications that specifically link domestic structure and its impact on state capacity to the shaping and implementation of the national strategies of foreign economic policy among developed countries.[18] Finally, stemming from the above studies, one of the contributors in this volume has suggested certain correlations and differentiations between the "regime type" (i.e., liberal democratic system, authoritative system, and state socialist system) and state capacity.[19]

In the field of China studies, there has never been a shortage of interest or focus on the role of the state. However, the new literature on state has brought in some fresh air as well. As far as this study is concerned, the inspiration can be seen in the way we set out the research agenda.

First, because the state plays such an important role, the renewed interest in the state calls for more scrutiny of the functioning or malfunctioning of the state. In China, as in other countries, it is no longer sufficient to treat the state as a monolithic whole. The internal workings, or conflicts for that matter, of a state carry as much importance for its governing ability as its dealings with external entities. For this volume, this means that our research has to go beyond either the totalitarian model that essentially treats the Chinese state as a monolithic entity, or the bureaucratic model that so far has limited its discussion of the "pluralization" of Chinese politics to bureaucratic in-fighting at the central ministerial level. We believe that a complete picture of the changing nature of the Chinese state will not emerge unless we include, and indeed pay greater attention to, sub-national actors such as provincial and lower levels of governments as well as non-traditional political actors such as enterprises and peasants.

Second, the emphasis on the dual role of state capacity in recent literature prompts us not to take the capacity of the Chinese state as a given but as a key variable. In so doing, however, we have introduced an important modification. Unlike the majority of recent studies of the state, this book does not take the traditional dichotomy of state versus society as the ultimate test of China's state capacity. Instead, given the fact that Chinese state socialism has been carried out with its "distinctions," we believe that the level of state capacity in the country since 1949 has been affected more by the center's ability to maintain coherence among the rank and file than its search for dominance over the society.

There are two basic reasons for this qualification. The post-1949 Chinese state was particularly successful in penetrating and then dominating Chinese society, eliminating the society as a potential counterweight to its rule. Since the consolidation of state control in the mid-1950s, few social institutions (such as the churches in the Eastern European countries) have been allowed to exist in China, let alone to function independently. No social institutions were capable of aggregating political or social demands and exerting tangible influence upon the national agenda. If they ever tried to do so (as exemplified somehow by the student movements in the 1980s), chances were that they would be crushed by overwhelming state power. While there is little question that various forms of resistance to the state--ranging from open resentment to hidden protest--do exist, and in a few cases could become very powerful, as far as basic constraints on the state are concerned, the only significant challenge to central control so far has come from within the state itself.

While the Chinese state was so successful in rooting out competition from the society, it ironically produced a monstrous governing system so large and complex that the act of maintaining sufficient coherence among the rank-and-file has become the state's Achilles' heel. To stay on top, the center has to have the ability to direct various state agencies to work for its goals, to centralize resources to a point sufficient to sustain these goals, and to make and enforce rules among various inferiors to ensure adequate compliance. It is this task and its success or failure that determine the overall level of the state capacity in China. The most important consequence of the reform so far, we argue, has not been the creation of an independent and self-sustaining society capable of competing with the state monopoly, but rather the dramatic degrading of the level of coherence of the state itself. Although uneven and perhaps not entirely irreversible, the trend toward a more fragmented state system and increasing autonomy among lower levels of the state agency has resulted in serious erosion of China's state capacity.

Moreover, while the center has to have power and resources to ensure its control, it has to do more than issue orders and use coercion upon its inferiors. It has to offer incentives as well. Decentralization from time to time has thus served a dual role for the Chinese state. It helped buy local support and reduced the costs of running everything from the center alone. In this regard, China's centrally-initiated decentralization often served as a needed ruling adjustment by the center.

The problem with such efforts at decentralization (including the latest one), however, is that it is easier said than done. More often than not, having no easy alternative to advance their own interests and not trusting that the center's decentralization offer would last long, the localities respond by taking excessive advantages of it. In addition, the lack of a constitutionally-guaranteed framework and an institutionalized process of implementing decentralization opens the door for loopholes, with the frequent flip-flop of central policies penalizing those who did not take advantage (or did not take advantage early enough) of the center's moves.

As a result, the stakes in decentralization are much higher in China's case than they are in other states. Whether the center is capable of keeping central-local relations on track depends on how well it conducts this limited decentralization. And because the center relies on localities to maintain its dominance over Chinese society, the result of such decentralization efforts inevitably affects the central regime's capacity to govern. The recent decentralization has further underscored this dilemma. Since China is moving toward a market system, the center needs to adjust its relations with localities before its relations with Chinese society can be redefined. In other words, localities served both as the recipient of the decentralization offer and the "point men" to help redefine state-society relations. To be sure, there are many other factors that may contribute to the change of Chinese state capacity, such as the ongoing transition in the nation's leadership, an emerging Chinese civil society, the changing Chinese military and its role in the nation's politics, as well as external challenge or influence. Looking forward, however, it is not exaggerating to say that the capacity for the Chinese state to rule has become overwhelmingly dependent on how the latest round of central-local readjustment is played out, and on whether a new central-local relationship emerges before the old one completely collapses. It is in this sense that the study of China's central-local relations goes far beyond the literate definition of the phrase; it touches upon the Chinese state's capacity to govern.

Structure and Findings

To help advance our understanding of the changing capacity of the Chinese state in light of the above arguments, this book is organized into three parts. In addition to this introduction, Part One provides a general background and identifies some key issues and problems involved in China's central-local relations. It consists of three chapters, ranging from an overview of the long and cyclical process of centralization-decentralization in China since 1949, to an examination of the nation's central-local relations during the reform era from the perspective of the interaction between market and state, and finally to the evolving institutional context within which China's decentralization has been taking place.

Part Two traces the changes that have occurred in the so-called "functional" areas. These four areas include the efforts and implications of decentralizing China's fiscal administrative system, the nation's decollectivization and its effects on the rural areas, the changes in state and enterprise relations, and the overhaul of the nation's foreign trade system. Since the reform process in general and decentralization in particular have been known for their width and depth, separate examinations of each of these areas are needed to generate a comprehensive picture of how much change the decentralized reform has already brought about.

Finally, in Part Three, the focus turns to comparative (regional differentiations) and case studies (Guangdong Province and Shanghai Municipality). This section offers insights into how decentralization has been received at the cross-regional and provincial levels in the reform process. In our view, the way in which specific regions or provinces are responding to the reform and the variations in their performance tells more than anything else about the changing nature of China's central-local relations.

To be sure, the general division of labor as described above is not intended to limit each chapter's scope of research, nor does it attempt to produce mutually complementary and coherent arguments. In fact, as all chapters clearly demonstrate, the key arguments of each chapter reflect the author's own conclusions rather than some well-coached consensus. Nevertheless, a ride through the key findings will show that the thrusts of these chapters often point in the same direction.

In Chapter One, Zhao Suisheng illustrates how, over the three decades between 1949 and the late 1970s, China's centralized system gradually devolved into a more decentralized one. This "progressive decentralization," as the author calls it, was the result of two distinct but related developments. One was the center's shift from relying on ideological and institutional control to relying increasingly on material incentives to motivate local governments and reduce the burden of coordination. The other factor was the difficulty of recentralizing the previously decentralized command structure. The former allowed localities greater say in policy-making and implementation while the latter reduced the center's freedom to retract results associated with decentralization. Zhao nevertheless cautions that without constitutional guarantees, these changes may lead to more intensified bargaining, and thus greater instability, in China's central-local relations. They will not automatically end the nation's unitary system.

In Chapter Two, Jia Hao and Wang Mingxia examine China's central-local relations from a perspective of the interaction between market and state. From a broad economic and political context, they argue, the progress of China's decade-long economic reform and the opening to the outside world has generated certain market mechanisms and the dynamics of domestic competition (particularly inter-provincial), made the localities a major driving force behind further reforms, and positioned the localities as equally important players (with both power and "legitimacy") vis-a-vis the center in China's political economy. Yet institutional problems within the state have constituted the major problem in the nation's further development. Accordingly, instead of stagnation, the real danger for China is development-generated structural instability. While certainly dictating a much broader institutional innovation, this conclusion first and foremost demands a "historic compromise" between the nation's center and localities characterized by "thinking federal." Seizing this transitional "window of opportunity" may contribute to China's economic development, political modernization, and the process of national integration.

Although the question of who controls how many economic resources is fundamental to understanding China's decentralization, the contest between the center and the localities for economic resources does not take place in an institutional vacuum, argue Gong Ting and Chen Feng in Chapter Three. The authors analyze three aspects of the institutional reorganization in China's reform era: institutional design, institutional function, and institutional differentiation. They find that the post-Mao administrative reform departs from the earlier experiments and has had a significant impact on China's changing central-local relations. The changes have contributed to the formation of a more "cellular polity" and made post-Mao decentralization hard to reverse. However, the problem of accommodation between decentralization to local governments and decentralization to enterprises remains, since the former may not always lead to a better environment for the latter.

Chapter Four attempts to trace the trajectory of changing central-local relations in China by reconstructing patterns of fiscal politics between the nation's central government and the provinces over the reform era. Wang Shaoguang shows how the central government's hold over financial resources has eroded, why the state has lost its battle over the control of crucial economic resources to the competing localities, and what have been the direct and indirect economic, social, and political consequences of the loss of central fiscal control. In the course of presenting the historical process through which China's central government's once nearly monolithic power has deteriorated into a fragile "weak state," the author also tests two hypotheses: (1) under the authoritarian state socialist system, the central government's extractive capacity is circumscribed mainly by the evasive tendency of local governments; and (2) the decline of this capacity contributes to the general crisis of the Chinese state socialist system.

In Chapter Five, Luo Xiaopeng explores the dynamics of China's rural reforms and the development of localism, which means the growing economic policy-making power of local governments vis-a-vis the central authorities. Despite the fact that the central leadership ruled out family farming at the beginning of rural reforms in 1978, the household responsibility system (HRS), initiated by destitute peasants, finally overwhelmed the ideological and political barriers to become a dominant rural policy in China. The post-Mao power struggle allowed some provincial leaders to facilitate this breakthrough, and resulted in an unprecedented decentralization of rural economic policies. Economically, rural reforms have broken the socialist "reform cycle" by creating a huge market for the partially reformed state industrial sector. This economic process not only sustained the continuing marketization process, but also promoted localism throughout China. An analysis of the impacts of marketization at the provincial level serves to clarify the decisive contribution of rural reforms to the fundamental changes taking place in central-local relations in China.

In Chapter Six, Xiao Geng explains how state capacity in China has been adversely affected both by the growing industrial productivity gap among different provinces and the related decline in revenue controlled by the center. While the two represent rather different aspects of the economic reform program, they share the same root--problems associated with state-owned enterprises. Xiao argues that it is the level of development of the non-state sector that fueled the enlarging gap among the coastal, inland, and western provinces, since the productivity level of the state sector exhibits little cross-regional variations. Accordingly, those provinces with a larger non-state sector tend to do well, but not necessarily to the benefit of the center. On the other hand, the center stands to lose more revenues as state-owned enterprises divert more and more money (potential sources of state income) to such local uses as the welfare of their employees. The center, Xiao maintains, would be better advised to focus on "encouraging development of the non-state sector" than trying to rearrange central-local fiscal relations.

The chapter by Zhang Amei and Zou Gang examines the process of decentralization in the foreign trade sector since 1979, in which they detect a progressive trend toward greater local responsibilities and influence. Most importantly, they argue, there has been a fundamental change in the way decisions are made and implemented. Before the reform, local governments' bargaining with the center reflected more of a local dependence (paternalistic in nature) on the center. Since the reform, however, changes in three key areas have made central-local relations regarding foreign trade either competitive rivalries or partnerships. Local governments can now bargain from a position of strength with clear-cut local interests in mind. They bargain not only over the share of benefits foreign trade may bring but also the rules that limit their freedom and that of the center. Finally, while gains and losses under bargaining are not absolute, indications are that local governments have clearly gained more than central ministries. These changes are fundamental because they have actually ended the center's traditional foreign trade monopoly.

As one of the salient outcomes of China's economic reform process, regional inequality is believed by many to have been greatly exacerbated due to the general reform policy that favors coastal development. However, Huo Shitao's research on regional income reveals that regional inequality in China was actually reduced from 1980 to 1987. This striking result is further buttressed by his two other empirical findings: first, that the "hidden hand" of the central government contributed enormously to this result through use of equalizing investment and tax policies; and second, that equalizing regional imbalances has now become a huge burden on the central fiscal capacity. Based upon these analyses, Huo further argues that in a country where the distribution of resources is largely imbalanced, China's economic reform requires an imbalanced strategy of development. Inequality is therefore a "necessary evil" that can be reduced only after the nation reaches a certain level of economic development, rather than eliminated artificially at an earlier stage.

Peter Tsan-yin Cheung's chapter focuses on Guangdong, the star province of China's decade-long reform, which has substantially expanded its autonomy. Major changes have taken place between the center and Guangdong in the administrative, political, fiscal, and policy dimensions. While certain mechanisms for central control remain, the capacity of the province, especially over economic matters, has increased significantly at the expense of the center. The key reasons for this, as Cheung argues, have to do with the way Guangdong has played the political resources it possesses within the central government, the emergence of a strong local leadership committed to reform, and the sheer fact that the abundant resources Guangdong accumulated during the reform process have made it a heavyweight in China's political economy. However, the gains on the part of Guangdong may not be a prototype for other provinces, since the changes in Guangdong's relations with the center were based on political and economic expediency, rather than a carefully designed and institutionalized framework of power-sharing.

Using Shanghai as an example, the last chapter of this volume provides another detailed case study of China's changing central-local relations. Lin Zhimin examines how the recent reform in general, and fiscal decentralization in particular, affected Shanghai's relations with the center. The municipality had been slow to respond to the earlier round of fiscal decentralization and had to pay a stiff price for that. However, even in this traditional stronghold of central planning and control, things began to change gradually but steadily. Using a combined strategy of "crying wolf" and making promises to get concessions, Shanghai was able to strengthen its position vis-a-vis the center. The process accelerated in the second half of the 1980s and led to a surge in Shanghai's influence over the distribution of local revenues, expenditures, and fiscal management. In conclusion, Lin argues, the local gains made during the recent reform period appear to depend as much on the quality of local strategies as on central policies.

Our Goals

Stemming from a political economy point of view, this volume focuses on describing, explaining, and evaluating the changing central-local relationship in China. Given the nature and scope of the subject, it is hard to touch upon every aspect of the changes (for instance, this study does not directly cover the political and nationality aspects of the issue). Nor is it easy to treat each chosen topic in its entirety. However, in the limited space that follows, we try to accomplish two goals. First, we want to present our readers with a comprehensive picture of what has happened in China's central-local relations during the decade-long economic reform, which we believe is essential to understanding the state of affairs in China and to predicting the nation's future. Second, we want to outline what we perceive as the patterns of transformation in a state socialist country, especially in the area of central-local relations. Our hope is that these patterns will further comprehension of the logic and complexity of such regime transformation--not only in China but in other state socialist countries as well.

Notes

1. In this volume, while mainly used to mean provincial, the word "local" alternatively refers to both provincial and sub-provincial governmental or non-governmental entities. In some other studies, Chinese provinces, autonomous regions, and municipal cities (Beijing, Shanghai, and Tianjin) are all referred to as provincial governments, while cities and counties at the sub-provincial level are referred to as "local" entities, and both levels of government are referred to as "subnational." See *China: Revenue Mobilization and Tax Policy* (A World Bank Country Report, 1990), p.72.

2. Aside from numerous Chinese sources on this topic, recent literature in English includes Arthur Waldron: "Warlordism Versus Federalism: The Revival of a Debate?" See *The China Quarterly*, March 1990, No. 121, pp.116-128

3. John King Fairbank, *China, a New History* (Cambridge, MA: Harvard University Press, 1992), p.247.

4. Andrew G. Walder, *Communist Neo-Traditionalism, Work and Authority in Chinese Industry*. (Berkeley: University of California Press, 1986).

5. Carl Riskin, "Neither Plan Nor Market: Mao's Political Economy", in William P. Joseph, Christine P.W. Wong and David Zweig, ed., *New Perspectives On the Cultural Revolution*. (Cambridge: Harvard University Press, 1991).

6. Ibid., p.137.

7. For a discussion of the differing impact of market and centralization, see, World Bank: *World Development Report 1991: The Challenge of Development*, Oxford University Press.

8. Although the phrase "socialist commodity economy" was adopted in 1987 by the 13th Congress of the CCP, it was not until 1992 that the phrase "socialist market economy" was formally adopted by the 14th Congress of the CCP.

9. *New York Times*, February 14, 1993.

10. *Renmin Ribao* (People's Daily), Overseas edition, February 20, 1993.

11. *Jiefang Ribao* (Liberation Daily), Shanghai, December 16, 1992.

12. This trend was particularly evident in Deng's recent moves. He used his tours to Guangdong and Shanghai to call for a new round of reform, rather than giving instructions to the central bureaucrats and asking them to come up with plans first.

13. *Shijie Ribao* (World Journal), New York, various issues in February 1993.

14. See, in particular, Peter B. Evans, in Dietrich Rueschemeyer & Theda Skocpol, ed., *Bringing the State Back In*. (New York: Cambridge University Press, 1985).

15. Joel Migdal, *Strong Societies and Weak States: State-Society Relations and State Capabilities in the Third World*. (Princeton: Princeton University Press, 1988), p.4.

16. For social transformation in third world countries, see, Atul Kohli, *The State and Poverty in India: the Politics of Reform* (New York: Cambridge University Press, 1987), and Migdal, 1988.

17. For the effectiveness in implementing domestic policies in advanced industrial societies, see, Peter A. Hall, *Governing the Economy: the Politics of State Intervention in Britain and France* (New York: Oxford University Press, 1986).

18. For the effects on international competitions, see Peter J. Katzenstein, ed., *Between Power and Plenty: Foreign Economic Policies of Advanced Industrial States* (Madison: The University of Wisconsin Press, 1978), and G. John Ikenberry, ed., *American Foreign Policy: Theoretical Essays*, especially part four (Glenview, IL: Scott, Foreman and Company, 1989).

19. Wang Shaoguang, "Building a Strong Democratic State: On Regime Type and State Capacity." *Papers of the Center for Modern China*, No.4, February 1991, pp.1-36.

PART ONE

Historical Perspective and Overview

1

China's Central-Local Relationship: A Historical Perspective

Zhao Suisheng

The People's Republic of China is a unitary state. Formal authority is constitutionally held by the central government. Provincial and local officials are appointed by the center, not elected by local citizens. The nation's constitution and political structure do not guarantee political powers for local governments. Although this unitary state structure has never been seriously challenged, the traditional central-local relationship, which took shape in the 1950s, has become a target of change ever since.

When describing the traditional center-local relationship, both Chinese scholars and government officials often use the family metaphor. The nation's economy was like an extended traditional family economy. The central authority was *jiazhang* (family head), who was responsible for the livelihood of the whole family and controlled all family resources. Local governments were like *haizi* (children) in the family, who were looked after by their *jiazhang*. They were expected to work hard for the prosperity of the family and contribute their income to the family pool. *Haizi* obeyed *jiazhang* out of commitment to the family ideology or a sense of moral responsibility, and were subject to the discipline of the family.

In the family-style unitary state, the administrative system of China was, in some Chinese scholars' words, a "*chuizhi xitong*" (integrated vertical system) in which "a hierarchical administration was supposed to integrate central authority, local authorities and enterprises."[1] All political, social, and economic powers were supposed to be bound up and concentrated within the central authority. Although local governments exercised direct administration over the localities, functions of the central authority and local governments often overlapped. Several Chinese scholars described this functional integration in the following way: "The central authority was responsible for balance and distribution of commodities, materials, investments, financial revenues, credits and loans, and foreign exchange at the top level, whereas local governments were responsible for the same affairs at lower levels."[2] In other words, within the functionally integrated system of China, while local governments were responsible for local social and economic development, their formal role was to implement centrally-made policies.

The strength of the integrated vertical system was supposed to be its ability to mobilize resources for rapid economic development. The central government, which controlled material resources and monetary funds, made decisions based on its assessment of the long-term needs of the society as a whole, not on the particularistic interests of individual actors, regions, or enterprises. In reality, nevertheless, the system produced numerous problems which hampered China's overall economic progress. One of the problems was economic inefficiency. The vertical system usually gave the central authority, especially central functional ministries, excessive control over the provinces. All important decisions had to be made in Beijing. Even the acquisition of fixed property worth as little as one hundred yuan required specific approval from the relevant central ministry.[3] This frequently resulted in delay and frustration in decision-making and implementation. Another problem was "ministry autarky".[4] James Wang indicated that tight control over the supply of materials and allocation of resources produced "centralized, ministerial, independent kingdoms, which interfered with provincial and local administration, drew up ill-conceived plans, and made repeated revisions of the plans." He believed that "this resulted in the neglect of priorities and the waste of raw materials."[5]

Consequently, the integrated vertical system was a major target of change from the late 1950s until the beginning of the reform era in late 1970s. During this period, while the unitary nature of the state was never seriously challenged, the central administration's authority was reduced. Decentralization had weakened the center's capacity to control local governments and encouraged local governments to pursue their own interests. What were the major instruments used by the center to control local governments in the unitary state of China? How had decentralization proceeded since the founding of the People's Republic in 1949 until the late 1970s? How should the decentralization be interpreted? And what features can we see in this process of the decentralization? These are the questions that this chapter seeks to answer.

The Control Instruments in a Unitary State

In the unitary state of China, the central authority exercised its power over local governments mainly through three coercive instruments: ideological requisiteness, party discipline, and the central planning mechanism.

The Ideological Requisiteness

Ideological requisiteness was a traditional control instrument used by the central government of China to make local governments comply with central policies. During the early period of the People's Republic, Chinese communist leaders relied heavily on both traditional Chinese doctrines and communist principles as ideological weapons to govern the nation.

The ideology was typically expressed by the statement that a "natural harmony of social interests" existed within the Chinese people. The central government and the Chinese Communist Party (CCP) represented the nation's highest interest.[6] According to this ideological appeal, Chinese people, including the provincial and local governments, were exhorted to defer to the center, subjugating their interests to state needs, their parochial preferences to the national good. It implied that local officials were called upon not only to accept but to internalize the values of the center. This was expressed in a slogan of the 1950s that "*quanguo yi panqi*" (all the nation was one chess game). There ought to be an identity of goals and a unity of will between the center and the localities. As mere pawns in the nation's chessboard, the rules of the game required that localities have no mind and preferences of their own. A unitary player, the center, made the moves alone. Very often, the localities were required to sacrifice for the good of the nation as a whole.[7]

Ideological requisiteness was a very powerful force during the early period of the People's Republic. While a nation for thousands of years, China had also experienced countless wars among regional rulers and warlords throughout its history. The country had often been divided. One of the greatest accomplishments that the Chinese Communist regime claimed was reunification of the nation. With the inauguration of the People's Republic on October 1, 1949, China was unified (except for Taiwan) and at peace for the first time in decades.

This historical background led Mao Zedong, immediately after the Communist Party took power over the nation, to state in his *On People's Democratic Dictatorship* that one of the most prominent goals of the communist regime was to maintain national political and economic unity. This unity was, according to Mao, based on a common goal represented by the Communist Party. Mao told the Chinese people that there were no fundamental conflicts of interest among the people. The government at different levels pursued the same goal: protecting the interests of the people.[8]

Mao and the official ideology presented by him did not encourage the pursuit of personal or local interests, or any form of compromise with these interests. In principle, governments at all levels were to discover under party leadership the objectively correct line of the historical moment and guarantee its wholehearted implementation by every government official. The correct line would lead to national unity, strength and prosperity, and the development of socialism. This was frequently a dominant theme in the rhetoric of government and party officials and encoded in propaganda exhortations such as: To pursue the party line, all government officials should maintain a *quanju guannian* (comprehensive perspective on the whole nation). Another such maxim was that local interests must give way to the national interest or, as it was expressed in Chinese, *jubu fuchong quanju*--the parts are subject to the whole.[9]

Party Discipline

Party discipline was the second instrument that the center used to control local governments. The Chinese Communist Party emerged from the revolutionary years as a highly disciplined and tightly knit organization with a membership of nearly five million. The imperatives of two decades of armed struggle had imparted a military-like discipline to its organization and to the behavioral habits and cast of mind of its members. The party members were guided by the Leninist principle of "democratic centralism," which meant that discussion of any issue within the party must be followed by unified implementation of whatever decision was reached at the top.[10] It in fact required that all party members submit to the decisions of the party center.

As Mao Zedong explained the Communist Party's system of democratic centralism, "The Communist Party not only needs democracy but needs centralization even more."[11] He added that, in the system of democratic centralism, "The minority is subordinate to the majority, the lower level to the higher level, the part to the whole, and the entire membership to the Central Committee."[12]

Deng Xiaoping followed Mao Zedong and talked about party discipline in similar terms: "Individual party members must be subordinate to the party organization, the minority to the majority, the lower party organization to the higher, and all party constituent organizations and members must be subordinate to the Central Committee."[13]

Party discipline functioned as a coercive instrument to enforce compliance from local governments mainly through two institutional devices. One was the system under which party organs overlapped and often arrogated the functions of government organs. Functioning as a quasi-government long before the formal establishment of the People's Republic, the party provided the main organizational base, leadership, and methods of mass organization as the new government took shape. While there might be some distinctions between the party organization and the formal administrative organs of the government, the leaders of the party usually held the key positions in the formal governmental administration. For example, Mao Zedong was both the party chairman and the chairman of the People's Republic for many years. The pattern was repeated down to the provincial and local levels. Party secretaries either formally held official posts in the governments or were placed in positions that supervised the administrative work of nonparty functionaries.

The second device was the *nomenklatura* system, through which the party's Central Committee had sovereign control over the appointment, promotion, transfer, and removal of party secretaries and top governmental officials at provincial and local levels. To prevent the development of strong local and regional loyalties and to maintain central control over local governments, the top provincial officials were often transferred from one to another province or from a provincial post to a ministry post in the central government.[14]

The importance of party discipline as a control instrument can be seen from a speech of Deng Xiaoping. At the central work conference of January 1980, he said that the party had become the ruling party and the core force uniting the whole country, bringing to an end countless divisions and little kingdoms. China was led by the CCP. This principle could not be shaken. Otherwise, China would have regressed into divisions and confusion.[15] In August 1980, Deng Xiaoping once again said that "In a big country like China, without a political party whose members possess a high degree of political consciousness, sense of discipline, and spirit of self-sacrifice ... it would be inconceivable that the ideology and strength of hundreds of millions of people could be united to build socialism." He underscored the point later:"China would be certain to fall to pieces and be incapable of achieving anything without the leadership of the CCP."[16]

The Central Planning Mechanisms

The third control instrument in the unitary state of China is the central planning mechanism, which was the single most important feature of the PRC system. Immediately after the 1949 victory of the communists on the mainland,[17] a powerful State Financial and Economic Commission was set up to take charge of national economic activities. "*Tongyi lingdao, tongyi guanli*" (unified leadership and unified administration) as a principle of the economic system replaced "*tongyi lingdao, fenshan jingying*" (unified leadership and decentralized operation) which prevailed in the "liberated areas" (*jiefang qu*) of war time.[18] In March 1950, the Government Administrative Council issued a "Resolution on Unifying State Financial and Economic Works," according to which all financial revenues and expenditures, material distribution, and cash management were highly centralized.[19] The State Planning Commission was established in 1952 and the First Five-Year Plan was launched in 1953. The integrated vertical system was thereby formed during the early period of the PRC.[20]

The vertical system worked through three central planning mechanisms: (1) physical planning of production, (2) centralized allocation of materials, and (3) budgetary control of revenues and expenditures. The central ministries directly controlled major enterprises, distributed funds and materials, and supervised fixed investment through a centralized budgetary allocation. A province generating more revenues could not necessarily spend more. The center set compulsory financial targets for the provinces and had complete budgetary control over provincial government expenditures. Through the central planning mechanisms, the central government controlled most of the nation's material and financial resources. A local government was normally beholden to the center for raw materials for its plants, a market for its goods, and budget revenue for its programs.

Progressive Decentralization

While these three traditional control instruments functioned effectively in the early period of the PRC, they gradually lost the ability to ensure compliance from local governments as a result of progressive decentralization that took place beginning in 1957.

The Integrated Vertical System in the Early 1950s

China copied its central control system from the Soviet Union and established a unitary state system during the early years of the People's Republic. The supreme executive organ set up in 1949 was called the Government Administrative Council (*zheng wu yuan*). In 1954, under a new constitution, its name was changed to State Council (*guo wu yuan*). The country was initially divided into six "greater administrative regions" (*da xingzhengqu*) which were placed under military administrative control.

Below these regions, the provincial administrative level consisted of the provinces, province-level autonomous regions (*zizhiqu*), and the municipalities of Beijing, Shanghai, and Tianjin. Under the provincial level, there were over two thousand counties (*xian*) and some cities (*shi*). The Communist Party organization paralleled this administrative subdivision, and often party and government positions were occupied by the same persons. The party played the main role in formulating and overseeing the execution of basic national policies.[21]

In the economic field, the central planning system was established soon after the People's Republic was founded. The integrated system played an important role in the reconstruction of the national economy during the early period of the People's Republic, laying down the base for the next forty years' evolution of the Chinese political and economic system under Communist rule.

The Origins of Decentralization

Decentralization in China denoted the devolution of central control of administrative authority and economic resources to lower levels. It was employed not to reduce the coercive central-local relationship but primarily to encourage the lower levels of government to fulfill or surpass the ambitious goals set by the center. Meanwhile, local control of resources remained strictly limited.

While the vertical system created in the early 1950s gave the center the upper hand over local governments, it also created problems of coordination and motivation on the central side and problems of initiative on the local side. As all major important decisions had to be made in Beijing, even the acquisition of fixed property worth as little as one hundred yuan needed specific approval from the central ministry. Chinese called the problem "*tiaotiao zhuanzhen*" (vertical dictatorship or ministry autarky).[22] This frequently resulted in delay and frustration in decision-making and implementation. These problems became more and more serious as the economy increased in size and complexity. Central decisions were often based on inadequate or erroneous information, while local governments possessing information were powerless to use it. In the meantime, as local expenditures were determined by the center and bore no relation to local revenues, the localities could not be motivated to increase their revenues and to engage in local development efforts.[23] In view of these problems, a Chinese scholar explained that the reason why China embarked on decentralization in 1957 was that "Chinese leaders at that time found that the overconcentration of power fettered the initiatives of the local governments and hindered the development of production."[24]

Wu Jinglian, another Chinese scholar, argued that the decentralization of 1957 was carried out "in a political atmosphere of anti-revisionism," and therefore was a deliberate deviation from the Soviet model.[25] Susan Shirk suggests a different explanation: that because of the strong party base in the provinces, whenever a party leader perceived that rival leaders were blocking his policy initiatives by their control over the central bureaucracy, he attempted to build support for his initiatives by "playing to the provinces." Mao launched the administrative decentralization to win provincial support for policies promoting revolutionary transformation in 1957.[26]

The Decentralization of 1957-58

Regardless of its motives, the radical decentralization that took place in 1957 was a significant attack on the integrated economic system. The first call for decentralization was put forward by Mao Zedong in his speech at the enlarged meeting of the CCP Politburo on April 25, 1956: "Our territory is so vast, our population is so large and the conditions are so complex, that it is far better to have the initiatives come from both the center and the local authorities than from one source alone."[27] Mao also criticized the Soviet model and said that "We must not follow the example of the Soviet Union in concentrating everything in the hands of the central authorities, shackling the local authorities and denying them the right of independent action."[28] Mao advocated enlarging the powers of the provinces and localities and also called more vaguely for increasing the authority of individual enterprises.

Following Mao's instruction, in late 1957 and 1958, a series of State Council directives were announced to decentralize the planning and management system for industry, commerce, and finance. The State Council issued a "Resolution on Improving the Industrial Management System" in 1957.[29] A further resolution on "Improving the Planning Management System" was jointly issued by the Central Committee of the CCP and the State Council in 1958.[30] Implementation of these resolutions resulted in the devolution of control over 88 percent of the centrally-administered enterprises down to provincial or municipal authorities. The rest of the enterprises were also placed under the dual leadership of both the center and provincial authorities.[31] In addition, local governments were empowered to approve all locally financed large- and middle-sized investment projects, to plan local production, to distribute materials, and to collect revenues.[32]

As a result, the number of enterprises administered by the central ministries was reduced from more than 9,300 in 1957 to less than 1,200 in 1958. In addition, the number of industrial products controlled by the

State Planning Commission was reduced from more than 300 categories in 1957 to 215 categories in 1959.[33]

The decentralization in 1957 was followed by the Great Leap Forward in 1958. As indicated by Wu Jinglian, this radical decentralization was the "organizational base of the Great Leap Forward in 1958."[34] Because of this linkage, it was logical that the failure of the Great Leap Forward interrupted the first decentralization reform. In addition to the failure of the Great Leap Forward, the decentralization also backfired because it resulted in localism, which was strongly opposed by the majority of the nation's central leadership. As James Wang indicated, "A direct consequence of the 1957 decentralization under the Great Leap was the emergence of the provinces as independent entities... Each wanted to build its own self-sufficient industrial complex."[35] This trend of localism was regarded as a dangerous tendency for the newly-founded People's Republic.

The Readjustment in the Early 1960s

When the strategy and tactics of guerrilla warfare applied during the Great Leap Forward led to an economic disaster which cost China "almost a decade of economic growth,"[36] a period of economic readjustment began in 1960.

The economic readjustment process included recentralization. Authority over resource allocation with regard to industry, commerce, finance, and labor, which had been handed down to local governments in 1957, was now recentralized. The CCP Central Committee issued a "Resolution on Readjusting the Management System" in January 1961 and later a "Resolution on Improving the Economic Management System" in August of the same year.[37] The documents stressed "*quanguo yipanqi, shangxia yibenzhang*". The whole nation is one chessboard and all levels of the administration use one accounting book.[38] During the readjustment period, almost all large- and middle-sized enterprises which had been transferred downward in 1957-58 were returned to the jurisdiction of central authorities. The recentralization was accomplished after completion of the readjustment in 1963. At that time, the degree of centralization had become even greater than it was before 1957, especially with regard to financial planning.[39]

The Decentralization in the 1960s and 1970s

The return to rigid centralization brought back the same problems that had disturbed the economy and some Chinese leaders, such as Mao Zedong, before the 1957-58 campaigns.[40] Hence, a second decentralization wave took place in 1964. The authority to approve investments in nineteen non-industrial sectors of the economy, including agriculture and animal husbandry, forestry, irrigation, fishing, commerce, banking, communications, and transportation, were devolved to the local governments in 1964. Local governments were permitted to distribute the output of the "smaller industries in five sectors" (including the small steel and iron industry, cement industry, fertilizer industry, coal industry, and machinery industry), and were also given some power fo handle the allocation of funds and materials in 1965.[41]

The decentralization that had started in 1964 continued during the Cultural Revolution period beginning in 1966. This was because, after the wide-ranging purge of the political establishment at all levels of government, "with neither market nor central planners to co-ordinate the economy, Mao sought to minimize the need for coordination by means of *zili gengsheng* (self-reliance)."[42] The self-reliance implied a principle of local initiative and non-dependence. According to this principle, the Central Planning Conference held in February 1970 called for each provincial government to establish an independent and comprehensive industrial system. On March 5, 1970, the State Council issued a document which directed that most of the enterprises administered by the center should be transferred to provincial governments, while the rest should be placed under dual central-provincial leadership.[43]

In the meantime, a system of financial, material, and investment sharing (*dabaogan*) was proposed in the Fourth Five-Year Plan Outline issued in March 1970.[44] The financial *dabaogan* stipulated that provincial governments would submit a fixed proportion of their revenue to the center and retain the rest. The material allocation *dabaogan* reduced the number of categories of centrally-controlled materials from 579 in 1966 to 217 in 1972. The investment *dabaogan* allowed local governments to retain enterprise depreciation funds (*zhejiu jijing*) for their improvement. Prior to 1966 all the depreciation funds were submitted to the center. A central document issued in 1971 provided that all depreciation funds (with the exception of those managed by the Second Industrial Ministry and the Water and Electrical Ministry) should be retained by local governments. These funds increased rapidly and amounted to 10 billion yuan in 1975.[45]

While the *dabaogan* experiment in the 1970s provided strong material incentives for local initiatives, it brought some new problems. Take the financial *dabaogan* as an example: Since each province had a different financial capacity, the *dabaogan* system increased the interregional difference in their revenues. To avoid this problem, the center had to establish differential revenue-sharing rates with individual provinces. Of the large share of revenue collected by the provinces, a disproportionate amount was raised by the richer ones. The center extracted a large percentage of this and a smaller proportion of revenue raised by middle-income provinces, and, then transferred some of these funds as subsidies to the poorest regions. In spite of this redistribution, the decentralization in the early 1970s greatly changed the central-local relationship and gave local governments considerable control over their own resources.

Consequences of the Progressive Decentralization

By the onset of the post-Mao reforms in the late 1970s, China had already experienced "*liangxia liangshang*"--two periods of "sending down" (i.e., two decentralizations) and two of "taking up" (i.e., two recentralizations)--in central-local relations. While this process seemed like a centralization-decentralization-recentralization cycle, the overall trend was toward greater decentralization. The vertically integrated system established during the early 1950s was already under heavy assault. Despite periodic attempts at recentralization, the central-local relationship has never returned completely to the old pattern.

This progressive decentralization has undercut the efficacy of the central authority's coercive instruments and undermined the center's capacity to enforce compliance from local governments. The mysterious "natural harmony of interests" which legitimized the ideology promoting the deference of local governments to the center was challenged by the conflicting parochial interests revealed in the decentralization process. The loss of ideological legitimacy was compounded by the laxness of party discipline and the paralysis of the central planning mechanisms.

(1) In order to function, the old ideology required that local leaders highly and positively commit to the official appeal that the central authority represents the highest interests of the Chinese people. Nevertheless, pre-reform decentralization revealed conflicting interests not only between the center and the localities but also among different localities. The campaign to repudiate "*tiaotiao zhuanzheng*" (the vertical dictatorship) and the exposure of the great power struggle among the ruling party during the Cultural Revolution also demoralized local leaders, however faithful they had been to the center, and gradually eroded the official ideology. It therefore became more and more difficult for the central authority to appeal to a natural harmony of interests among the people to enforce compliance from local governments.

The coastal provinces were mostly dissatisfied with the redistributive aspects of the ideology, which required reallocation of the revenues they generated in favor of the less developed areas. For their parts, the less developed inland provinces also complained about the centralized aspect of the ideology, which required them to sacrifice local manufacturing development in favor of industrial projects in the coastal provinces. Taking advantage of the decentralization, coastal provinces underfulfilled and overspent their fiscal targets, while less developed provinces protected their local markets for their own factories by means of administrative blockades, and nurtured their infant consumer goods industries by excluding high-quality merchandise from coastal and other traditional manufacturing centers.[46]

By the late 1970s, although the central authorities still talked in ideological terms about coordinating the national economy like one big chessboard, local governments in pursuit of parochial interests had already divided up the board. The power of ideology was no longer sufficient to carry out recentralization programs and to override parochial interests in favor of central control over economic resources or financial targets.

(2) By the early 1980s, as a cumulative result of the progressive decentralizations since the late 1950s, party discipline as a coercive instrument to enforce compliance from local governments had also been loosened. Although the central leaders expressed concerns and talked about strengthening it, the laxness of party discipline had become an irreversible trend, as both of the party's institutional devices--party organs which arrogated the functions of the government agencies and the *nomenklatura* system through which the party controlled the appointment and removal of government officials--had been weakened during the decentralization process.

With decentralization of the nomenklatura system came the localization of provincial leaders. To prevent the development of strong localistic and regional loyalties, the top provincial leaders used to be brought in mostly from the outside--the center or other provinces. Nevertheless, by December 1981, 43 percent of the 58 provincial leaders were either natives of the province of appointment or had spent most of their working lives there. The localization of provincial leaders had further weakened central control over localities.

(3) The most noticeable change in the pre-reform decentralization process was the paralysis of the central planning mechanisms, as the powers of resource allocation, investment, and budgetary responsibilities were decentralized. Christine P. Wong observes that "the emerging picture reveals a system that has become progressively decentralized through the Cultural Revolution period, with local authorities gaining control over major portions of financial and material resources--a trend that accelerated in the post-Mao period."[47] In retrospect, each decentral-

ization widened the power base of local leaders and gave them stronger leverage over the central authorities.

Conclusions

From 1957 until the end of Cultural Revolution, progressive decentralization had to a great extent changed China's traditional "family" relationship between the center and localities. It became difficult for *jiazhang* to maintain the extended "big family" relationship as ideology and party discipline had gradually lost their coercive power. It also grew harder for *jiazhang*, who controlled fewer material resources, to enforce its coercive power. As a negotiated relationship began to emerge, *haizi* began to complain that *jiazhang* mistreated them. They also requested that *jiazhang* divide the family up and allow the *haizi* to go off on their own. The post-Mao reform measures, such as financial *fenzhao chifan* ("eating in separate kitchens") introduced in the early 1980s, were to a certain extent a consequence of the changing central-local relationship developed earlier.

However, pre-reform era decentralization had by no means reached the stage of disintegration of the "big family" itself. After all, the center's aim had been only to maintain the "family ties" by finding a fine way to resolve the *haizi* initiative problem. It was clear from the frequency of complaints among Chinese leaders that excessive centralization stifled local initiative while excessive decentralization produced chaos and detracted from the pursuit of national interests.[48] What the pre-reform Chinese leaders wanted to find was a happy medium between the two.

It is true that the trend of progressive decentralization in the pre-reform era had produced a division of power between the central and local authorities--a nascent form of federalism. However, not only had this "federalism" been introduced within the framework of a unitary state but also the division of power had no constitutional guarantee. The outcome of the changing central-local relationship after the pre-reform decentralization may thus be conceptualized as "federalism without a federal constitution."[49] The primary characteristic of federalism is "a constitutionally guaranteed division of power between the central government and the governments of the member units or component units of the federation. It is usually accompanied by decentralization, that is, substantial autonomy for the members of the federation."[50] While the pre-reform decentralization had given more powers to the local government, and the center's capacity to control local government had been greatly weakened, the form of a unitary state had been maintained, and the decentralization process had not been guaranteed by any constitutional or even legal system. This was like introducing federalism to China without attempting to establish a federalist constitutional framework. Even today, after a decade-long reform process that has changed China's central-local relations even more profoundly, the fact that decentralization is still not constitutionally guaranteed implies that the central government remains potentially all-powerful. Therefore, while this chapter has argued that decentralization had already become an important aspect of China's central-local relations by the end of the pre-reform era, the central government's coercive power has by no means completely lost its relevance. The current Chinese central-local negotiatory relationship simply means that the center has to take the economic interests of the localities into serious consideration when any decision concerning the latter is to be made.

Notes

1. Lou Jiwei, Xiao Jie, and Liu Liqun, "Guanyu Jingji Yunxing Muoshi yu Caizheng Suishou Gaige de Ruogan Sikao" (Some Ideas About Patterns of Economic Operation and Fiscal Revenue Reform), in Wu Jinglian and Zhou Xiaochuan, ed., *Zhonghuo Jingji Gaige de Zhengti Sheji* (The Integrated Design of China's Economic Reform), (Beijing: China Zhanwang Publishing House, 1988), p. 115.

2. Ibid.

3. Zhou Taihe, ed., *Dangdai Zhongguo de Jingji Tizhi Gaige* (Economic Reform in Contemporary China), (Beijing: Chinese Social Science Publishing House, 1984), p. 84.

4. James C. F. Wang, *Contemporary Chinese Politics* (Englewood Cliffs, N.J.: Prentice-Hall, Inc., 1985), p. 144.

5. Ibid.

6. For a study of how the natural harmony doctrine survived the transition from Confucianism to Marxism in the People's Republic of China, see Andrew Nathan, *Chinese Democracy* (New York: Alfred A. Knopf, 1985), pp. 45-66.

7. Zhongguo Jingji Tizhi Yanjiuhui (Research Association of China's Economic Reforms), ed., *Zhongguo Jingji Tizhi de Xin Moshi* (New patterns of the Economic System in China), (Beijing: People's Publishing House, 1984), p. 171.

8. Mao Zedong, "On the People's Democratic Dictatorship", in *Selected Works of Mao Zedong* (Beijing: Foreign Language Press, 1961), Vol. 4, pp. 411-424.

9. Zhongguo Jingji Tizhi Yanjiuhui (Research Association of China's Economic Reforms), ed., *Zhongguo Jingji Tizhi de Xin Moshi* (New patterns of the Economic System in China), (Beijing: People's Publishing House, 1984), p. 186.

10. Hu Hua, ed., *Zhongguo Shehuizhuyi Geming and Jianshe Jiangyi* (Notes on China's Socialist Revolution and Reconstruction), (Beijing: Chinese People's University Publishing House, 1985), p. 69.

11. Mao Zedong, "Rectify the Party's Style of Work", in *Selected Works of Mao Zedong* (Beijing: Foreign Language Press, 1965), Vol. III, p. 44.

12. Ibid.

13. Deng Xiaoping, "The Present Situation and the Tasks Before Us", in *Selected Works of Deng Xiaoping* (Beijing: Foreign Language Press, 1984), p. 256.

14. The provincial governorship and the central ministership are at the same rank in the Chinese official ranking system.

15. Deng Xiaoping, op. cit., pp. 224-258.

16. Deng Xiaoping, "On the Reform of the System of Party and State Leadership", in *Selected Works of Deng Xiaoping* (Beijing: Foreign Language Press, 1984), p. 324.

17. Ma Hong, ed., *Xiandai Zhongguo Jingji Shidian* (Dictionary of Events in Contemporary China), (Beijing: Chinese Social Science Publishing House, 1982), pp. 20-22.

18. Zhou Taihe, op. cit., p. 214.

19. Fang Weizhong, ed., *Zhonghua Renmin Gongheguo Dashi Ji: 1949-1980* (Chronicle of major events of the PRC: 1949-1980), (Beijing: Chinese Social Science Publishing House), 1982, p. 13.

20. Liu Guoguang, ed., *Zhongguo Jingji Fazhan Zhanlue Wenti Yanjiu* (A Study of Strategical Issues on the Economic Development of China), (Shanghai: Shanghai Renmin Chuban She, 1984), p. 489.

21. Ma Hong, op. cit.

22. James C. F. Wang, *Contemporary Chinese Politics* (Englewood Cliffs, N.J.: Prentice-Hall, Inc., 1985), p. 144.

23. The problems of overconcentration of power in the center have been a major subject of debate among Chinese leaders, economists and economic officials. For one description of the debate, see Liu Guoguang, *Lun Jingji Gaige yu Jingji Tiaozheng, di Yixie lilun he Shiji wenti de tiantiao* (Economic Reform and Economic Readjustment--Views on Some Theoretic and Empirical Issues), (Nanjing: Jiangsu People's Publishing House, 1983).

24. Zhou Taihe, op. cit., p. 220.

25. Wu Jinglian and Zhou Xiaochuan, op. cit., p. 3.

26. Susan Shirk, "Playing to the Provinces: Deng Xiaoping's Political Strategy of Economic Reform", in Studies in *Comparative Communism*, Vol. 23, No. 3/4, Autumn/Winter 1990, p. 254.

27. Mao Zedong, *On the Ten Major Relationships*, Beijing: Foreign Language Press, 1977, p. 13.

28. Ibid.

29. Fang Weizhong, op. cit., p. 201.

30. Ibid., p. 227.

31. Zhou Taihe, op. cit., p. 220.

32. Zhou Taihe, op. cit., pp. 222-224.

33. Zhou Taihe, op. cit., pp. 70-72.

34. Wu Jinglian and Zhou Xiaochuan, op. cit.

35. James C. F. Wang, op. cit., p. 145.

36. Carl Riskin, *China's Political Economy: The Quest for Development since 1949* (Oxford: Oxford University Press, 1987), p. 133.

37. Fang Weizhong, op. cit.

38. Zhou Taihe, op. cit., p. 227.

39. Zhou Taihe, op. cit., p. 124.
40. Liu Guoguang, op. cit., p. 491.
41. Zhou Taihe, op. cit., p. 232.
42. Carl Riskin, op. cit., p. 203.
43. Zhou Taihe, op. cit., p. 136.
44. Zhou Taihe, op. cit., p. 138.
45. Zhou Taihe, op. cit., p. 143.
46. Zhang Zhenbin, "Difang Zhengfu zai Qiye Yinyunzhong de Jingji Xinwei" (The Economic Behaviors of Local Government in the Enterprise Operation), *Jingji Yanjiu* (Economic Research), August 1991, p. 51.
47. Christine P. W. Wong, "Ownership and Control in Chinese Industry: The Maoist Legacy and Prospects for the 1980s", in U.S. Congress Joint Committee, *China's Economy Looks Toward the Year 2000*, Vol. 1, (Washington D. C.: U.S. Government Printing Office, 1986), p. 572.
48. Chen Yizi, *Zhengzhi Tizhi Gaige Jianghua* (Talks on the Reform of the Political System), (Beijing: People's Publishing House, 1987), p. 55.
49. Zhao Suisheng, "The Feeble Political Capacity of a Strong One-Party Regime--An Institutional Approach toward the Formulation and Implementation of Economic Policy in Post-Mao China (Part Two)", in *Issues and Studies*, Vol. 26, No. 2, February 1990, p. 58.
50. Arend Lijphart, *Democracies: Patterns of Majoritarian and Consensus Government in Twenty-one Countries* (New Haven: Yale University Press, 1984), p. 169.

2

Market and State: Changing Central-Local Relations in China

Jia Hao and Wang Mingxia

A nation's central-local relations can be examined in a number of ways. This chapter examines China's central-local relations from the perspective of the interaction between the market and the state.[1] This angle has been chosen for two reasons. First, it is our judgment that the roots of China's changing central-local relationship since the late 1970s lie with economic reform, opening to the outside world, and the profound chain effects related to both. Among them, a market mechanism has emerged to play an important part. On the one hand, the market has fundamentally shaken China's old central command economic system, which over decades constituted the very basis of the nation's state socialist polity. On the other hand, it has also generated the dynamics of competition among provinces and regions in the country. Accompanied by economic development and institutional innovation in the localities, the changes that the market mechanism has brought in have also profoundly altered China's central-local power structure. Analyzing the interaction between market and state thus constitutes an important dimension of examining China's changing central-local relations.

Our examination has also been illuminated by some new findings and theoretical syntheses of market and state in comparative perspectives.[2] For instance, as the World Bank's *World Development Report 1991: The Challenge of Development* suggests, "the central issue in development"--the interaction between governments and markets--is not a question of intervention versus laissez-faire, which is "a popular dichotomy, but a false one." Nowadays it is generally agreed that competitive markets are undoubtedly the best way yet found to efficiently organize the production and distribution of goods and services. Yet, markets cannot operate in a vacuum. The full play of the market mechanism necessitates legal, regulatory, physical, and social frameworks--roles and functions that can only be provided and protected by the state. The relationship between market and state thus also concerns a society's institutional development (often referred to as the process of "institutionalization"). This "market-friendly" approach to development stresses the complementarity of markets and governments: when the market and the state work in opposition, the results can be disastrous; if the two are adequately brought together, evidence suggests that the whole is greater than the sum.[3]

Focusing on the Chinese situation, in the following analysis we will argue that: China's decade-long economic reform and opening to the outside world have generated certain market mechanisms and the dynamics of domestic competition (particularly inter-provincial and inter-regional), made the localities a major driving force behind reform, and positioned the local forces as equally important players (with both power and "legitimacy") vis-a-vis the center in the Chinese political economy. Yet the institutional weaknesses of the Chinese state, such as the nation's fragmented process of policy-making and implementation, its ineffective monitoring and law-enforcement mechanisms, and the repeating, vicious economic cycle resulting from a lack of control of macroeconomic policy, all pose major problems for China's further development. Consequently, the real danger for the nation is not stagnation, but structural instability generated by economic development.

Two Different Views

How do we judge the impact of China's decade-long economic reform on its central-local relations? Where does China stand today and what direction is it heading? Generally speaking, there are two different responses to the above questions. Some scholars argue that China's economic changes during the last decade can be generalized as a "disintegrating reform," centered on "*fenquan rangli*"--administrative decentralization and allowing interests to be shared by provincial and local entities. Scholars in this group favorably assess the impact of reform, which they believe has resulted in a significant weakening of the nation's old-fashioned command economy and greater local autonomy.[4] In their view, the reform has transformed Chinese society in the following important ways: (1) the trend of regional economic pluralization has become irreversible; (2) the weakening of economic centralization has also brought the development of the nation's "political pluralization"--the relative autonomy of local authorities from the center; and (3) the relative autonomy of local governments constitutes a stabilizing mechanism for the local economy, which will be particularly important in saving China from future crisis. If in future the Chinese central government loses control, the "stability of the country will have to be sustained by the local governments collectively." Accordingly, scholars of this group propose as "an urgent task" the "transfer of even greater power to the local governments", helping local governments learn how to integrate various local forces and to coordinate and cooperate on inter-provincial relations.[5]

Scholars of the second group view the results of Chinese economic reform more critically.[6] They argue that China's economic reform has done little to reduce the role of public authorities (government at various levels) in economic activities. The thrust of their criticism is that, given the organizational nature of the "multi-level hierarchies" in China's economic and political systems--mainly composed of the three tiers of central government, local governments, and enterprises--"*fenquan rangli*" and other reform measures did not bring about a straightforward transfer of resources and decision-making power from the nation's central government to economic agents (particularly the state-owned enterprises).[7] Instead, during the reform process, provincial and local governments "captured" and expanded their control over the enterprises.[8] The reform process has thus not led to the withering away of the traditional command economy. Instead, it has resulted in a "smaller-sized command economy" centered on China's local bureaucracies and controlled by "local mandatory plans," leaving little room for the play of market forces.[9] One critical consequence of this development is that the central government lacks the necessary resources and authority to carry out adjustments in the macro- economy and has allowed the emergence of an "aristocratic economy" ruled by local "dukes" and "princes."[10] The increased strength of the localities has thus "significantly weakened China's state capacity."[11]

Finally, scholars of the second group further contend that, while becoming pivotal political players in deciding the nation's future course, Chinese local leaders have turned out to be the major barrier in the way of moving the reform process either backward or forward. On the one hand, due to vested interests, local leaders are a powerful force in sustaining the existing reform policies and resisting recentralization. On the other hand, the economic alliance between local bureaucrats and enterprise managers creates both economic and political obstacles to further economic changes, leaving China's reform in "gridlock."[12]

While the opposing schools concur that China's economic reform process has devolved substantial resources and policy-making authority from the center to the localities and thus has significantly altered the old central-planning economic system, they disagree on how to evaluate its implication for the nation's central-local relations, and, in turn, where the process is heading. Both views and some of their basic arguments should be further examined.

Implications of Economic Reform: How To Assess?

In our opinion, the critical view of Chinese economic reform underestimates the profound implications of the basic reform approach centered on the country's administrative decentralization. Stemming both from the historical background of China's "Cultural Revolution" that led to a radical reorientation of the national elites' thinking, and the economic circumstances at the time, China's economic reform since the late 1970s chose decentralization as its breaking point.[13] It has been carried out "as a means of using locally available information more effectively, allowing local preferences greater influence over local spending decisions, and providing material incentives to local governments and enterprises to pursue growth objectives, as they would be the main beneficiaries of increased incomes."[14] Seen by some as "the single most important event" in the reform process, fiscal decentralization adopted between the late 1970s and the early 1980s has thus "changed not only the resource distribution between the central and local governments but also the property rights structures" (through retained revenues by the provinces).[15] With their power base and personal interest increasingly related to the reform process, the provincial and local leaders in general have become unprecedentedly reform-minded.[16]

The decentralization approach and the changes in the property rights structure, combined with the stimulus of opening to the outside world, have allowed a dynamic market mechanism and competitive environment to emerge in the country. Working together, these factors have fundamentally altered China's central command economic system and the power structure between the center and localities. To support our argument, in the following section we will examine the implications of China's reform for central-local relations from four aspects: rural reform, opening to the outside world, the new dynamic of inter-regional competition (as well as cooperation) in the country, and, finally, the emergence of the localities as a major driving force behind the reform process.

The Impact of China's Rural Reform

Judged by many as the most successful of China's reform programs, rural reform started in the late-1970s and centered on specifying and enforcing property rights in the form of the "household contract responsibility system." Rural reform was characterized by the abandonment of governmental intervention in collective properties, which, in turn, were decollectivized. The specifying and enforcing of property rights, along with decentralization, contributed greatly to rural commercialization.[17] From 1978 to 1990, the proportion of agricultural procurement regulated by state prices dropped from 94.4 percent to 25.2 percent, while the proportion regulated by the market increased from 5.6 percent to 52.2 percent. (The remainder was regulated by "the state-guided price").[18] During the same period, with the exception of cotton and half of the nation's commercial grains, the prices of other major agricultural items, such as meat, sugar, vegetables, fruits, edible oil, and sea foods, all became regulated by the market.[19] A fundamental change occurred when the markets in rural areas developed swiftly, since this created huge supply and demand for the urban industrial sector. This result is regarded by some as a crucial factor that helped China to break the "vicious reform cycle" encountered in other state socialist countries.[20] Decollectivization and marketization then promoted China's agricultural productivity and increased per-capita real income.[21]

One of the most important "chain effects" of rural reform has been the dramatic development of China's township and village enterprises (TVE's). From 1979 to 1990, the number of TVE's increased from 1.52 million to 18.50 million, and their total employment more than tripled (from 29.1 million to 92.6 million people).[22] During the same period, the gross output value of TVE's increased from 54.8 billion to 846.2 billion renminbi yuan, a 15.4-fold increase.[23] By the end of 1991, even in China's biggest industrial city of Shanghai, the output of TVE's accounted for one fourth of the city's gross industrial output.[24] Operating entirely beyond the control of state planning, TVE's have become the major driving force behind the growth of China's industry and the nation's whole economy.[25] As a Chinese scholar put it, by placing little emphasis on reforming old organizations but instead pinning hopes on the growth of a nascent private sector, "the massive entry of nonstate enterprises has led to a dramatic increase in competition, which is key to the efficacy of reform."[26]

Since the vast majority of the Chinese populace are peasants or rural residents (constituting one-seventh to one-sixth of the total world population), the foundation of the nation's entire command economy was shaken once market mechanisms were unleashed in the rural areas.

Opening to the Outside World

Another dramatic change is the external link and stimuli generated during China's decade-long opening toward the outside world. The dawn of China's opening was marked by special policies designated for Guangdong and Fujian Provinces in 1979 and the establishment of four Special Economic Zones (SEZs) in 1980. Since then, China's opening process has extended further to include not only the coastal areas but also the previously isolated border and inner regions. This has expanded the nation's opening in all dimensions.

The opening process has both altered China's isolation from the outside world and fundamentally transformed the country's formerly autarkic economy. With GATT probably the only remaining exception, China today enjoys full and active memberships in all the principal economic organizations worldwide (such as the World Bank and IMF) and in the Asian-Pacific Region (such as the Asian Development Bank and the Asian-Pacific Economic Conference). From 1978 to 1990, China's foreign trade quadrupled (from $20.64 billion to $115.44 billion) and its exports enjoyed a 6.37-fold increase (from $9.75 billion to $62.09 billion),[27] while the country's foreign exchange reserves reached a record high of $42.67 billion at the end of 1991.[28] During this period, China's total foreign trade and exports as a percentage of GNP increased from 9.9 percent to 31.4 percent and from 4.7 percent to 17.5 percent respectively,[29] even higher than in some industrialized countries.

The reform and economic opening have also brought a huge amount of foreign capital into China, along with equally needed management expertise and technologies. From 1979 to 1991, China introduced $121.47 billion in foreign funds through signed contracts or agreements, of which $79.63 billion was actually used.[30] China approved the establishment of 41,300 foreign-funded enterprises using some $51.4 billion, of which $22.95 billion was actually invested[31]--roughly equal to China's total investment in capital construction in 1989 and 1990.[32] By the end of 1991, 16,000 foreign-funded enterprise were already in operation, accounting for up to 5 percent of the nation's GNP and providing millions with employment.[33] When accompanied by the rapid growth of the country's overseas investment, foreign labor service, and international travel industry,[34] these developments demonstrate China's unprecedented integration into the global economy and its heavy reliance upon the world market. Moreover, China's adjustment of trade and monetary policies as well as improvement in its intellectual property rights--due to China's joining of international economic regimes and improving bilateral commercial ties with other countries--have all exerted a profound impact on the nation's institutionalization process.

The opening process has also led to an unprecedented interplay between Chinese localities and foreign entities. As observed in other countries, in an increasingly interdependent world, international trends strengthen the role of the localities, which are often more efficient mobilizers of resources and are better able to articulate particular interests seeking expression in the new environment.[35] For instance, with the central monopoly over foreign trade declining sharply, the number of companies allowed to conduct foreign trade mushroomed from 800 at the end of 1987 to more than 5,000 by the late 1990s. Since most of them are provincial or local companies over which the central government has little control, the center's already weakened foreign trade monopoly thus further shattered.[36] Finally, the emergence of what Robert Scalapino termed "NEAs" (natural economic areas)--to characterize the economic pairings between Guangdong Province and Hongkong, Fujian Province and Taiwan, Shandong and Liaoning Provinces with South Korea and Japan, and Northeastern and Northwestern China with the Republics of the former Soviet Union--have also stimulated the development of China's economy and the market mechanism on the one hand while strengthening the role of localities on the other.[37]

Dynamics of the Market Mechanism and Inter-Regional Competition

As a result of these changes, we have seen a domestic market mechanism swiftly developing in China.[38] Apart from the agricultural market mentioned earlier, statistics also show the number of China's state-allocated capital goods were reduced from 256 categories in 1978 to 24 in 1987, and to merely 17 in 1989.[39] Meanwhile, the industrial products covered by the state mandatory plan fell from about 40 percent of China's industrial gross output in 1984 to 17 percent in 1989.[40] By the end of 1991, less than 30 percent of the prices of all commodities and capital goods in China were decided by the state planning.[41]

As Karl Polanyi noted,[42] the most important effect of a market development lies in the fact that it provides an environment for domestic (particularly inter-regional) competition. A recent comparative study in Japan, Korea, Singapore, the United States, and six European countries found that domestic competition, with access to larger foreign markets and more regional competition, was a key to the global competitiveness of the successful industries in those countries.[43]

As China's various provinces and regions gain greater autonomous power to allocate resources and pursue alternative economic policies, "surrogate laboratories" are provided for institutional innovation and policy experimentation. Along with the changing property rights mentioned earlier that allow retained revenues, provincial leaders are increasingly sensitive about local interests and their own performance. Rapid development not only strengthens the economic power and political influence of the region, it also enhances the status and reputation of the local leaders. In this respect, it is illuminating to mention the earlier examples of former Sichuan Governor Zhao Zhiyang and former Anhui Governor Wan Li, as well as some later examples such as former Guangdong Governor Ye Xuanping, former Shanghai Mayor Zhu Rongji, and former Tianjin Mayor Li Ruihuan--all of whom were promoted to the central government after making economic achievements in their own region.

On the other hand, lower rates of output or a broadened gap in the living standard could exert enormous pressure (both from the center and within the region) on the leaders whose province (or region) are lagging behind. For instance, there is a sharp contrast between neighboring Henan and Shandong Provinces due to their disparate performances during the last decade. Throughout the 1980s, the annual growth rate of Henan Province's Total Social Output Value was consistently 2.5 percent less than that of Shandong, although the two are very similar in population size, natural resources, and original level of economic development.[44] The other example involves Hunan and Guangdong Provinces. Before reform there was little difference between the two in terms of economic development. Yet today the former's GNP accounts for only half of the latter's. Consequently, after waging a "Pig War" in 1985 and conducting a grain sanction against Guangdong in 1988, the leadership of Hunan finally decided in 1991 to revitalize its reform process by sending a "study delegation" to Guangdong and reinvigorating its cooled reform experiments.[45]

For scholars who argue that the decline of China's central planning has not led to a market economy, but rather has been replaced by a "smaller-sized command economy" centered on local bureaucracies, a typical example given is the situation in Shanghai. Until 1988, although only 18 percent of Shanghai's gross industrial output fell under the state mandatory plan in the wake of administrative devolution, in many industrial sectors--especially textiles, metallurgy, and some machine-building enterprises--production (including above-quota output), sales price, and the price of the raw materials were almost 100 percent planned by the municipality.[46] However, changes in the city since the late 1980s indicate that the earlier situation was only transitional.

The nationwide reform environment put Shanghai under growing financial pressure and introduced fierce competition from other provinces. During the five years from the mid- to late-1980s characterized by the city's "efficiency sliding," the realized profits of Shanghai's industries fell from more than 8 billion to a little more than 3 billion yuan.[47] Shanghai's leading position in the late 1970s in terms of GNP and gross output value of industry among Chinese provinces dropped to number 4 and 7 respectively in 1990.[48] This situation put great pressure both on the city's leadership and the rank and file. Various opinion surveys during the period show that more than 90 percent of the city employees felt "the only way out" was a more radical reform program.[49] Ultimately, the Shanghai authorities decided in early 1991 to push the city's state-owned industries into the market. The municipality cut its purchases from the textile industry by 50 percent and only supplied half the industry's raw materials.[50] Since September 1991, the city authorities have furthered reform efforts and decided to push the state-owned industries in the city out of the present standstill within three to five years.[51] Initiating a radical experiment in one tenth of the city's state-owned enterprises by dropping their mandatory production plans completely, these enterprises are now allowed to make independent decisions, even on such long taboo practices as stock-holding, dismissal of employees, demotion of managers, mergers, and bankruptcy.[52] Shanghai's experience is by no means exceptional, as similar situations have occurred in cities such as Xuzhou, which first tried reform experiments in the state-owned enterprises, Benxi, and China's capital city of Beijing.[53]

With regard to another major defect in China's economic reform criticized as "local protectionism", it has been argued that each of the country's 30 provinces, autonomous regions, and municipalities occupy "a separate sphere of influence," pursuing their own development without coordinating with each other or with the center. Operating according to the local interest, these regions of China have carried out various forms of protectionism, restricting sales of some raw materials to and importing certain commodities from other regions--including reported inter-provincial or inter-regional "wars" over silkworms, wool, tea, tobacco, coal, cotton, pigs, and grain.[54] As far as protective measures are concerned, local governments may issue lengthy regulations requiring numerous permits and "quality-control tests" or simply impose high taxes to exclude non-local commodities. They may also exact fines against local enterprises that buy and sell products without approval or instruct local banks to deny loans to those enterprises.[55] Thus, some scholars argue, contrary to domestic rationalization of resource flows and regional specialization, the above practices result in an "aristocratic economy": a fragmented domestic market ruled by various "dukes" and "princes".[56]

While decentralization in China has been accompanied by some tendencies toward regional monopolies and protectionism, it has, on the other hand, significantly promoted regional competition[57] and cooperation--both of which help shape the nation's domestic market. For instance, in Southern China, marketization has reached an estimated 90 percent in Guangdong and Hainan Provinces and 80 percent in Fujian Province. The commercialization of Guangdong's economy has reached such an extent that the province nowadays sells two-thirds of its industrial products to other provinces or abroad.[58] For Shanghai's market, which has boasted annual retail sales of more than 40 billion yuan in recent years, half the products were imported from other provinces or abroad.[59] In Jiangsu Province more than 70 percent of industrial raw materials and products are imported or sold outside the province's boundary. Jiangsu also has more than one hundred inter-provincial or inter-regional markets, with the top forty accounting for 100 million to a billion yuan annually.[60] The evidence indicates that the situation is similar in some inland provinces. For instance, the annual retail sales of social commodities in Wuhan (the capital city of inland Hubei Province) have experienced a three-fold increase since the mid-1980s (reaching 11.3 billion yuan in 1991), of which 6.78 billion or 60 percent came from other provinces.[61]

It is interesting to note that, since the mid-1980s, economic cooperation among the regions has also been flourishing. Taking the early form of bilateral "cooperation agreements" between localities,[62] today China has more than 100 inter-provincial or inter-regional multilateral organizations (or unions) of economic cooperation in such fields as trade, investment, finance, and science and technology.[63] These include the Southwest Economic Cooperative Region which was established in 1984 and currently involves the five provinces (or autonomous regions) of Sichuan, Yunnan, Guizhou, Guangxi, Xizang (Tibet), and the two municipalities of Chongqing and Chengdu.[64] Shanxi, Gansu, and Sichuan Economic Cooperative Region was established in 1986 and now involves 12 parties. The Nanjing Association for Regional Economic Coordination was established in 1986 and now includes 18 cities and prefectures in Jiangsu, Anhui, and Jiangxi Provinces. By mid-1991, the Nanjing Association alone had set up more than 70 "horizontal networks" and created commodity, material, finance, and science and technology markets, which in turn reached more than 5,000 agreements on cooperative projects, created a capital base of more than 8 billion yuan, and traded commodities worth more than 300 billion yuan.[65]

While still developing in an inter-provincial or inter-regional way and obviously far from the final shaping of a nationwide market, this regional competition and cooperation explains, to a large extent, why the so-called "smaller-sized command economy" and "local protectionism" have not constituted the mainstream in China's reform process.

A Major Force for New Reforms

Finally, with the localities' economic power strengthened, have localities become, as some people suggest, "the major barrier to further economic reforms," causing a state of "reform gridlock" in China? Judging by the behavior of provincial and local leaders in recent years (particularly after 1989), we argue that the localities are not only opposed to rolling back the reform process, but also constitute a major driving force moving economic reform forward.

Since the economic austerity program was imposed by the Chinese central government in September 1988, roughly three stages can be defined in the interaction between the center and the localities: (1) the recentralization period from September 1988 to early 1990; (2) the relaxation of the austerity program from early 1990 to late 1991,; and (3) since late 1991, the beginning of a new wave of reform.

The austerity program imposed by conservative Chinese forces in September 1988 and intensified after the 1989 Tiananmen event met great local resistance, particularly from the coastal areas. Mainly due to the pressures exerted by provincial leaders at the party Plenum and the subsequent economic working conferences in late 1989, previous reform principles such as central and local revenue sharing, foreign exchange retention schemes, and the factory contract responsibility system were reaffirmed afterwards.[66] Later, in the face of resistance from local governments and mounting economic problems, the center was compelled to retreat further from its controversial recentralization program.

In March 1990, China's State Planning Commission announced that the state would continue policies favorable toward rural industry such as tax cuts and access to bank loans, marking a significant policy turnabout by the center.[67] In the meantime, the Shanghai Pudong New Area was allowed by the central government to adopt policies granted to the SEZs, aiming to improve comprehensive development in the middle and lower reaches of the Yangtze River and thus signaling "a new stage" in China's opening up to the outside world.[68] Finally, in late 1990 and early 1991, the Party Central committee and China's State Council held two working conferences to "rectify deviations" in policies advocated by the conservative central leaders who were calling for "developing and strengthening a new collective economy" in rural areas.[69] In addition, "the planned recentralization of financial revenues was not achieved, and the central government's allocation of materials increased only slightly. One by one, the center abandoned the policies directed at recentralizing economic authority."[70]

It is not only the coastal areas that enthusiastically advocate the reform process, but, pressed by the broadened gap of regional development and lured by the achievements of the advanced regions, even the inland and border localities have been pushing the reform and opening process ahead. For instance, at a national conference of the heads of the nationalities affairs commissions in February 1989 (just months after the beginning of the economic austerity program), the central government proposed a series of new policies aimed at expediting the reform and opening up the nation's minority areas. It included a "dual opening" program of that allowed these areas to look in two directions simultaneously: south and east to the coastal areas and developed countries; west and north to neighboring countries across the Chinese border.[71] In January 1991, with the inland/border areas asking for competition on an equal footing and the coastal areas asking for further opening, the center further delegated authority over foreign trade to all localities and abolished all export subsidies.[72] By late 1991, under mounting pressure from both the localities advocating further economic reform[73] and the macro-economic environment, the center had to adjust and lean toward a more reform-oriented approach. By claiming that "China has dismissed planning and marketing as norms to distinguish between a socialist and a capitalist economy,"[74] even the conservative Chinese leaders now concur that "the pace of reform should be speeded up and the scale of reform should be expanded,"[75] an apparent departure from the previous official line that espoused "deepening of reform"--a codeword signifying Beijing's indecision over how to proceed.

China's paramount leader Deng Xiaoping's trip to the nation's coastal areas and his strong endorsement of speeding up market-oriented reforms in early 1992 has been further used by the local leaders to push harder for their reform programs, with a reform "hurricane" sweeping the whole country.[76] Economic experiments have been carried out in fields such as stock-holding, finance (including security market and foreign banking), taxes, social insurance system (including unemployment insurance), housing, and medical care.[77] These new developments in recent years indicate that the prediction of reform "gridlock" or "stalemate" was misguided.

From the above analysis, it is fair to say that the localities have not only become articulate representatives of subnational interests and strong advocates of further reform, but also finally emerged as an important force in the country capable of balancing the center with their economic power, political influence, and "legitimacy". The question then arises: do the profound economic changes that have occurred in China under the influence of the market mechanism imply that the role of the state can be ignored, or do they imply that the center should be further weakened through devolving even more power to the localities, as some scholars argue? We believe these questions deserve to be studied carefully in light of new findings in comparative studies and the reality in China.

Institutional Problems and Structural Instability

As indicated earlier, the relationship between the market and the state concerns a society's process of "institutionalization." In order to improve the allocation efficiency and reduce transaction costs, institutions are the public bodies through which the state discharges its most fundamental responsibilities such as maintaining law and order, investing in essential infrastructure, raising taxes to finance such activities, and so on. It is also a necessary process for the state to tackle the problems of political instability, fragile social consensus, and weak governance that are inevitably accompanied by a developing society. Moreover, the broad concept of "institutionalization" goes further, extending to "the conventions that govern the way people deal with each other: property rights, contracts, and norms of conduct," since "people's values and ideologies affect institutions, and these in turn affect the economy."[78] It is this issue of institutionalization that raises the major problems of China's further development, largely because of China's fragmented process of national policy-making and implementation, and ineffective monitoring and law-enforcement mechanisms.

I. Fragmented Process of National Policy-Making and Implementation

In this section, the problems of China's growing "social burdens" on farmers, the tax collection process, and the banking system will be analyzed to highlight the fragmented nature of China's national policy-making and implementation process.

Growing "Social Burdens" on Farmers

An illuminating case of China's mounting institutional problems is that of the increased "social burdens" on Chinese farmers, which are imposed mainly by government agencies at various levels and have become "an outstanding problem" both in the nation's administration of rural affairs and in its agricultural development.[79] According to a report by the Chinese Agriculture Ministry at the end of 1991, the per-capita contributions of rural residents to the village and township level authorities in 1990 was 1.7 times greater than in 1985, 11.6 percentage points higher than the growth rate of their income over the same period. The overwhelming "social burdens" have thus made the country's farming less profitable and have badly hurt farmers' enthusiasm for production. In some areas, frustrated Chinese farmers have gone so far as to refuse to sell grain to the government or to pay agricultural taxes. The problem has led to "most tensions" between farmers and local authorities and has "become so bad that its is now impossible to ignore the seriousness of farmers' conditions."[80]

To ease the pressure of the farmers' complaints, China's State Council issued five circulars on the issue during the period from 1978 to 1991. The fourth decree (1990) stipulated that farmers' financial responsibilities should be strictly limited to 5 percent of their per-capita income in the township of the previous year, although with some local modifications (approved by county-level authorities) the ceiling could be "raised to some reasonable extent" in some better-off areas. But this leeway has evidently been abused by all levels of government. Statistics from China's Ministry of Agriculture reveal that in 1990 farmers' per-capita expenditure on authorized items already accounted for 8 percent of their net income in 1989. Unauthorized collection of fees, random apportionment, and fines ate away another 3.1 percent. Thus every farmer actually lost 11.1 percent of his net income compared to the previous year. Still, these figures are conservative since there were many items beyond the purview of central government statistics. To curb the deteriorating situation, the Chinese State Council issued its fifth set of regulations concerning the issue in December 1991.

The problem, however, is not likely to be temporarily eased, let alone solved. Ironically, it is the unitary system and the gigantic central government itself that constitutes the core of the problem.

To begin with, given the sheer size of the country (with the size and population of many of its 30 provinces equal to that of a middle-sized countries in the world) and huge regional disparity, China is just "too large to govern uniformly and effectively from the capital."[81] Consequently, it is hard for the center "to apply any kind of regulation across-the-board."[82] Just as a former Chinese insider points out, "when a regulation finally could be applied to everybody, it became so general and vague that the content's language was not precise and any implementation control became difficult."[83] This process inevitably leaves room for local manipulation and abuse of power. As Chen Junsheng, a high-ranking State Counselor in China, noted in a recent *People's Daily* article: "The lower departments, in a bid to seek profit for themselves, use central directives as pretexts to raise funds." Constituting a "classical situation" of the behavior of officials at various levels, one Chinese observer notes that, when "lower-level officials are told to raise funds by higher bureaus, some of these guys can't stand seeing all the money go back to the top, so they just increase the tax on the peasants and pocket anything they make over their quota."[84]

Moreover, without clearly defined jurisdictions both at the center and between the center and localities, invasion of the policy-making process by the huge central bureaucracies makes the problem even worse. As the previously mentioned report by China's Agriculture Ministry reveals, by the end of 1991, 148 documents increasing regulations and adding to the farmers' economic burdens were in fact issued by 48 ministries and commissions of the nation's State Council.[85] It is thus not surprising that the nation's Agriculture Minister Liu Jiang admitted recently (and was quoted by the official *People's Daily*): "The root of the peasant's financial burden rests in the governmental departments which oversee rural areas."[86] People must wonder, if the central government cannot clean its own backyard, how can it be effective in regulating its huge and distant subordinates? Lacking moral authority in such "policy-making," as an old Chinese saying goes, "those below follow the example of those above."

Finally, despite the decade-long economic devolution and the increasing awareness of local interests, the Chinese political system remains highly centralized. All local officials are in fact still chosen by their direct superiors, with ultimate political power at the center (particularly with the Chinese Communist Party). For instance, the party's Central Organization Department is in charge of assignment, dismissal, and transfer of all officials both at the vice governor and provincial party standing committee level and above in China's 30 provinces.[87] Politically, local officials at various levels are still often characterized by their "upward accountability," rather than a sense of responsibility for their constituencies.

Not surprisingly, after Chinese farmers rioted and protested over taxes and inflation in Sichuan, Jilin, Tibet, and Henan provinces in early 1993, the Chinese central government had to make another urgent call to reduce the financial burden of the nations' farmers.[88]

Tax Collection

China's lack of an effective system of central taxation is seen by some as one of the major systemic weaknesses that the current regime inherited from the country's imperial past, especially from the late Qing Dynasty period of the nineteenth and early twentieth century).[89] Normally, China's fiscal system is unitary and highly centralized, which in principle means that the central government directs expenditure policy and determines all aspects of tax policy. All taxes, with few exceptions, are national-level central taxes that formally accrue to the central government, which then shares the revenue with provincial and lower-level governments. The central government also provides significant formal limits to local government autonomy: on the one hand, provincial governments cannot, in principle, redefine the legal tax base, nor may they vary the nominal tax rates; on the other hand, subnational governments have few legal revenue sources of their own.[90]

In most countries the taxes are collected by the central government and then allocated to lower-level governments. In China, however, they are collected by the local governments and "shared-up" to the higher (provincial and central) levels. In this regard, China differs from many other countries in that the central government collects very few of its own taxes. Rather, local governments, typically at the municipal and county level, collect most of the revenues aside from customs duties and selected excises.[91] Because the system gives local governments unusual responsibility for administering the fiscal system, and because of the inevitable central-local asymmetry of management information, the localities have great leeway in assessing and collecting taxes, and, therefore, they can and do give tax relief without seeking central approval.

As a result, a World Bank study found that in China "subnational governments can substantially alter the level and pattern of effective tax rates paid by enterprises."[92] Not surprisingly, this reliance on local tax collection also gives local governments substantial control over the revenues they collect. In 1989, the local governments' share of total national revenue was 62.50 percent, while China's provincial and local governments accounted for 63.65 percent of the total direct expenditures of the country.[93] The localities use this discretion to promote economic development and other interests in their own jurisdiction, even though the preferences granted sometimes do not conform with the objectives of the central government and seriously impair its revenue collection. When comparing China with other countries, the World Bank report concludes: "Only a few countries in the world can claim as great a degree of expenditure or revenue decentralization and none can claim this degree of decentralization in tax administration."[94] This taxation system, in addition to the annual financial negotiation between the center and each province that features "one on one" talks and no formal rules, is thus "increasingly incompatible with China's emerging market system."[95]

Banking System

In the early and mid-1980s, China conducted reforms of its banking system to strengthen the central banking authorities and to grant some autonomy to commercial banks in their credit decisions. While they aimed at improving both microeconomic efficiency and macroeconomic control, these efforts "ended up largely with disappointment."[96] One of the major reasons for the failure is the local governments' effective control of the banks within their jurisdictions--wielding power over the careers and well-beings of bank directors and their families. Under the close supervision of local governments, banks in the localities have had limited scope for independent decision-making and are careful to heed the former's priorities. Thus, "giving banks autonomy actually means giving control of financial resources to local governments."[97] Acting in the interests of the local bureaucrats is often more important than state priorities or even the bank's own profits. This inevitably leads to excessive expansions of both local investment and consumption, over which the center has little control. It, in turn, has resulted in a situation in which the Chinese central government has frequently lost its grip over the nation's macroeconomic control.

The above institutional problems have contributed to phenomenal structural inflation in China. Because the center lacks control over revenue and bank loans, the two principle economic levers it must rely upon, the "expanding impulse" and "collective action"[98] by the local governments, enterprises, and common people to maximize consumption and investment inevitably get out of the control of the central government. Local credit expansion and the national budget deficit force the central government to pursue a loose monetary policy, which, in turn, further exacerbates the imbalances between aggregate demand and supply and the repeated symptoms of structural inflation. This is one of the fundamental reasons why, in just a decade-long reform period, China has experienced a repetitive cycle (although to different degrees) of overheated growth followed by an austerity program in the early, middle, and late 1980s, with the last stage leading directly to the national tragedy of 1989. Despite the economic retrenchment that took place between 1988 and 1991, there is no sign that the Chinese economy is any less under the shadow of this vicious cycle now. On the contrary, all signs show just the opposite.

In 1992, China's economy grew 12.8 percent. Worried about overheating, Beijing set more cautious targets in early 1993 of about 9 percent annual growth and about a 6 percent inflation rate. But the economic expansion continues to outpace the center's efforts to slow it down. National growth has remained at 13-14 percent through the first half of the year, with total output of rural industries from January to May of 1993 rising a shocking 72 percent over the same period last year. Frenzied business and investment have led to a boom in real estate development, local industrial zones, large luxury buildings, over-extended credit, and soaring prices that threaten to overwhelm China's underdeveloped infrastructural capacity. Among them, fixed asset investment soared a whopping 70.7 percent in the first three months of 1993, with more than three-quarters invested by local administrations--signaling both the expanded local autonomy and Beijing's inability to rein in provincial officials. The failure to restrict capital construction projects is soaking up credit and raw materials, contributing to supply shortages, transport bottlenecks, and demand-fueled increases in production costs.[99]

The expansion came with an average inflation rate in 35 major cities of 17 percent in mid-1993. This was the highest official rate since the 18.6 percent recorded in 1988--when price hikes ignited panic buying in cities and the government was forced to clamp down with an austerity program, which was followed by unprecedented social unrest. Under mounting pressure, the Chinese leadership in mid-1993 resorted to strict administrative measures to deal with the country's seriously overheating economy,[100] increasing the likelihood that the "boom-bust" cycle may repeat itself again.

II. Ineffective Monitoring and Law Enforcement Mechanisms

China's systemic flaws, described above, are reinforced by another organizational problem, related to the nation's largely ineffective monitoring and law enforcement mechanisms.

In mid-1993, as carried by state-run media, the Chinese central government publicly assailed local officials for mishandling market reforms and abusing fiscal powers, leading to economic anarchy.[101] The latest notice was issued by the Communist Party's Central Commission for Discipline Inspection and the State Council's Supervision Ministry, both watchdog agencies that are supposed to police the activities of Chinese officials at various levels. This move was designed to calm public concern over the nation's growing economic problems but was also a clear admission by the top leadership of its failure to rein in localities who increasingly ignore the center.

Demanding that "party and government officials at all levels should strictly abide by and execute" national economic directives, Chinese central authorities warn in their latest move that "those who violate discipline will be investigated and punished." But, as the following examination reveals, China's ineffective monitoring and law enforcement mechanisms in fact intensify the nation's problem.

Normally, China's monitoring system that supervises the performance of China's provincial and local bureaucracies consists of three separate channels: the legal, the administrative, and the Communist Party supervising systems. While the party system actually has the final authority and the administrative system is another example of bureaucratic duplication, the legal monitoring agencies in localities are in fact under "dual leadership"--subordinate not only to their superior judicial agencies but, more importantly, to the administrative organ at the same level they are supposed to monitor. It is therefore not surprising, when local government officials themselves are a part of or direct beneficiaries of policy deviations, that the monitoring system "breaks down rather easily."[102]

For the legal officials executing local monitoring functions, there are two major constraints leading to their dependence on the administrative organs at the same level. First of all, they owe their positions to the local leaders. For instance, although officials of the local courts and procurators are appointed by their superior agencies, they are in fact "recommended and nominated" by the personnel office of the Party Committee of the same locality, with the appointment by their superior office "only a procedure."[103] Second, since legal officials in localities depend heavily on local bureaucrats for their own welfare and family benefits (such as employment, housing, and mobility), they are extremely vulnerable to the demands and pressures imposed by the latter.

China's phenomenal "triangular debt problem" (the mounting pile of overdue inter-company debts) can be used as an illuminating example of the severe consequences of China's ineffective monitoring and law enforcement mechanisms. Termed by the nation's business circle "a cancer to the economy," the debt problem has mainly stemmed from the inefficiency of the Chinese state-owned sector. In recent years, chronic losses by about 40 percent of state-owned enterprises have reduced the central government's revenue by one third annually, far more than what is spent on either the nation's military or education.[104] While the debts were less than 5 billion yuan in the early 1980s,[105] by 1990 the country's banking system had to inject 50 billion yuan into enterprises as special loans for debt-paying, which reportedly eased 160 billion yuan in triangular debts. In the first half of 1991, however, such debts again shot to a record high of 250 billion yuan.[106] The situation finally reached such an extreme that in late 1991 the Chinese central government launched an all-out national campaign to curb the deteriorating problem.

"Everyone is trying to conceal problems from everyone else," China's monitoring system failed to detect the real situation in the first place. Factory managers hide problems from Government officials, and managers and local officials sometimes join together to hide problems from their superiors or foreigners. As a result, some revelations by Chinese newspapers show that the problem may be even worse than originally believed. For instance, an investigation in 1991 of the fiscal accounts of 257 enterprises in nine provinces and cities discovered that by overstating earnings or under-reporting losses, three fourths of the companies (202) had accumulated "hidden losses" of $257 million over the last four years, nearly twice the amount of losses they officially reported.[107]

Moreover, the institutional flaws of law enforcement have done little to help improve the situation; there is simply no legal framework to enforce loan repayment. With debts mounting and a growing number of companies refusing to pay on their loans, collecting debts has become one of the biggest headaches among company managers. Without legal protection for lenders and punishment of those debtors who simply refuse to pay back their loans, the awesome situation is vividly described by two popular sayings among Chinese business circles: "lending money is like spilling water on the floor," and "those who owe money are bold and self-assured, while those who want repayment must crawl on their knees and beg."[108]

We discussed above the impact of both the decade-long progress of China's economic reform and China's institutional weaknesses. Chinese experiences demonstrate once again what has happened in various other countries: while markets are an extremely important force for a nation's economic development, a "self-regulating market" implies another "stark utopia," as Karl Polanyi argued. Because, a "self-regulating market" demands nothing less than "the institutional separation of society" into economic and other spheres--such a society "could not exist for any length of time without annihilating the human and natural substance of society."[109] Therefore, institutions (hence the state) and markets must "grow up together."

However, by hurting farmers' productive enthusiasm, shattering macroeconomic foundations, and, most of all, weakening the state capacity, China's institutional problems hinder the prospect of a unified domestic market and, in turn, endanger the nation's future. Moreover, if the troubling judicial and legal problems exposed by the "triangular debt issue" are not dealt with appropriately, the society's economic activities can be paralyzed. However, without a sound system of business credibility, an economic system can hardly be sustained. Just like the editor-in-chief of a journal in Shanghai on debt problems observed, "the system of credit is breaking down. People no longer respect the need for credit ..."[110] It is hard to imagine that such behavior norm would not adversely affect economic and social development in the country. With the rapid advancement of the market mechanism on the one hand, and the intensifying institutional problems on the other, China today is facing a real danger of development-generated structural instability.

"Thinking Federal"

Based upon the consequences and current status of the decade-long reform of China's central-local relations, two possible future scenarios can be spelled out. First, for a period of time, the status quo of China's central-local relationship will be maintained, accompanied by a gradual trend toward further economic and political disintegration. As central authorities are increasingly weakened, the "endless cycle of centralization, decentralization, and recentralization" is not likely to continue.[111] On the one hand, it will be extremely hard for the center to reverse the decade-long reform process, particularly after its failed trial in 1988-1990. On the other hand, even if recentralization is forcefully carried out, it would be more likely than not to intensify the various problems faced by the nation today. As a result, either a forced recentralization will lead to an open central-local conflict, or the center will find it has little choice but to finally abandon attempts at recentralization.

Under the second scenario, the current situation will deteriorate dramatically, particularly when triggered by either a succession transition or other domestic crisis. It is worth noting that China today faces growing ethnic problems between the center and the border minority regions, particularly in Tibet, Xinjiang, and Inner Mongolia. The tensions stem both from ethnic (racial, linguistic, religious, and cultural) sources and political/economic factors. By taking advantage of the further weakening of the center and the growing non-ethnic central-local frictions (i.e. among the majority Han people), the ethnic central-local problem may get out of control. This prospect is looming larger due to the dismantling of the former Soviet Union and the creation of the newly independent ethnic Republics in Central Asia and Mongolia. Finally, the unfolding of central-local relations on the mainland will also influence China's resumption of sovereignty over Hong Kong and the future of mainland-Taiwan relations.

To take the above scenarios one step further and view China's situation from the perspective of long-term social development, the outlook is even more troublesome. Today, as a country in the process of modernization and social transformation, China has to deal with both the systemic failure of state socialism and the problems commonly faced by other developing countries. Together, they have significantly weakened China's central authority (and hence the state capacity) at a time when economic development and political modernization all demand, one way or the other, the strengthening of both based upon a revitalized ruling legitimacy. We therefore argue that it would be premature to simply propose that the role of the state be ignored and the center be further weakened through devolving even more power to the localities. China's dilemmas are to a large extent the outcome of the nation's centralized and unitary system. They are not likely to be dealt with appropriately, let alone solved, within the framework of the current system and the traditional ways of thinking (such as the continuation of the decentralization and recentralization cycle). Nor is a positive development likely to occur simply by chance. While certainly dictating a much broader systemic innovation, such a development demands new ways of thinking, among them a new perspective on the relationship between the center and localities.

With regard to the central-local relationship in today's world, the major comparison with a unitary system is the federal one. Interestingly, it is in this regard that China once again poses a "distinctiveness" issue, as probably the only big country--with sizable territory, a large population, and social complexity (race, religion, language, and cultural)--that still adheres to a unitary system. As a matter of fact, given the dual pressures throughout the world for larger political units capable of fostering economic development and improving security on the one hand, and for small political units more sensitive to their constituents and capable of expressing local interests on the other, it is not surprising that the federal solution is even more appealing today.[112] Post-War history has witnessed a "proliferation of federal experiments" in Asia, Europe, Africa, and Latin America.[113] According to Daniel J. Elazar, of the more than 160 politically sovereign states now in existence, more than one-third are engaged in formal arrangements using federal principles in some way within their boundaries or in partnership with other polities.[114]

Federalism stands for organizing a polity on a "more democratic basis" than that of the modern nation-state. The latter emerged in Europe in the sixteenth-century based upon the notion that sovereignty lies with the state and is exclusive: a national government can claim to be sovereign and hence have unlimited, residual, and final powers. It thus inevitably stands in principled opposition to the diffusion of any political power and to the accommodation of diversity through overlapping jurisdictions. Rather than clinging to the old European view of the sovereign state, federalism maintains "sovereignty to be vested in the people." This fundamental notion of popular sovereignty maintains that "the consent of the governed is the only legitimate basis" for any government. The various units of government--whether federal, state, or local--therefore could exercise only those powers explicitly delegated to them. Moreover, in today's interdependent "global village," all states are, economically and politically, dependent upon each other. It is in these respects that federalism provides an alternative method of coping with the problems of the modern nation-state.[115] Based upon the notion of popular sovereignty, the simplest possible concept of a federalist system can thus be termed "self-rule plus shared rule."[116] The existence of more than one government over the same territory has become an increasingly common phenomenon. Today, more and more states have accepted this concept in exchange for other desired advantages (for instance, economic development and social justice). The transformation from a unitary system to a federalist one in European countries such as Spain and Belgium are good examples. The European Community is another prominent example of how the acceptance of limitations on state sovereignty in certain spheres can be traded for greater benefits in economic and social domains. Finally, it is worth noting that, after a decade-long reform process, some advanced regions of China have also started to ask for the power of local legislation to promote political and legal institutionalization, such as Shenzhen municipality has proposed since early 1992.[117] All of these developments demonstrate that the classic center-periphery model of statehood is increasingly being challenged by the new model, which views the national polity as a matrix of overlapping and interlocking units, powers, and relationships.[118]

Specifically, a federal system is first and foremost a "*constitutional* division of powers" between the central (or national) government and the constituent (provincial or state) governments, with each given substantial yet separate functions based on a constitution. Different from both unitary and confederate polities, in a constitutional framework of federalism, neither the constituents nor the central government receives its powers from the other; rather, both derive them from a common source--a *constitution*. Moreover, instead of an ordinary process of administration or legislation, this federal distribution of power can only be changed by a constitutionally regulated procedure. Indeed, for the sake of political stability, most federalist countries have made this kind of change extremely difficult. Finally, both levels of government operate through their own agents and exercise power directly over their citizens.[119] Based upon the above foundation, the federal and local governments in a federalist polity will not only have the ruling legitimacy granted by their relative constituencies, but can also act within a more clearly defined jurisdiction, which ultimately will be more stable and efficient than China's current unitary system, characterized by the rule of man.

To apply federal principles to China's situation requires the notion of "thinking federal"--that is, rather than being obsessed with a monistic and centralist perspective, one should be open to both the ideas and norms of constitutionalism, republicanism, and power sharing between the center and the localities, which are essential to federalism.[120] Compared with federal principles, the prevalent way of Chinese thinking since 1949 has been a mentality of "*dayitong*" (a grand, unitary, and centralized China), with its roots inherited from the nation's historical legacy.[121] Moreover, the Chinese leaders' way of thinking also demonstrates that the issue of central-local relations inevitably involves a larger question about the most basic political structures of the country.[122]

Just like there is no one "obvious and obviously best democratic model," the terms "federalism" and "federal arrangements" suggest that there is more than one way to apply federal principles. In other words, using federal principles does not necessarily mean adopting a specific federal system as it exists in any federal state. As a matter of fact, the essence of federalism is not to be found "in a particular set of institutions" but rather "in the institutionalization of particular relationships among the participants in political life."[123] Judging by the federal experiences in various countries, as long as the proper relationships are created, a wide variety of political structures can be developed that are consistent with federal principles.

China might need "the will to federate" since its long political culture does not favor the notion. Yet, as happened in some other countries, the process may still be stimulated by a "particular situation" which makes the introduction of federal arrangements "the best and most acceptable solution."[124] As Arend Lijphart argued, political modernization does not just mean a transition to democracy; in practice, it also means a transition to a particular form of institutionalization.[125] Consequently, people have to make important choices among institutional alternatives of a new polity, which is by no means an easy job. But it is of crucial importance to consider and evaluate all of the available options at the outset. This is because the success of the process depends heavily on the *kind* of democratic institutionalization that is adopted, and also because once a new constitutional framework and a set of basic institutions are in place, they are hard to change.[126]

To conclude, a "historical compromise" between the center and localities in China characterized by "thinking federal" may offer a historic "window of opportunity" for the nation. Grasping this opportunity will contribute to China's further economic development, political modernization, and the process of national integration.

Notes

1. In this chapter, while it mainly means provincial, "local" is also alternatively used to refer to both provincial and sub-provincial governmental and non-governmental entities.

2. Based on China's distinctive political and economic systems, historical legacy, and cultural background, it is often argued that a comparative study of political economy between China and other countries is difficult, if even possible. "Comparative analyses across national economic systems are very difficult because of the many cultural and historical differences among people."--see Thomas R. Dye, "Economic Growth and Reform in China's Provinces, Municipalities, and Regions," in James A. Dorn & Wang Xi, ed., *Economic Reform in China: Problems and Prospects* (Chicago: The University of Chicago Press, 1990), pp. 223-238. Yet, it is our view that some general comparison of the central-local relations between China and other countries can at least provide a frame of

reference and thus shed light on China's current situation. We further argue that, while one should not be blind to China's distinctiveness, apprehending the trend(s) of other countries' central-local relations and their experiences in coping with related problems will undoubtedly be beneficial for China.

3. The viewpoints about the relationship between market and state are generally borrowed from World Bank's *World Development Report 1991: The Challenge of Development*, (World Bank and Oxford University Press, 1992), pp. 1-2, and p. 134.

4. Li Xianglu, "Why the Guiding Principle of 'Fenquan Rangli' is Correct," *Zhishi Fenzhi* (The Chinese Intellectual), Vol. 6, No. 1, Spring 1990, pp. 3-6; Wang Runsheng, "Zhongyuan Delu Buyouren: Growth and Decline of the Relative Power of the Center and Localities," *Mingzhu Zhongguo* (Democratic China), No. 8, February 1992, pp. 57-59.

5. Li Xianglu, ibid.; see also Zhang Xin, "On Regional Economic Autonomy" (I) and (II), *Zhishi Fenzhi* (The Chinese Intellectual), Vol. 6, No. 3, Spring 1991, pp. 43-47, and Yang Xiaokai, "Lessons from the Reforms of China's Economic System," *Papers of the Center for Modern China*, No. 1, November 1990, pp. 23-40.

6. Wang Shaoguang, "Building a Strong Democratic State: On Regime Type and State Capacity," *Papers of the Center for Modern China*, No. 4, February 1991, pp. 1-36, see also chapter 4 in this volume; Chen Kang, "The Failure of Recentralization in China: Interplay Among Enterprises, Local Governments, and the Center," in Arye L. Hillman ed., *Markets and Politicians: Politicized Economic Choice*, (Holland: Kluwer Academic Publishers, 1991), pp. 109-229; and Huang Yasheng, "Web of Interests and Patterns of Behavior of Chinese Local Economic Bureaucracies and Enterprises During Reform," *China Quarterly*, September 1990, pp. 431-458.

7. Chen Kang, "The Failure of Recentralization in China," op.cit.

8. Christine P.W. Wong, "Between Plan and Market: The role of the Local Sector in Post-Mao China." *Journal of Comparative Economics*, Vol. 11, 1987, pp. 385-398; also Yu Bing, "China in 1989: A Distorted Authoritarian State in Crisis," in Jia Hao, ed. *The Democracy Movement of 1989 and China's Future*, (Washington, D.C.: The Washington Center for China Studies, 1990), pp. 27-45.

9. Huang Yasheng, "Web of Interests"; see also Chen Kang, "The Failure of Recentralization in China," op. cit.

10. Shen Liren and Dai Yuanchen, "Formation, Defect and Origins of the Economy Divided by Dukes or Princes under the Emperor in China," *Jingji Yanjiu* (Economic Research), No. 3, 1990.

11. Wang Shaoguang, "Building a Strong Democratic State," op. cit.

12. David M. Lampton, "China's Biggest Problem: Gridlock, Not Revolution," in Study Papers by the Joint Economic Committee of the Congress of the United States, Vol. 1, April 1991, *China's Economic Dilemmas in the 1990s: The Problems of Reforms, Modernization, and Interdependence* (Washington, D.C.: U.S. Government Printing Office, 1991), pp. 65-69; also Huang Yasheng, "Web of Interests," op.cit., pp. 431-32 and 457; and Chen Kang, "The Failure of Recentralization in China," op.cit. p. 227.

13. Jia Hao and Lin Zhimin, "Reforms and the State Capacity:The Changing Central-Local Relations in China (Introduction)," in *Political Science and Internation-*

al Relations, journal of the Chinese Scholars of Political Science and International Science, Inc., April 1992, p. 14; see also the Introduction to this volume.

14. Chen Kang, "Economic Reform and Collective Action in China," *China Report* (The Washington Center for China Studies), Vol. 3, No. 3, May 1991, p. 11.

15. Shi Zhengfu, "Why Economic Reforms Failed Everywhere but China--A Public Choice Perspective," manuscript, pp. 28-29. It is worth noting that the specification and enforcement of property rights in China is different from that of other countries. In the Chinese situation, particularly during the reform era, the right of using and transferring properties are often separated; see Yang Xiaokai, Wang Jianguo, and Ian Wills, "The Impact of Property Right Changes on the Commercialization and Productivity in Rural China," *Papers of the Center For Modern China*, Vol.3, No.1, March 1992, pp. 1-40; see also S. Cheung, "The Contractual Nature of the Firm," *Journal of Law and Economics*, Vol. 26, No. 1, pp. 1-21, April 1983.

16. See also Luo Xiaopeng's chapter in this volume.

17. Yang Xiaokai, et.al., "The Impact of Property Right Changes," op. cit.

18. Li Ping, "Price Reform: The Progressive Way," *Beijing Review*, May 4-10, 1992, pp. 18-21, Table (p. 21).

19. New China News Agency, February 1, 1992, see *Shijie Ribao* (World Journal), Feb. 9, 1992, p. 6.

20. On differences in reform course between China and other socialist countries, see Du Rensheng's comments of June 1, 1992, *Shijie Rebao* (the World Journal), June 3, 1992, p. 10; also Luo Xiaopeng's chapter in this volume.

21. During the 1979-1990 period, agricultural gross output increased 6.1 percent annually and the average annual increase in per capita consumption rose 6.4 percent; see Chinese National Statistical Bureau, ZHONGGUO TONGJI NIANJIAN (Statistical Yearbook of China, 1991), (Beijing: Chinese Statistical Press), p. 21, Table 2-3.

22. Ibid., p. 377, Table 9-55 and 9-56.

23. ZHONGGUO TONGJI NIANJIAN, op. cit., p. 378, Table 9-57; in 1991, for the first time the output value of township and village industry exceeded 1,000 billion yuan (US$189 billion); see "China Enters 1992 with More Confidence," *Beijing Review*, January 13-19, 1992, p. 7.

24. *People's Daily*, Overseas ed., February 10, 1992, pp. 1, 3.

25. The output of TVEs, as a percentage of China's GNP, increased from 14.6 percent in 1980 to 47.8 percent in 1990; see ZHONGGUO TONGJI NIANJIAN, op. cit., p. 18, Table 2-2, and p. 378, Table 9-57.

26. Chen Kang, "Economic Reform," op.cit., p. 12

27. ZHONGGUO TONGJI NIANJIAN, op.cit.

28. *People's Daily*, April 21, 1992, p. 1.

29. ZHONGGUO TONGJI NIANJIAN, op.cit., p. 20, Table 2-2, and p. 615, Table 15-1.

30. *People's Daily*, April 21, 1992, p. 1.

31. Dai Yannian, "Speed Up Reform, Open the Doors Wider," *Beijing Review*, March 9-15, 1992, pp. 7-9.

32. *Zhongguo Xinwen* (China News), "Open Policy Brings Achievements," see *Beijing Review*, December 30, 1991-January 5, 1992, p. 27.

33. *People's Daily,* Overseas ed., December 20, 1991, p. 1.

34. From 1979 to 1991, China approved 1,008 enterprises investing overseas, in the form of solely Chinese-owned ventures, joint ventures, or cooperatives. Among them more than 800 of them are in operation, with exported overseas labor totalling 500,000. See *People's Daily,* Overseas ed., April 10, 1992, p. 1. In 1991 China also hosted 4.7 million foreign travellers and earned $ 2.8 billion from the travel industry, *People's Daily,* Overseas ed., January 17, 1992, p. 8.

35. Daniel J. Elazar, *Exploring Federalism* (Tuscaloosa: The University of Alabama Press, 1987).

36. See Zhang Amei and Zou Gang's chapter in this volume.

37. See also *People's Daily,* Overseas ed., February 19, 1992, p. 1.

38. Li Rongxia, "Economic Rectification Meets Its Goals," *Beijing Review,* January 6-12, 1992.

39. Y. Zhang, "Four Major Achievements in the Ten-Year Economic Reforms," *People's Daily,* Overseas ed., October 4, 1988; also *Jingji Ribao* (Economic Daily), October 16, 1989.

40. Dai Yannian, "Speed Up Reform," op. cit.

41. Li Peng, "Chinese Economy in the 1990s," *People's Daily,* Overseas ed., February 1, 1992, p. 4.

42. Karl Polanyi, *The Great Transformation: The Political and Economic Origins of Our Time* (Boston: Beacon Press, 1944), p. 60.

43. Michael E. Porter, *The Competitive Advantage of Nations* (New York: Free Press, 1990).

44. *People's Daily,* Overseas ed., December 31, 1991, p. 3.

45. Ibid.

46. Dong Funai, "The Reform of Economic Mechanism and the Reform of Ownership," *Jingji Yanjiu* (Economic Research), No. 7, 1988; also Sheryl WuDunn, "As China's Economy Thrives, the Public Sector Flounders," *The New York Times,* December 18, 1991, pp. A1, A14.

47. *People's Daily,* Overseas ed., February 17, 1992, p. 3.

48. For 1990 figures, see *People's Daily,* Overseas ed., January 23, 1992, p. 1.

49. *People's Daily,* Overseas ed., February 17, 1992, p. 3.

50. Ibid.

51. *People's Daily,* Overseas ed., February 17, 1992, p. 3; see also "Reforms Revive Big State Firms," *Beijing Review,* January 13-19, 1992, pp. 16-17.

52. *People's Daily,* Overseas ed., January 29, 1992, p. 3; *Economic News,* see "Reforms Revive Big State Firms," *Beijing Review,* January 13-19, 1992, pp. 16-17; also *People's Daily,* Overseas ed., February 17, 1992, p. 3.

53. As of early 1992, 229 large or medium-sized state-owned enterprises in Beijing entered the new wave of reform experiments, accounting for 66 percent of all large or medium-sized state-owned enterprises in the city. See *People's Daily,* Overseas ed., February 18, 1992, p. 1.

54. Chen Kang, "The Failure of Recentralization," op. cit.

55. Lena H. Sun, "Economic Guerrilla Warfare Thriving in China," *The Washington Post,* November 7, 1990, pp. A10, A11.

56. Shen Liren and Dai Yuanchen, "Formation, Defect, and Origins," op. cit.

57. Examples include "Guangdong Cookie Dominating Shanghai," and "Kaige yinxiang Lost Hegemony", which reported that "Kaige" car radio made in Shanghai, once dominant nationwide, only accounted for 28 percent of 1992 orders of the "Santana" automobile factory also in Shanghai. See *People's Daily*, Overseas ed., March 9, 1992, p. 3.

58. *People's Daily*, Overseas ed., May 30, 1992, p. 1; and *Shijie Ribao* (World Journal), January 9, 1992, p. 10.

59. *People's Daily*, Overseas ed., April 21, 1992, p. 1.

60. *Shijie Ribao* (World Journal), March 11, 1992, p. 10.

61. *People's Daily*, Overseas ed., May 9, 1992, p. 1.

62. See Zhang Amei and Zou Gang's chapter in this volume.

63. *Shijie Ribao* (World Journal), May 9, 1991, p. 10.

64. *Shijie Ribao* (World Journal), Sept.6, 1991, p. 10.

65. *Shijie Ribao* (World Journal), May 9, 1991, p. 10.

66. Huang Yasheng, "Web of Interests," op. cit.

67. In mid-1989, the Chinese central government adopted policy changes which apparently discriminated against TVE's in favor of state-owned firms. No new bank loans were allowed to be extended to TVE's and zero growth in total lending was imposed, while central control over materials allocation was increased. See Chen Kang, "Economic Reform," *China Report* (The Washington Center for China Studies), Vol. 3, November 3, May 1992, p. 12, originally published in *Jingji Ribao* (Economic Daily), November 6, 1989, and *Zhongguo Ribao* (China Daily), March 17, 1990.

68. Li Rongxia, "Economic Rectification Meets Its Goals," *Beijing Review*, January 6-12, 1992, pp. 16-22.

69. Wen Tiejun, "Organizational Cost and Institution-Building--A Survey Report on Laixi County (Shandong Province)"; paper presented to CSPSIS 6th Annual Conference (San Diego), August 1991.

70. Chen Kang, "The Failure of Recentralization," op. cit.

71. Lu Yun, "Expediting Development in Minority Areas," *Beijing Review*, March 27, 1989, p. 7.

72. China's foreign trade companies must now act on their own, compete on an equal footing, and assume sole responsibility for their profits and losses. See *People's Daily*, Overseas ed., December 23, 1991, p. 3; see also Wang Maolin (Party Secretary of Shanxi Province), "Actively Explore Opening Policy Suited to the Characteristics of the Inland Provinces," *People's Daily*, Overseas ed., December 27, 1991, p. 2.

73. *Zhongyang Ribao* (Central Daily), January 5, 1992, p. 4.

74. "Markets Creation: A New Wave," *Beijing Review*, Dec. 2-8, 1991, p. 7.

75. Quoted from Li Peng, Reuter, January 11, 1992, see *China News Digest* (News Global), January 14, 1992.

76. *South China Morning Post*, May 7, 1992.

77. Li Rongxia, "Economic Rectification Meets Its Goals," *Beijing Review*, January 6-12, 1992, pp. 16-22; also *People's Daily*, Overseas ed., January 11, 1992, p. 1; *People's Daily*, Overseas ed., January 31, 1992, p. 3.

78. World Bank, *World Development Report 1991*, op. cit., p. 134.

79. As recently disclosed in China's official *Zhongguo Ribao* (China Daily) and further reported in "New Rules Protect Farmers' Income," *Beijing Review*, January 13-19, 1992, pp. 37-38.

80. Ibid.

81. Kenneth Lieberthal, "The Dynamics of Internal Politics," in Study Papers by the Joint Economic Committee of the Congress of the United States, Vol. 1, April 1991, *China's Economic Dilemmas in the 1990s: The Problems of Reforms, Modernization, and Interdependence* (Washington: U.S. Government Printing Office), pp. 15-28.

82. Zhou Qiren, "Rural Development and Market Economy: A review of the Ten-year Reform," *A Changing China* (A Publication Sponsored by the North American Coalition for Chinese Democracy), Vol. 1, No. 2, Spring 1991, pp. 3-6.

83. Ibid.

84. Japan Economic Newswire, June 21, 1993.

85. The practical figure would probably be doubled if one includes also those documents created by various local authorities. See also footnote 79.

86. Japan Economic Newswire, June 21, 1993.

87. Yan Huai, "A Survey of Political Organization in China," *China Report*, August 1991, Vol. 2, No. 4, by the Washington Center for China Studies, pp. 1-36.

88. Japan Economic Newswire, June 21, 1993.

89. Kenneth Lieberthal, "The Dynamics of Internal Politics," op. cit. p. 17. "... the Qing dynasty in its later years lacked an effective system of central taxation. It depended for revenues on a foreign-administered customs apparatus [this has been changed] and on a domestic tax farming system. The PRC as of 1990 still does not directly collect central taxes from individuals and units. Instead it farms out tax collection to the country's 30 provinces and autonomous regions and negotiates revenue agreements with each of them."

90. *China: Revenue Mobilization and Tax Policy* (A World Bank Country Report), 1990, p. 78 and Table 3.2 on p. 79. For instance, from 1980 to 1985, purely local taxes in China ranged from only 11.8 percent to 19.0 percent of the expenditures of the localities.

91. It was calculated by the World Bank in *China: Revenue Mobilization and Tax Policy* (1990) that China's municipal and county government tax bureaus directly assess and collect about 70 percent of all taxes. Op. cit., p. 80.

92. Yan Huai, "Survey of Political Organization," op. cit.

93. World Bank, *China: Revenue Mobilization and Tax Policy*. Op. cit., calculated from Table 6-12, p. 221.

94. Ibid., p. 80, footnote 6:"The comparable ratios for the United States--which is a decentralized fiscal system by world standards--are 43 percent of taxes collected and 42 percent of expenditures made by state and local governments." Originally from Roy Bahl, "The Design of Intergovernmental Transfers in Industrialized Countries," *Public Budgeting and Finance*, Winter 1986, Vol. 6, No. 4, pp. 3-22.

95. World Bank, *China: Revenue Mobilization and Tax Policy*. Op. cit., p. 21.

96. Zhou Xiaochuan and Zhu Li, "China's Banking System: Current Status, Perspective on Reform," see Bruce Reynolds (ed.), *Chinese Economic Reform* (Boston: Press, 1988), pp. 116-17.

97. Chen Kang, "The Failure of Recentralization," op. cit., p. 215.
98. Chen Kang, "Economic Reform," op. cit.
99. UPI, April 19, June 15, and June 21, 1993.
100. UPI, June 17, 1993.
101. UPI, June 22, 1993.
102. Huang Yasheng, "Web of Interests," op. cit., p. 444.
103. Zhang Yi, "Tudi He Tuhuangdi" (Land and the Local Emperor), *Zhongguo Zuojia* (Chinese Writer), 1987 (14) pp. 73-100; see also Zhou Xueguang, "Bringing the Missing Link Back in: Local Bureaucracy in China's Political Dynamics," *Revue Europeenne des sciences sociales,* Tome XXVII, 1989, No. 84, pp. 169-189.
104. To bail out those money-losing enterprises, government subsidies rose from $8.4 billion in 1988 to $10.9 billion in 1990.
105. *Zhongyang Ribao* (Central Daily News), January 8, 1992, p. 4.
106. *Zhongyang Ribao* (Central Daily News), April 18, 1992, p. 4.
107. Reported in early December 1991 in the official *People's Daily.* See also Sheryl WuDunn, "As China's Economy Thrives, the Public Sector Flounders," *The New York Times,* December 18, 1991, pp. A1, A14.
108. Ibid.
109. Karl Polanyi, *The Great Transformation,* op. cit.
110. Sheryl WuDunn, "As China's Economy Thrives, the Public Sector Flounders," *The New York Times,* December 18, 1991, pp. A1, A14.
111. Zhao Suisheng, "Institutional Defects of Central-Local Relations and Economic Policy Implementation in Communist China," (unpublished manuscript, pp.1-37). See also his chapter in this volume.
112. Ronald L. Watts, "Federalism, Regionalism, and Political Integration," Chapter One in David Cameron, ed., *Regionalism and Supranationalism: Challenges and Alternatives to the Nation-State in Canada and Europe* (Montreal: The Institute for Research on Public Policy and Policy Studies Institute, 1981), pp. 3-19.
113. Daniel J. Elazar, *Exploring Federalism,* op.cit., p. 3.
114. Ibid., p. 8.
115. Daniel J. Elazar, *Exploring Federalism,* op. cit.
116. Daniel J. Elazar, *Exploring Federalism,* op. cit., p. 6.
117. Interview with former Shenzhen Mayor Zheng Liangyu, see *Zhongyang Ribao* (Central Daily News), May 7, 1992, p. 4.
118. Daniel J. Elazar, *Exploring Federalism,* op. cit. p. 225.
119. James MacGregor Burns, J.W. Peltason, and Thomas E. Cronin, (12th ed.), *Government by the People,* (Englewood Cliffs, NJ: Prentice-Hall, Inc., 1984), p.42.
120. Daniel J. Elazar, *Exploring Federalism,* op. cit., pp. 12 and 192.
121. Lieberthal argues that the Chinese leadership since 1949 has remained wedded to the traditional notion that China should be a unitary (as opposed to federal) state. Arthur Waldron contends that its roots should be traced to as early as the *junxian* versus *fengjian* debate in the Qin (B.C. 221-207) and Han (B.C. 207-A.D. 24) Dynasties. Arthur Waldron, "Warlordism Versus Federalism: The Revival of a Debate?" *The China Quarterly,* March 1990, No. 121, pp. 116-128.
122. For instance, Mao Zedong had noticed the merits of federalism. He contended: "Our Constitution stipulates that the localities have no right to make laws and the power of legislation lies with the [Chinese] National People's

Congress." "This was also learnt from the Soviet Union." "The states in America have the right to make legislation, and their laws may even conflict with the federal Constitution. ... It appears that the financial and tax laws in various states are different as well. America is a highly advanced country. The fact that it took only a hundred some years to reach its current level of development is very noteworthy." "... There must be some reasons for America to have become such an advanced country. Its political system deserves study. It seems that we should also give more power to our localities. It is disadvantageous for socialist construction if the power of the localities is too limited." However, Leninist "democratic centralism" and a hatred of the Western "bourgeois political system," prevented Mao from applying the federalist principles. See Bo Yibo, *Retrospect of Certain Important Policy-making and Events,* (Beijing: The Publishing House of the Chinese Communist Party School, 1991), pp. 486-489.

123. Daniel J. Elazar: *Exploring Federalism,* op.cit.

124. Daniel J. Elazar: *Exploring Federalism,* op.cit., p. 195.

125. Arend Lijphart maintains three institutional options are especially important: the choice between parliamentary and presidential forms of government, the choice of the electoral system (with proportional representation and majoritarian methods like plurality being the main alternatives), and the choice between federal-decentralized and unitary-centralized government. See Arend Lijphart, "The World Shops for a Ballot Box: A Comparative Perspective on Democratization," in *Political Science and International Studies,* by The Chinese Scholars of Political Science and International Studies, Inc., October 1991, pp. 12-15; also see Arend Lijphart, "Constitutional Choices for New Democracies," *Journal of Democracy,* Vol. 2, No. 1 (Winter 1991), pp. 72-84.

126. Ibid.

3

Institutional Reorganization and Its Impact on Decentralization

Gong Ting and Chen Feng

This chapter examines China's institutional reorganization[1] since the late 1970s, which has had a significant impact on the nation's central-local relations. Although the question of who controls what economic resources is fundamental to understanding China's ongoing decentralization process, the contest between center and localities for economic resources does not take place in an institutional vacuum. In our view, institutional readjustment is important for analyzing China's post-Mao decentralization on two fronts: (1) it provides an administrative framework from which to understand economic decentralization; and (2) it is a significant component of China's changing central-local relations.

Administrative reform has been an important theme in post-Mao China. The reorganization of governmental institutions, the shift of institutional functions between the center and local governments and between governmental and non-governmental organizations, the differentiation of the party from the government, and the separation of the government from enterprises, all have a significant impact on central-local relations. We argue that China's ongoing decentralization is more than a process of redistributing controlling power over economic and fiscal resources between the center and localities. It also involves a broad reshuffling of political and administrative powers, which has made the post-Mao era differ significantly from the nation's previous decentralization efforts.

This chapter begins with a conceptual construction of how to measure institutional decentralization. It then examines the organizational changes that have taken place during the process of institutional decentralization in post-Mao China, and concludes with a discussion of the implications of institutional decentralization for overall power redistribution between the center and localities in China's future development.

Measuring Institutional Decentralization

Traditional measurements of decentralization focus on the degree of decentralization taking place. Rondinelli and Cheema distinguish four types of decentralization: deconcentration, delegation, devolution, and debureaucratization.[2] While attempting to portray different models of decentralization, these four types represent a spectrum with deconcentration at the least decentralized pole and debureaucratization (privatization) at the other. Rondinelli admits, however, that all government structures consist of some combination of these forms of decentralized administration.[3] As often as not, the four-fold distinction evokes considerable debate about which category a particular example fits into and which model best describes the features of decentralization.[4]

Other scholars evaluate central-local government relations according to the position of local governments in the political system, i.e., the functions, access, and discretion of local authorities.[5] This measurement offers a more precise conceptual framework for cross-national comparisons. Its precision, however, brings other problems. For one thing, it limits attention to formal authorities and institutions in contrast to other possible forms of decentralization. A second, yet related, problem is that it treats the relationship between the center and localities as a kind of zero-sum game: an advance or retreat for one side constitutes a retreat or advance for the other. In fact, however, increases in the responsibility, discretion, and access of local governments may not necessarily reflect or induce decreasing power at the center.

This study proposes an alternative conceptual framework to measure changes in central-local relations. It involves a careful examination of three main characteristics in the institutional framework of central-local relations:

Institutional Design. By institutional design, we mean the formal and informal organizational arrangements which affect central-local relations. This includes not only the organizations within well-defined geographical or political boundaries (e.g., the center, provinces, counties, and towns), but also those decision-making institutions at the national level (e.g., the legislature, central ministries) and specialized organizations across local jurisdictions (e.g., special economic zones), since they all impact on changing central-local relations.

Institutional Function. We will also examine the functions of central and local institutions. Instead of formal responsibilities, however, we focus our attention on the broad functions or power embodied in the formal responsibilities. There are always distributions of tasks within a government--for example, national defence is the responsibility of the center; primary and secondary education are generally the responsibility of the localities. We are not going to examine these concrete tasks. Rather, we will look at how authority and power actually shift with the reallocation of these tasks between center and localities.

Institutional Differentiation. Institutional differentiation refers to the extent to which administrative institutions are specialized. In a broad sense, it denotes both horizontal and vertical inter-institutional relations. Under many circumstances, the degree of institutional differentiation affects central-local relations: the more integrated the administration, the less decentralization it can achieve.

Changes in Institutional Design of the Central-Local Relations

Two prominent features traditionally dominated China's institutional design: hierarchy and extensiveness.

China's vanguard-led 1949 revolution and the centralized economic planning that followed produced a highly hierarchical bureaucracy. The administrative organization of the country consisted of three levels: the central administration (*zhongyang zhengfu*), regional and local governments (*difang zhengfu*), and grass-roots working units (*jiceng danwei*). However, decisions made at the center were usually channeled down vertically through the so-called "systems" (*xitong*) or "branches" (*tiaotiao*). Each system represented a distinct function or line of work, and was organized in a vertical order with specialized institutions and personnel at each level of the administrative hierarchy.[6] Responsibilities were centered in the national ministries. Instructions and directives travelled downward and outward to localities.

In this chain of "vertical leadership" (*chuizhi lingdao*), local government was the weakest link. This was because centralized control over economic activities had been the single most important feature of the Chinese management system. The importance of central control can be seen from the following: (1) central ministries directly controlled major enterprises;[7] (2) central ministries distributed funds and major resources; and (3) the state supervised fixed investment through a centralized budgetary allocation. Centralized control based on three main mechanisms--physical planning of production, centralized allocation of resources, and budgetary grants of fixed investment--left little room for regional and local governments to function automatically.[8] As a result, regional and local governments acted merely as the intermediaries between the center and grass-roots work units, with very limited decision-making role for themselves. The hierarchical order of the "systems" also made horizontal communication and coordination between government agencies difficult, as these agencies were often components of different systems and only accepted top-down instructions. Thus, as Lieberthal and Oksenberg have observed, the Guangdong Electric Power Bureau had difficulty developing formal and direct ties with the local railway district or the provincial coal department, because they belonged to different ministerial hierarchies.[9]

At certain times, the central administration relied more heavily on regional governments (*kuaikuai*) to implement its policies--such as in the early 1950s and during the Great Leap Forward of the late 1950s. This, however, did not significantly change the hierarchical nature of China's administrative structure: plans were still made at the center; information continued to flow down through vertical channels; and, more importantly, all areas were under the control of the party's visible hand through its local committees.

A second character of China's traditional institutional design was its extensiveness. During the process of transformation from a revolutionary organization into a professional bureaucracy, China's administration went through regularization and professionalization.[10] Administrative institutions proliferated accordingly. When the People's Republic was founded, only about 35 central ministries and other bodies existed under the State Administrative Council (the predecessor of the State Council). However, most of the institutional reorganizations in subsequent years followed the same pattern of replacing one ministry by several.[11] By the end of 1981, institutional expansion had reached its peak. In the State Council alone,[12] 100 agencies existed, including 52 ministries, 43 general bureaus, and five general offices. In addition, more than 40 *ad hoc* agencies had been established to coordinate between ministries and bureaus. Not surprisingly, as the government's structure became more and more unwieldy, efficiency and coordination deteriorated.

The Chinese leadership was not unaware of the problem. It proposed several "organizational simplification" campaigns (in 1952, 1958, and 1961). But all these pre-reform institutional reorganizations did not break the cycle of institutional streamlining-swelling-streamlining-swelling. Two factors accounted for this. First, these "organizational simplification" campaigns only changed the size of government bodies, rather than their functions. Economic management still remained in the hands of the state apparatus. Government agencies were set up on the basis of production specialization (e.g., the Ministry of Textile Industry, the Ministry of Geology and Mineral Resources, the Ministry of Chemical Industry, the Ministry of Aeronautics and Space Industry, the Ministry of Forestry, and the Ministry of Electronic Engineering). When a specialization became important in national economic planning, a new ministry had to be created to manage it. Consequently, government agencies in charge of industrial affairs grew most rapidly.[13]

Second, "organizational simplification" only reduced the number of state institutions, rather than their entrenched power and authority. In China, government agencies engage in many things that could otherwise be done by enterprises themselves. Instead of decentralizing managerial authority, "organizational simplification" merely moved the power of one institution to another, or shifted the authority of several institutions to one institution.[14]

Since 1982, however, post-Mao administrative reforms have brought some important changes to China's institutional design, and we will now examine these in turn.

Institutional Reorganization at the Center

The State Council has undergone two major structural reforms in the post-Mao era. The first took place in 1982, and the second in 1988.

The 1982 reform package included: (1) the dismantling of State Council commissions which had acted as overlords to each of the hierarchical "systems"; (2) reduction of the total number of State Council institutions from 100 to 61 by abolishing or merging agencies with similar or overlapping functions; and (3) diminution of the State Council staff by 34.7 percent, from a total of 49,000 to 32,000.[15]

Though it streamlined the government, the 1982 reorganization did not focus enough attention on the reform of governmental functions. As a result, bureaucratization revived quickly in the years following the reform. It was characterized by three "increases": (1) the increase of formal government institutions: by 1986, the number of ministries and other agencies under the State Council, once reduced to 61, again reached 71; (2) the increase of temporary or *ad hoc* agencies: in the 1982 reform, agencies of this type dropped from 44 to 30, but only five years later, the number doubled again;[16] and (3) the increase of administrative expenditure: according to official statistics, the nation's administrative expenditure increased by 105 percent from 1982 to 1987.[17]

These problems compelled a second large-scale reorganization of the central state apparatus in the late 1980s. The First Session of the Seventh

National People's Congress in 1988 approved further reform of the State Council. The 1988 institutional reorganization demonstrated some new reform patterns which had important implications for central-local relations. First, it focused on the downward shift of government functions. This included transferring macro-managerial functions from national administrative institutions to specialized agencies at different levels, and micro-managerial functions from government agencies to non-governmental agencies. Second, it converted several central ministries into general corporations (*zonggongsi*). These corporations are no longer administrative agencies (*xingzheng danwei*) which exercise centralized control over local companies and factories. They are expected to earn their keep as economic entities (*jingji shiti*). Such arrangements weakened the vertical administrative relationship based on "systems." The 1988 reform was also incomplete, however. It left some unfinished business, partially because of the interruption of the 1989 Tiananmen Incident. For example, the reform did not greatly affect the government size. The number of the central ministries was only reduced from 72 to 65. As we will see in the following pages, the impact on the size of local governments was even less. In addition, the intervention of central ministries in local affairs rebounded quickly after the 1988 decentralization. In one reported case in 1991, a provincial government was urged by 18 official documents from different central institutions to increase its agencies and staff in some fields.[18]

Development of Urban-Based Regionalization

The post-Mao reform era has also witnessed a bewildering array of new regional institutional reforms, triggered by disappointment over the persistent shortcomings of centralized management as well as the demands of economic development.

China's vertical administration has long been organized into a five-tier structure: the center (*zhongyang*), provinces (*sheng*), prefectures (*diqu*); counties (*xian*) or cities (*shi*); and towns (*zhen or xiang*). The economic reforms begun in 1978 facilitated agrarian commercialization, the development of township and village enterprises, and the urbanization of rural China. China's reformers attempted to reorganize the size and shape of local areas to prepare for further modernization and urbanization. Their basic aim was to strengthen the economic and administrative capabilities of the cities, make them the cooperative junctures of vertical and horizontal socioeconomic development, and thereby boost regional modernization. The leadership hoped that urban-based regionalization would help decentralize the overly top-heavy central control over the nation on the one hand, and solve the chronic problem of urban-rural disparity on the other.

Regional reorganization took several forms:

Creation of New Cities. As urbanization developed, it became necessary to create new cities. While in 1978 China had only 190 cities, by the end of 1991 the number had grown to 476, with an average of more than 20 new cities emerging each year.[19] The newly-created cities differed from the old ones in several aspects. First, they were no longer the products of population growth.[20] Instead, the level of socioeconomic development was taken into consideration when creating a new city. For example, a town could be converted into a city when its non-rural population reached 60,000 and its GNP rose to more than 200 million *yuan* a year. Likewise, a county could become a city when it limited its rural population to under 40 percent of the total and raised its GNP level to 300 million *yuan*.[21] Cities also began to undertake more active functions as socioeconomic centers of surrounding areas, rather than merely acting as intermediaries between the center and localities. According to the government, the purpose of this strategy was to decentralize administrative power in the following ways: (a) by transforming cities into open, multifunctional, socialized, and modernized centers of economic activities; (b) by relinquishing control over enterprises to the cities; and, (c) by solving the question of how core cities should exercise leadership over their enterprises. The cities were supposed to provide important social services for enterprises such as information, technology, communication, and transportation, and also provide a check against excessive enterprise autonomy through their formal administrative functions.[22] The economic and administrative importance of cities also lay in the fact that they incorporated various economic entities in the hinterlands into their own production and trading circuits.

Establishment of Metropolitan Regions. An important effort of China's regional reorganization, begun in 1982, was to develop the so-called "city-managing-county" (*shiguanxian*) system. By re-allocating area administrative authority and, sometimes, redrawing area administration boundaries, adjoining rural counties and prefectures were brought into the economic orbits of the core cities. By the end of 1988, 711 counties (accounting for 36.7 percent of the nation's total) had been put under the direct jurisdiction of 168 cities. The rationale behind the development of the "city-managing-county" system was, in Jonathan Unger's analysis, "to erase the miniature rural area satrapies that had previously interfered with free commerce; under the new arrangement, the industrial cities were to become the hubs of regional development, unimpeded by the skein of local administrative barriers."[23]

Preferential Treatment for Some Core Cities. Since 1983, several major cities have been put on a "separate list of core cities" (*zhongxin chengshi danlie*) in the national planning system. This new device gave some major cities special and preferential treatment in their economic, technological, and social development. In 1983, seven cities were on the list--Wuhan, Guangzhou, Shenyang, Chongqing, Dalian, Harbin, and Xian.[24] Two more (Qingdao and Ningbo) were added in 1987, bringing the total to nine. These cities were granted the same economic management authority held by provinces, and, therefore, are no longer subject to economic interference from their respective provinces (although administratively they are still subordinate to the latter). Compared with the three municipalities directly under the central government (Beijing, Shanghai, and Tianjin), these nine cities had the same economic power but less administrative autonomy.

Establishment of Regional Economic Zones. Beginning in 1983, the Chinese government started to promote the development of regional economic zones. Today, these includes the Yangtze Delta Zone centered on Shanghai, the Pearl River Delta Zone centered on Guangzhou, the Beijing-Tianjin-Tangshan Economic Zone, the middle-Yangtze Commercial Zone centered on Wuhan, and the Bohai Gulf Economic Cooperative Zone including Tianjin, Dalian, Qingdao, and some other cities.[25] These regional economic zones were used to promote so-called "horizontal linkages" (*hengxiang lianxi*), or "horizontal cooperation" (*hengxiang xiezuo*). Cities and enterprises in the same economic zones enjoyed cheaper labor and raw materials, cooperative production, and preferential trading.

All these changes in institutional design had some unanticipated effects on central-local relations. First, reforms in 1982 and 1988 simplified the institutional setting of the central administrative organizations but have had less impact at the local levels. Local government agencies were either less affected or were restored faster than those at the center after the institutional streamlining. Consequently, by 1985 the average number of government agencies at the provincial level for the first time exceeded that of the institutions at the center. (See TABLE 3.1).

According to recent statistics, each province has an average of more than 70 agencies now. The total number of government agencies at the country level and above has reached more than 30,000, accommodating some 40 million personnel.[26]

Anhui province provides a good example of this institutional growth at the regional level. From 1983 to 1988, its government agencies increased from 47 to 66 at the provincial level, from 33 to 55 at the prefecture level, and from 45 to 62 at the city level. Government personnel increased accordingly by 44.7 percent. In the same period, the province's administrative expenditure soared from 2.53 million *yuan* to

TABLE 3.1 Institutions under State Council and at Provincial Level (Selected years, 1952-1985)

Year	No. of Institutions under the State Council	Average No. of Institutions at Provincial Level
Before the Cultural Revolution		
1952	42	25
1953	42	30
1954	64	40
1956	81	50
1957	80	45
1958	68	47
1959	60	49
1964	77	47
1965	79	60
After the Cultural Revolution		
1976	52	45
1978	76	50-60
1981	100	80
1982	61	35-40
1985	67	70

Sources: Su Shangrao, "The Evolution of the Central Institutions in China," *Zhongguo Xingzheng Guanli* (Chinese Administrative Management), No. 23, May 1987, p. 32; and Wang Feng, "The Evolution of the Provincial Level Institutions," *Zhongguo Xingzheng Guanli*, No. 30, December, 1987, pp. 32, 42-45.

4.45 million *yuan*, with an annual average increase rate of 12 percent--much faster than increases in revenue income.[27] Another example is Shanxi province. The number of government agencies at and above the county level reached 5,473 by the end of 1986, exceeding the authorized number by 22.5 percent. At the provincial level alone, temporary agencies increased from 39 to 85 during the period of 1983-1986.[28] As a result, the issue of institutional streamlining of government was again raised by the party leadership at the 14th National Party Congress held in October 1992, with local governments clearly one of the targets.

Second, vertical institutional relations became more complicated. As mentioned already, the government structure in the past was quite linear, constructed from the top to the bottom in five tiers. As FIGURES 3.1 and 3.2 show, however, central and local administrative relations became more diverse and fragmented following the reform, especially with the development of new regional organizations. In addition to provinces, prefectures, counties, and towns, there were regional economic zones, core cities, and metropolises, extending beyond the traditional hierarchy. As the hierarchical order became less clear, central control over local organizations was lessening.

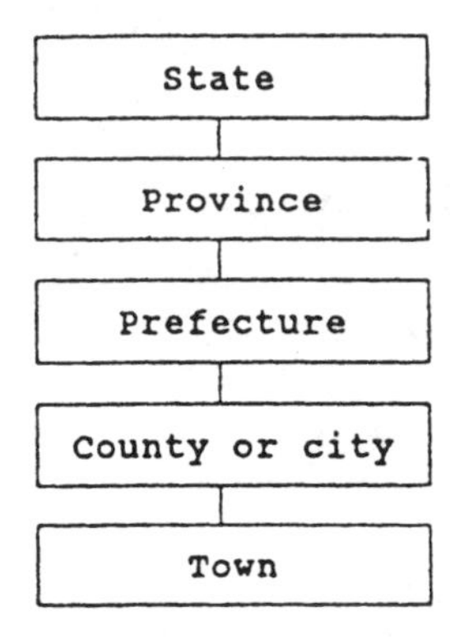

FIGURE 3.1 Vertical Administrative Structure before the Reform

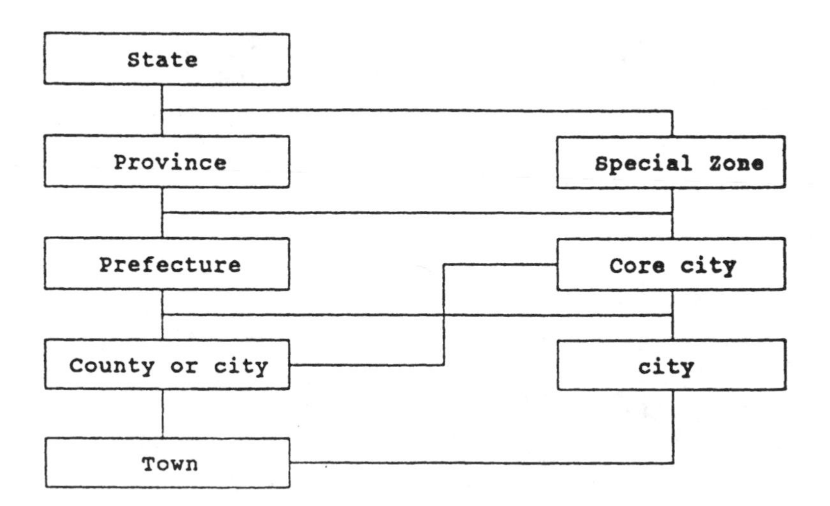

FIGURE 3.2 Vertical Administrative Structure after the Reform

Reallocation of Institutional Functions

Before the reform, the importance of local governments in the Chinese political system derived from the fact that they were important vehicles for the party to mobilize popular energies to serve the state--often interpreted as the central government. Thus, local governments were to faithfully deliver and implement decisions and programs made at the center. Although local governments also supervised and coordinated public undertakings in their respective regions, in general their position in China's pre-reform political system was passive and subordinate in character. The center, for example, reserved the legislative power, according to the so-called "one-level legislation" (*yiji lifa*) system where all the local levels (from the province down to the township level) had no power to make laws. In addition, local executive organs were held responsible and accountable to the administrative bodies at their immediate higher level; they were "administrative organs of the state under the unified leadership of, and subordinate to, the State Council."[29] Moreover, the center exercised authority over cadre appointments, removals, and transfers for two levels down along the administrative hierarchy (*xiaguan liangji*). This meant that the center controlled any change of leading cadres at both the provincial and prefecture levels.

Since the reform, these functional relationships between the center and localities have changed significantly.

Legislative Function

In July 1979, the second session of the Fifth National People's Congress issued two important laws: *The Organic Law of Local People's Congresses and Local People's Governments of the People's Republic of China* and *The Electoral Act of Local People's Congresses and Local People's Governments of the People's Republic of China*. The two laws improved the legislative functions of the local levels in several important ways by: (a) allowing the People's Congresses at and above the county level to establish their standing committees as the authoritative organ in a respective region, thus, enhancing the local leadership;[30] (b) changing the "one-level legislation" into "two-level legislation" (*liangji lifa*), as the laws granted provincial People's Congresses the legislative power as long as their statutes do not contravene the Constitution, laws, policies, and orders of the state;[31] and (c) creating citizen constituencies for delegates to local people's congresses through more direct and competitive elections.[32] These changes helped to make local people's congresses more responsible and accountable to their constituencies than to higher level authorities. These new measures were later incorporated into the country's 1982 Constitution.

Executive Function

For the first time in the history of the People's Republic of China, the 1982 Constitution described the executive function of local governments in relatively clear terms:

> Local people's governments at and above the county level, within the limits of their authority as prescribed by law, conduct the administrative work concerning the economy, education, science, culture, public health, physical culture, urban and rural development, finance, civil affairs, public security, nationalities affairs, judicial administration, supervision and family planning in their respective administrative regions.

Reforms since 1978 have significantly amplified local executive power. The most noticeable changes have taken place in the economic sphere, as the center relaxed its control over resource allocation, gave greater autonomy to the local authorities over investment, and decentralized managerial power over enterprises.

Decentralization of Allocation Power. Planned allocation of resources has gradually declined since 1979. According to a recent World Bank report, between 1979-1989 the number of raw materials controlled by the center fell from 256 to 27, and the proportion of capital goods embraced by the state's mandatory plan was reduced from 80 percent to 20-30 percent.[33] Local governments undertook the major responsibility for material allocations in their own areas. They could also obtain resources and products through exchange and cooperative bargaining with their neighboring regions.

Decentralization of Investment Power. Economic reforms also led to the delegation of investment power from the center to localities. Before 1984, all investment projects valued at more than 10 million *yuan* were subject to the center's approval. Starting in 1988, however, the State Planning Commission only reviewed those projects valued at more than 50 million *yuan*. The rest were left under the jurisdiction of provincial authorities.[34] In addition, the local government's control over banks and local taxes also allowed them to intervene in investment activities.

Decentralization of Managerial Power. While local administration has become more articulated, the national government's ability to intervene in micro-economic management has sharply declined. According to some statistics, of more than 400,000 industrial enterprises in the country in 1980, only some 190 were managed by the central authorities.[35] These enterprises usually dealt with crucial sectors of the economy, such as military production, transportation, electric power, and posts and telecommunications. A great majority of enterprises came under the control of local authorities. Local governments also enjoyed more tax power than before. In 1992, seven provinces and cities were selected to experiment with tax system reform. In these areas, tax revenues would be divided into those of the center, those of the local authorities, and those shared between them.[36]

Personnel Management Function

The linchpin of personnel management in China is the *nomenklatura* system.[37] The system defines the jurisdictions of different governing bodies in cadre appointment and dismissal. It also includes institutions and processes for making appropriate personnel changes. Reform of the *nomenklatura* system has been an important step in decentralizing China's personnel management. In 1984, the party's central leadership decided to transfer a major part of its cadre management authority to lower levels. The center thereafter has only taken care of major leading cadres at and above the level of vice minister and vice governor, as well as presidents of key universities and colleges. Thus, the number of cadres at the center's disposal fell by almost two-thirds (from 13,000 to 5,000).[38] The party center also required lower-level party committees to follow suit by reducing their personnel management jurisdiction from two levels to one level down the administrative hierarchy. Undoubtedly, the new system has given more discretion to each level of local leaders to exercise their own authority in civil service management.

With the decentralization of personnel management came the localization of provincial cadres.[39] In the past, a majority of provincial leading cadres were "outsiders"--that is, they came to the province from the center or other provinces.[40] In December 1981, for example, only 43 percent of 58 provincial leading cadres (i.e., provincial party secretary and governor) were natives of the province of appointment or had spent most of their working lives there. But with the reforms, the party's top leadership appeared more willing to promote local cadres, rather than to assign "outsiders" to leading provincial positions. By June 1989, local cadres held 70 percent of the leading provincial positions.[41] More recently, another important sign of the growing importance of local power in terms of personnel is that five provincial and municipal leading cadres became members of the powerful Politburo at the 14th Party Congress.[42] As a result, the current Politburo includes eight new people that have local experience.[43]

Institutional Differentiation

Inter-institutional relations in China during the pre-reform period were opaque. Due to the highly concentrated power structure, it was often difficult to distinguish the authority and functions of the party from those of the government, and that of the government from those of enterprises. Under the banner of "the party's unified leadership" (*dang de yiyuanhua lingdao*), power was concentrated in the hands of the ruling Chinese Communist Party. The "unified leadership" often turned into leadership by individuals. Note, for example, Deng Xiaoping's own analysis:

> Historically, we ourselves have repeatedly placed too much emphasis on ensuring centralism and unification by the party, and on combating decentralism and any assertion of independence. And we have placed too little emphasis on ensuring the necessary degree of decentralization, delegating necessary decision-making power to the lower organizations and opposing the over-concentration of power in the hands of individuals. We have tried several times to divide power between the central and local authorities, but we never defined the scope of the functions and powers of the Party organizations as distinct from those of the government and of economic and mass organizations.[44]

The government's jurisdiction included enterprises. In pre-reform China, government agencies, especially those at the central level, directly managed enterprises. They produced mandatory plans, controlled resources and supplies, set prices, absorbed all revenues and costs, and regulated all labor.

This highly integrated political system had led to power abuses and administrative pathologies such as sluggishness and ineffectiveness. It also impeded reform efforts to decentralize government authority. Two main factors account for this. First, the party monitored and supervised government agencies at different levels through its own hierarchical system parallel to that of the latter. Thus, it considered any attempt to change the power structure as detrimental to party rule and harmful to the socialist system. Second, before there was clear definition of power and functions between the government and enterprises, any decentralization effort could only be "administrative decentralization" in character. That is, decentralization became a mere readjustment of the authority between government agencies rather than an assumption of authority by enterprises. No matter to whom the enterprises were subordinate, they would have no autonomous power of their own. As some critics point out, "administrative decentralization" is certainly an important component of reforming central-local relations, but it alone cannot bring about enterprise autonomy.[45] The purpose of decentralization, after all, is to give enterprises more incentives, opportunities, and authority to develop their managerial capabilities as real economic entities. As discussed below, since 1980, reformers have taken some important measures to adjust inter-institutional relations.

Separating the Party from Administration

The 1982 Constitution stated that "all political parties, ..., must abide by the Constitution and the law. ...No organizations or individuals may enjoy the privilege of being above the Constitution and the law." Technically, this subjected the Chinese Communist Party to the law of the state. The constitutional limitation on the power of the party was accompanied by some important measures. First, the party gradually abolished those departments within it that duplicated government agencies. These departments had been established to supervise their counterparts in the government. For example, the party's central committee and provincial committees all had their own departments to manage industry, economy and trade, culture and education, and rural work. There were also industry secretaries, agricultural secretaries, education secretaries, and secretaries of legal affairs on party committees. These positions were gradually abolished during the reform in order to reduce the interference of the party in daily administration.[46]

Second, the party also reduced concurrent government offices held by leading party cadres. Before the reform, party secretaries usually concurrently held the leading positions of the government at the same level. Thus, the first secretary of a party provincial committee was at the same time the governor in that province. The head of a commune was usually also the secretary of the commune's party committee. During the reform, the power of party secretaries lessened as the Director Responsibility System (*shouzhang fuze zhi*) was introduced at the grass-roots level. In factories, party committees gradually withdrew from the domain of daily administration, while managers assumed authority over plant production and operations. In rural areas, village and township governments were established to replace the people's communes, which had combined all the activities of the party, administration, and production in the past. At the provincial level, the number of positions concurrently held by party cadres was dramatically reduced. For example, in October 1978 all 29 of China's provincial governors concurrently held the position of first secretary of their respective provincial party committees, while only one province (Anhui) still had this arrangement by June 1989.[47]

Another important but lately aborted measure in separating party functions from government administration was the proposal to eliminate all the party core groups (*dangzu*). Party core groups were established in the subordinate organs of the State Council, mass organizations, and important government institutions at provincial and prefecture levels, to supervise government institutions. One of their functions was to exercise significant control over cadre appointments, promotions, and dismissals. The 13th Party Congress in 1987 endorsed the plan to "gradually abolish" these party core groups over several years, but the plan was aborted after the Tiananmen Incident in 1989, with the Party Constitution revised at the 1992 14th Party Congress to reemphasize the importance of party core groups.[48]

Separating Administration from Enterprise

As mentioned above, enterprises in China were long regarded as appendages to administrative organs and were deprived of independent decision-making power. More often than not, to "decentralize power" in the past only meant a change of masters for enterprises--either making them more dependent on a central authority or more reliant on local powers. In contrast, the reform since 1978 has sought to "invigorate" enterprises by relieving them of their previously dependent status.

One important measure was to distinguish ownership (*suoyouquan*) from management (*jingyingquan*). The State Council's "*Provisional Regulations on Further Extending the Decision-Making Power of State Industrial Enterprises*" in 1984 set a series of new policies in this regard. Enterprises were still owned by the state, but they enjoyed important operational rights: (a) they could produce for the market after fulfilling their quotas; (b) they could sell these products as well as overstocked items and goods rejected by state purchasing agencies; (c) they could vary the price of marketed goods by up to 20 percent on either side of the state price or negotiate prices with purchasers; (d) they could choose their suppliers of state distributed materials; and (e) they could bypass the state distribution network and buy raw materials directly from producers. Other expanded powers involved the use of retained profits, the leasing and sale of surplus equipment, personnel and wage matters, and the formation of joint ventures that cut across official administrative divisions.[49] These discretionary powers turned enterprises into "independent management units" (*duli jingying danwei*).

A second measure, as mentioned earlier, was the establishment of the "Director Responsibility System", which created an administrative system headed by a factory director (or manager) to ensure the coordinated and effective functioning of the enterprise.[50] Under the system, the enterprise manager assumes responsibility for factory production, operation, and administration, and is empowered to determine long-term and annual plans, major technological improvements, administrative personnel and employment. The Second Plenary Session of the Sixth National People's Congress in May 1984 formally discussed and adopted the "Director Responsibility System." Only one month later, more than 200 enterprises began to experiment with the system. The passage of the three sets of regulations governing enterprise organizations[51] in 1986 finally formalized the system. By the end of 1987, the system existed in virtually all enterprises.

Efforts were also made to change the functions of government agencies to "invigorate enterprises." From 1986 to 1987, 16 medium-scale cities conducted spot-testing institutional reforms. The purpose was to redefine and reallocate the functions of government agencies after the separation of administration from enterprises. In the process, many government institutions found that they had taken on many tasks which should have been the responsibility of enterprises themselves. For example, the Economic Committee of Zigong City divided its power into 492 concrete responsibilities. Among them, 246 were given back to enterprises; others rightfully belonged under the jurisdiction of other sectors. After reallocation, the committee was left with only 124 responsibilities (about 25 percent of its original workload), and this, in turn, helped reduce its size and promote efficiency.[52]

Conclusions

China's administrative reform is a response to the needs of economic modernization in the post-Mao era. It is a top-down program sponsored by reformers who saw administrative readjustment as an important dimension of economic reform. The reform measures have not only deepened economic decentralization, but also demonstrated some important tendencies which depart significantly from pre-reform decentralization efforts. First, there is a tendency towards legalization of the duties and rights of local governments. Local governments, for the first time, are granted constitutionally-defined authority, although this is still vague according to some critics.[53] The division of authority between the center and localities has been institutionalized in the form of laws. Although it would be naive to think that these new legalities are unrescindable in China's political context, they do provide a legal basis from which local governments can defend their interests or bargain with the center.

Second, the Chinese administrative system has tended to become more cellular in nature. Two developments have broken down the previous hierarchy of central-local relations. One is the spread of "horizontal organizational linkages" (*hengxiang zhuzhi lianxi*), which have rendered the center's vertical control more difficult than before. The other is the expansion of enterprise autonomy. Unlike the pre-reform period, the current decentralization has been accompanied by efforts to separate the party from administration, and administration from enterprises. With its power being further fragmented, the center's control is being reduced tremendously in scope.

Finally, there is a tendency for localities to become independent players after the readjustment of central-local relations. Instead of waiting passively for instructions from the center, local governments have been actively searching for powers and rights for themselves. Driven by local interests, they now dare to bargain with the center for more authority.

All these developments signal the emergence of what David Lampton has called the "cellular polity" in China.[54] However, problems have arisen as well. First, in the process of decentralization, some important economic managerial powers have actually been grabbed by local administrators, instead of being further transferred down to enterprises. This has led to a dual performance pattern on the part of local governments. On the one hand, they request delegation of power from the center in the name of decentralization. On the other, they enhance their own control over enterprises and continue to intervene in local economic activities by administrative means. This pattern may well remain until there is a strict separation of local administrative authority from that of enterprises. Second, tensions occur as local administrators protect local interests by creating man-made barriers (e.g., market protection measures, raw materials embargoes) against other regions. Contests between the center and localities will become keener when the former tries to reassert control while the latter resists. The problem is not with the competition between different administrative units (center, province, city, country, etc.), but with the lack of rules to guide competition. Thus, while the Chinese leadership has to push ahead with the shift from "decentralization to local authorities" to "decentralization to enterprises," it must also learn how to manage decentralized power relations by legal means. To a large extent, the future development of China's central-local relations lies at the intersection of the solutions to these two problems.

Notes

1. By institutional change, we mean innovations and rearrangements pertinent to political and administrative devices, functions, and procedures.

2. Dennis A. Rondinelli and Shabbir G. Cheema, eds., *Decentralization and Development: Policy Implementation in Developing Countries*, (Beverly Hills, CA: Sage Publications, 1983).

3. Dennis A. Rondinelli, "Government Decentralization in Comparative Perspective: Theory and Practice in Developing Countries," *International Review of Administrative Sciences,* No. 2, February 1981, p. 139.

4. Diana Conyers, "Decentralization: A Framework for Discussion," in Hasnat Abdul Hye (ed.), *Decentralization, Local Government Institutions, and Resource Mobilization* (Comilla, Bangladesh: Bangladesh Academy for Rural Development, 1985), pp. 22-42.

5. Edward C. Page & Michael J. Goldsmith, eds., *Central and Local Government Relations: A Comparative Analysis of West European Unitary States* (London: Sage Publishers Ltd., 1987).

6. Doak A. Barnett, *Cadres, Bureaucracy, and Political Power in Communist China* (New York: Columbia University Press, 1967), p. 7.

7. Center-controlled enterprises increased from 2,800 to 9,300 during 1953-1957, and reached 10,503 in 1965. See, Wang Huning, "The Changing Central-Local Relationship in China: Its Political Implication," *Fudan Xuebao* (Fudan Review), No. 5 (May 1988), pp. 1-8, 30.

8. The World Bank, *China: Long-Term Development Issues and Options* (Baltimore: The Johns Hopkins University Press, 1985), p. 178.

9. Kenneth Lieberthal & Michel Oksenberg, *Policy Making in China: Leaders, Structures, and Processes* (Princeton: Princeton University Press, 1988), p. 142.

10. Yinmaw Kaw, *Government Bureaucracy and Cadres in Urban China under Communist Rule, 1949-1965* (Ph.D. dissertation, Cornell University, 1968); Harry Harding, *Organizing China: The Problem of Bureaucracy, 1949-1976* (Stanford: Stanford University Press, 1981).

11. Although the Great Leap Forward and the Cultural Revolution brought disorder and reduced the size of the state apparatus, they were both followed by immediate and rapid restoration of institutions.

12. Not including the party agencies at the center.

13. Han Zhulin, "Small Government, Big Society," *Shehui Kexue* (Social Sciences), No. 3 (March 1989), pp. 30-33.

14. Ren Xiao, "The Dynamics and Process of Administrative Reforms in China, 1982-1988," *Zhengzhixue Yanjiu* (Journal of Political Science), No.6 (June 1989), p. 17.

15. John P. Burn, "Reforming China's Bureaucracy, 1979-1982," Asian Survey, 23:6 (June 1983), pp. 707-714; Xia Hai, "Correctly Evaluating the 1982 Institutional Reform," *Zhongguo Xingzheng Guanli* (Chinese Administrative Management), No.24 (June 1987), pp. 23-24.

16. He Guanghui, "The Blueprint for the Institutional Reform of the State Council." *Liaowang* (Outlook), April 4, 1988, pp. 10-11.

17. Ren Xiao, 1989, op. cit., pp. 23-24.

18. Liu Jinghuai, "China Will Carry Out Institutional Reforms in a Comprehensive Way" (in Chinese), *Liaowang* (overseas edition), September 21, 1992, p. 3.

19. *People's Daily,* September 19, 1992.

20. In the past, population growth was the major factor in the creation of new cities. For instance, the central government stipulated in 1955 that a city could be created when the population of a town exceeded 100,000 (Gao, 1988: 30). Gao Yan, "Replacing Counties with Cities: Urbanization with Chinese Characteristics,"

Zhongguo Xingzheng Guanli (Chinese Administrative Management), No. 35, May 1988, pp. 29-31.

21. Ibid.

22. Cities must supervise the fulfillment of state planned output quotas and the proper use of state distributed materials.

23. Jonathan Unger, "The Struggle to Dictate China's Administration: The Conflict of Branches vs. Areas vs. Reform," *The Australian Journal of Chinese Affairs*, No. 18, July 1987, pp. 21-23.

24. *People's Daily*, September 21, 1985.

25. The Chinese government is reportedly designing an economic framework for the 1990s based on seven major regions. *People Daily*, September 26, 1992.

26. *Liaowang*, September 21, 1992.

27. Yu Chaohui and Zhang Jialin, "The Size and Staff of the Government Agencies in Anhui Province," *Zhongguo Xingzheng Guanli* (Chinese Administrative Management), No. 56, February 1990, pp. 30-31.

28. The Statistical Bureau of Shanxi Province, "Too Fast Increase, Too Much Burden," *Lilun Xuekan* (Journal of Theoretical Studies), No. 10 (October 1987), pp. 10-12.

29. *The Constitution of the People's Republic of China* (Beijing: Foreign Languages Press, 1982), p. 79.

30. Before the reform, the People's Congresses at local levels did not have their own standing committees and were therefore unable to effectively deal with problems of their own constituencies.

31. *The Constitution of the People's Republic of China*, op. cit., p. 73. Local legislation proliferated after 1979, especially in the first several years thereafter. From November 1979 to June 1982, 355 local laws were passed in provinces and municipalities directly under the central government, as well as autonomous regions. Of these, 37.2 percent dealt with the local economy; 30.7 percent were concerned with political and legal affairs; and another 26.6 percent impacted education, science, technology, and public health. In the 1983-1989 period, more than 1,000 laws were issued in localities. Statistics are available in Xin Chunyin, "A Preliminary Study of the Jurisdiction of the Local Legislative Power in China," *Faxue Zazhi* (Journal of Legal Studies), No. 23, February 1984, pp. 31-32; Kevin J. O'Brien, *Reform without Liberation; China's National People's Congress and the Politics of Institutional Changes* (New York: Cambridge University Press, 1990), p. 161.

32. The electoral act of 1979 introduced direct elections for the People's Congresses at the county level and provided that all levels were to have competitive elections. It stipulated that at the county level and lower, candidates should number one and one-half to two times more than positions; and at above-county levels, 20-50 percent more candidates were required. See, the Legislative Affairs Commission of the Standing Committee of the Chinese National People's Congress, *The Laws of the People's Republic of China* (1979-1986), two volumes (Beijing: Foreign Language Press, 1987).

33. The World Bank, *China: Between Plan and Market* (Washington DC: The World Bank, 1990), p. 60.

34. This trend has been partially reversed since early 1990: projects valued at more than 30 million *yuan* must have the approval of the State Council, except in a few industries such as chemicals.

35. Liu Reizhong & Wang Chende, "Reasons for the Growth of the Economic Role of Local Governments at Present: An Analysis," *Zhongguo: Fazhan yu Gaige* (China: Development and Reform), No. 1, January 1988, p. 44.

36. For some minority areas, the distribution ratio would be 2:8 between the center and the locality. *People's Daily*, June 20, 1992.

37. John P. Burn, *The Chinese Communist Party's Nomenklatura System* (New York: M.E. Sharp, Inc., 1989).

38. *People's Daily*, July 20, 1983.

39. The phrase "provincial leading cadres" refers to the heads of the party and administration at the province level, or more accurately, the first party secretary and the governor of a province.

40. This "outsider in" appointment of provincial leading cadres had been an important institutional way for the center to avoid factionalization of local politics since imperial China.

41. Our statistics are based on the biographical data provided in Wolfgang Bartke, *Who's Who in the People's Republic of China* (2nd ed.) (Munchen, the Federal Republic of Germany: K.G. Saur Verlag, 1987); *Who's Who in China: Current Leaders* (Beijing: Foreign Languages Press, 1989).

42. These five new members of the Politburo are: Chen Xitong, the Party Secretary of Beijing, Wu Bangguo, the Party Secretary of Shanghai, Tan Shaowen, the Party Secretary of Tianjin, Xie Fei, the Party Secretary of Guangdong and Jiang Chunyun, the Party Secretary of Shandong.

43. Another three newly-elected members of the Politburo had worked as leading local cadres before assuming a post in the center. They are: Zhu Rongji, Vice Premier, and the former Mayor of Shanghai, Hu Jingtao, the former Party Secretary of the Tibetan Autonomous Region, and Li Lanqing, Minster of Foreign Trade and the former Vice Mayor of Tianjin.

44. Deng Xiaoping, *Selected Works of Deng Xiaoping* (Beijing: Foreign Languages Press, 1984), p. 312.

45. Lou Jiwei, "We Should Avoid the Road of Further Local Decentralization," in Wu Jinglian & Zhou Xiaochuan, eds., *A Systematic Design of the China's Economic Reform* (Beijing: Prospect Press, 1988), pp. 204; Yang Chutang and Cui Xiangning, "The Reform of Center-Local Relations," *Zhengzhixue Yanjiu* (Journal of Political Science), No. 27 (May 1989), p. 27.

46. Zhao Ziyang's Speech on the Preliminary Meeting of the Seventh Plenary Session of the 12th Chinese Communist Party Central Committee; *People's Daily*, November 11, 1987.

47. This statistic is based on data provided in Ma Qibin, *The Chinese Communist Party at Forty, 1949-1989* (Beijing: The Press of the Chinese Communist Party Historical Documents, 1989), pp. 573-576.

48. *People's Daily*, October 17, 1992.

49. For details, see *The Selected Important Works Since the Third Plenary Session of the Eleventh Chinese Communist Party Central Committee* (Beijing: People's Publishing House, 1987), pp. 207-210.

50. Jiang Yiwei, "Overall Reorganization is a Constructive Reorganization," (Part III), *Jingji Guanli* (Economic Management), No.5 (May 1982), p. 6.

51. These regulations are "Regulations on the Work of Factory Directors in Industrial Enterprises Owned by the Whole People"; "Regulations on the Work of Basic-Level Organs of the Chinese Communist Party in Industrial Enterprises Owned by the Whole People"; and "Regulations on Staff/Worker Congresses in Industrial Enterprises Owned by the Whole People." For the texts of these documents, see *Enterprise Management* (Qiye Guanli), No. 11 (November 1986), pp. 10-19.

52. Geng Liang, "A Comprehensive Report on the Spot-testing of the Medium-Size City Institutional Reform," *Jingji Yanjiu Cankaoziliao* (Reference Materials on Economic Studies), No. 75, (May 1987), p. 7.

53. Yang and Cui, 1989, p. 27; Xu Fengchao and Zhang Tianping, "Rationalization of the Power Distribution Between Center and Localities," *Zhongguo Xingzheng Guanli* (Chinese Administrative Management), No. 50, August 1989, p. 9.

54. David M. Lampton, ed., *Policy Implementation in Post-Mao China* (California: University of California Press, 1987), p. 14.

PART TWO

Functional Dimensions

4

Central-Local Fiscal Politics in China

Wang Shaoguang

Just like a human being cannot live without blood, a state cannot function without revenue. The extraction of fiscal resources is a precondition for the implementation of all other government programs. In this sense, the capacity to extract revenue is the most fundamental capacity of any state.

In general, the state is inclined to extract as much revenue as it can from taxpayers. However, it is also subject to various constraints that limit its capacity to extract more revenue. In the non-state socialist system, according to Margaret Levi, the state's "relative bargaining power," "transaction costs," and "discount rates" have determinant effects on its revenue production capacity. Those constraints are generally imposed by societal forces.[1] In the authoritarian state socialist system, however, organized societal forces are virtually nonexistent. The state doesn't have to negotiate with any private citizen in making its revenue policy, and it thereby pays little, if any, "transaction costs" for negotiating an agreement on the policy and for implementing the policy. What restrains the extractive capacity of the state thus is merely "discount rates"--its concern over securing future revenue. Sensible policy-makers would "extract revenue up to the point at which further extraction would put future output at risk."[2]

Does this mean fiscal politics does not exist in the state socialist system? Far from it. Although fiscal politics between the state and society is largely nonexistent, fiscal politics between the central government and local governments (at the provincial level and below) assumes prominence. The local government has a dual "personality" under the centralized fiscal system of state socialism. On the one hand, the local government acts as a "tax collector," collecting taxes from taxpayers within its jurisdiction (mainly state and collective enterprises, not individuals). On the other hand, it is a "taxpayer" itself, paying a certain amount or proportion of the revenue it generates locally to the central authorities. As a "tax collector," the local government is predatory. But as a "taxpayer," it has to deal with the no less predatory central government. Fiscal politics between the central and local governments results in the former trying to maximize its collection and the latter trying to minimize its contribution. The central government's revenue-producing capacity is thus constrained by its relative bargaining power vis-a-vis local governments and its calculation of the costs and benefits of attempted actions.

This chapter attempts to trace the trajectory of changing central-local relations by reconstructing the patterns of China's fiscal politics between the center and the provinces over the last 15 years. It will show how the central government's hold over financial resources has eroded, why the central state has lost its battle over the control of crucial political resources to competing local governments, and what have been the direct and indirect economic, social, and political consequences of the loss of central fiscal control. In the course of demonstrating how the once nearly monolithic power of the Chinese state has deteriorated into a fragile "weak state," I hope to test two hypotheses:

1. Under the authoritarian state socialist system, the central government's extractive capacity is circumscribed mainly by the evasive tendency of local governments.
2. The decline of this extractive capacity contributes to the general crisis of the Chinese state socialist system.

Decentralization

Since Mao's death in 1976, the Chinese economic system has undergone significant changes. The essence of the economic reform may be summarized by the phrase "*fenquan rangli*," that is, to devolve central control over resources and decision-making power to local governments on the one hand and enterprises on the other.[3] Deng Xiaoping chose this fiscal policy as the basis of his overall reform program.[4] Many have interpreted Deng's fiscal decentralization as a voluntary concession, aimed at narrowing the scope of state intervention and strengthening the role of the market. This is probably right. Unlike Mao, who had advocated decentralization as an alternative to both central planning and the market, Deng viewed decentralization as a way for China to move away from a command economy and to head in the direction of a market economy. But Deng's intention to replace the planned economy with a market economy was only part of the reason he initiated fiscal decentralization in 1980 and further expanded local and enterprise autonomy in the ensuing years. In fact, in 1980, the reformist central leadership had very few options other than fiscal decentralization.

In December 1978, the Chinese Communist Party convened the Third Plenary Session of the 11th Party Central Committee. The plenum set out to solve various problems affecting people's daily life that had accumulated for years. It was decided, among other things, to raise prices by a wide margin for basic farm produce and agricultural sideline produce, to reduce or remit agricultural taxes in some poor regions, to import a large amount of grain from abroad, to arrange jobs for millions of educated youth who had been sent down to the countryside, to raise salary levels for state employees, to restore the bonus system, to build more houses for urban residents, and the like. All of these measures were imperative for winning popular support for the reform drive, but they entailed a great burden on the state budget. In 1979, China ran a deficit of 20.6 billion yuan, almost three times as large as the previous peak of 7.1 billion in 1960. The next year saw yet another big deficit of 14.2 billion. Together, deficit in these two years was as high as 34.8 billion, exceeding the total deficit in the previous 29 years (24.8 billion).[5] It is not hard to imagine how anxious the central planners were when facing such big numbers.

How to make up the deficit? One way was to print bank notes. The total volume of new paper money issued in the two years (1979-1980) was 13 billion yuan more than the normal increase. This, however, ran the risk of inflation. Ultimately, the government had to find ways either to increase its revenue or to cut its expenditure, or both. In China, state enterprises, rather than individuals and private firms, were the main contributors to budget revenue. Some enterprises were run directly by the central government, but more were under the control of local governments at various levels. Local governments in effect possessed proprietary rights over their "own" enterprises. This was not a phenomenon observed in the former Soviet Union or in the former state socialist countries in Eastern Europe.[6] Due to China's unique form of central-local shared control of enterprises, local governments tended to resist the center's encroachment on local sources of revenues as much as they could. To increase revenues or cut expenditures, the central government thus had to negotiate with the provincial governments. The central government could not expect to increase revenue by recentralization without triggering strong local resistance. At a time when the reformist central leadership desperately needed the support of provincial leaders for their reform programs, it would be no less than political suicide for the center to provoke such local resistance. To choose the path of least resistance, the reformist leadership adopted the "eating-in-separate-kitchens" reform in 1980.[7] The scheme had two advantages: it required localities to bear more financial responsibilities while at least guaranteeing central income at current levels. The center hoped that decentralization would give local governments sufficient incentives to maximize budgetary revenues, thus making the fiscal "pie" bigger, which in turn would enlarge the absolute size of the center's own slice.

The 1980 fiscal decentralization was thus attributable not so much to the reformist leadership's voluntary decision to extract less than its capacity, as to its incapacity to maximize fiscal revenues in old ways. The decentralization reflected the central reformists' desire to increase revenue over time in a new way.[8]

Tug-of-War

This fiscal decentralization has fundamentally changed the institutional environment within which local governments make their decisions. Before the reform, the center mainly relied on administrative commands to create compliance among local governments. This was a method that induced compliance out of fear of sanctions. However, the method has two inherent drawbacks. On the one hand, for sanctions to be effective, the center has to build elaborate mechanisms of monitoring and enforcement into the structure of government. The marginal cost of universal enforcement could be prohibitively high if the center hopes to rely solely upon coercion to eliminate noncompliance. On the other hand, even if local governments comply passively, they would not have incentive to bring their potentialities into full play.

Deng's decentralization was aimed more at tapping the latent potentialities of local forces than at obtaining their passive compliance. Thus the reformist central leadership had to gradually replace mechanisms of administrative command with mechanisms of inducement. For such new mechanisms to work, the center needs to create an institutional environment where local governments find that the marginal benefits from compliance are larger than the marginal benefits from noncompliance. Employing inducement, however, is a very delicate task, which involves careful calculation and thoughtful institutional design on the part of the national government. A bad institutional design could produce undesired incentives and induce noncompliance rather than compliance. The "*fenquan rangli*" reform was such a defective design.

The "*fenquan rangli*" reform does not change the preference structure of local governments: their primary objective is still to enhance their own revenue base. What has changed are the following two things. First, local officials have become highly motivated to maximize local revenues. Before the reform, local governments had an organizational interest in increasing local revenues, but local officials as individuals did not have much personal interest in doing so. Back then, local revenues were used almost exclusively for capital investment; local officials' personal welfare was unrelated to the expansion of local revenues. After the reform, however, local revenues could be used to sponsor housing projects, to increase bonuses, to provide various forms of local collective welfare, and the like. The larger the volume of revenue under local discretion, the more the local people (at least some of them) would benefit. Since personal interests are now at stake, local officials tend to be energetic and innovative in expanding local revenues.

Second, what needs to be monitored has become so much more intricate than before that there are plenty of opportunities for local governments to take advantage of the central government. No matter what form of revenue sharing is adopted, it has to be executed according to some elaborate formulas. These necessarily require a larger volume and better quality of local information in order for central controllers to detect noncompliance. Since such information is hard to come by, local governments have a much better chance than before to augment their funds through various legal, quasi-legal, and illegal methods. Four strategies have often been used.

The first is to negotiate with the central government for favorable arrangements within the revenue-sharing framework. The provinces now are "cooking and eating in separate kitchens," namely, each of them is placed on a contractual agreement with the central government that stipulates either a revenue-sharing scheme or a lump sum payment (or subsidy) scheme. Such schemes are usually fixed for a number of years, and in some cases involve annual increments.[9] With more resources under their control since decentralization, the bargaining position of local governments in negotiating with the center over revenue-sharing has been generally strengthened. Therefore, throughout the 1980s, each time central-provincial contracts needed to be renewed, local governments were always able to strike better deals for themselves.

The second strategy used by localities to augment their funds is to take a noncooperative position whenever local governments consider central policies detrimental to their interest. This strategy is used to compel the center to make institutional changes favorable to local interests. To be sure, localities do not dare to openly challenge the authority of the central government. What they can do is to overtly comply, but covertly make no effort to enforce such central policies. They may even raise obstacles to the implementation of those central policies. The "taxes-for-profit" reform of the mid-1980s is a case in point. Introduced in 1983, the taxes-for-profit system was designed to reduce the negotiability of enterprises' financial obligations to the state treasury and to restore central fiscal strength. Most experts believed that the new system had the advantage of simultaneously promoting economic efficiency in enterprises and increasing state revenue. But it threatened the financial position of local governments by diminishing their patronage over local enterprises. Partially due to resistance from local governments, both profit margins and tax margins began to slope downwards beginning in early 1985 and continuing for twenty-two months in succession.[10] Facing such a grievous situation, the center had no choice but to give up the taxes-for-profit experiment in 1987. What replaced it was the tax contracting system.[11] Based on ad-hoc negotiations of profit or tax delivery responsibilities between enterprises and their supervisory bodies, the contracting system allowed local governments to continue to act as "patriarchs" in their regions.[12] A World Bank study revealed that no matter what form the contracting took, the effective rate of income tax tended to be significantly lower than under the tax-for-profit regime.[13] In other words, under the tax contracting system, the center received a declining share of enterprise income. The successful boycott of the taxes-for-profit reform demonstrates how local powers are now sometimes able to "veto" central decisions.

The third local strategy is to hold back as much local funds as possible from central extraction. Under the revenue-sharing regime, local governments have to share tax revenues that they collect locally with the central government. For this reason, they prefer to see local earnings retained as much as possible rather than subjecting such funds to formal taxes. As long as funds are kept within localities, they are within the reach of local governments. There are countless ways for local governments to help their enterprises retain more profits than they should. They may lower tax rates, authorize tax holidays, and grant tax relief for the benefit of local enterprises. Legally, local governments have only limited authority to grant such tax exemptions. But unauthorized exemptions have been so common and so widespread in recent years that it has become a big headache for the central government. Local governments may wink at local enterprises when they evade taxes. The level of tax evasion has reached colossal dimensions in recent years. Local governments may also be "munificent" in setting tax payment targets or profit remittance targets when negotiating with their subordinate enterprises over management contracts. The basic idea is to let local enterprises keep more profits.[14]

The fourth strategy used by localities to augment their income is to impose ad-hoc charges on local enterprises. Subnational governments' largesse in collecting formal taxes is coupled with their predatoriness in imposing various ad-hoc charges, or what is known in Chinese as *tanpai*, on enterprises. With no statutory basis, varieties of *tanpai* are authorized by local governments or their agencies. Whenever local authorities need funds, they impose some form of *tanpai* on local enterprises. To enterprises, these ad-hoc charges are exorbitant levies. But the central government does not receive a penny from the revenues generated by local governments in this way. Originally, *tanpai* was an innovation of rural cadres. After the decollectivization, accumulation funds of teams, brigades, and communes were no longer available to them. *Tanpai* was a new source of funds for supporting the operation of government and for feeding cadres at the grass-roots level. In the early 1980s, the central government issued numerous injunctions to stop *tanpai* from spreading in the countryside. Before long, however, *tanpai* made its way into cities. By the late 1980s, there were literally tens of thousands of forms of *tanpai*. For instance, the Chongqing Municipal Public Security Bureau alone imposed over 1,000 varieties of fees.[15] *Tanpai* has probably contributed more than formal taxes to revenues at some lower levels of government. Due to widespread complaints about the extent of *tanpai*, the central government has made numerous attempts to stop its rapid proliferation. This has proved to be a losing battle. In April 1988, the State Council issued a directive barring local governments from imposing *tanpai* on enterprises. An economist found in May 1989, however, that the Sichuan Provincial Government had imposed five new forms of *tanpai* after June 1988.[16] Moreover, a nationwide survey conducted in 1990 found that there were altogether more than 50,000 varieties of such charges,[17] from which local authorities extracted at least 20 billion yuan a year.[18] A large percentage of enterprises' extrabudgetary funds was sucked away by *tanpai*. Empirical studies suggest that somewhere between 20 and 60 percent of extrabudgetary funds originally retained in the name of enterprises eventually ended up in the pockets of local governments.[19] Many enterprises complain that the burden of *tanpai* is twice as heavy as that of formal income taxes.[20] The growing magnitude of *tanpai* is a sign that local governments have become strong enough to make rival claims over resources in defiance of the center's regulatory authority.

The Decline of Extractive Capacity

The evasive tendency of local governments has significantly weakened the central government's fiscal-extractive-capability, as is shown in the following four areas.

1. *Budget revenue as a percentage of national income has dropped by a wide margin.*

Because of the major government role in the economy, the level of budgetary revenue as a share of GNP is expected to be substantially higher in the state socialist setting than in the capitalist setting.[21] In 1978, on the eve of economic reform, government revenue as a ratio of GNP was 34 percent in China, already far below the levels achieved by the Soviet Union and East European countries.[22] After ten years of economic reform, the ratio had fallen to 19.8 percent in 1988, even lower than the average levels achieved by developed capitalist countries, middle income countries, and Third World countries.[23]

2. *Of the budget revenue, the central government's share has dropped by a wide margin.*

As Table 4.1 indicates, the Chinese central government's share of total budget revenue was generally higher than 60 percent before the reform. While the reform has no doubt enlarged the size of the fiscal "pie" and the size of the central government's "slice" in absolute terms, the central government's share has been shrinking.

In the former Soviet Union and former socialist countries of Eastern Europe, central revenue generally accounted for 70 percent of total revenue. Even in capitalist countries, it is rare for the ratio of central revenue to total government revenue to be lower than 50 percent. In the United States--a decentralized fiscal system by world standards--the federal government's tax income accounts for about 60 percent of total tax revenue while state and local governments together get only 40 percent.[24] As for expenditure, on average, the national governments' share accounts for about 70 percent of all government expenditures in industrialized countries, and 85 percent in Third World countries. In China, however, the central shares of government revenue and expenditure in the late 1980s were only 45 and 36 percent respectively, well below these averages. No wonder a World Bank study exclaims: "Only a few countries in the world can claim as great a degree of expenditure or revenue decentralization [as China]."[25]

Table 4.1 Central Government's Share of General Government Revenue and Expenditure (in percentages)

	Revenue	Expenditure
Pre-1980	--	57.8
1980	66.1	--
1981	58.5	50.8
1982	--	48.1
1983	--	48.2
1984	56.1	46.6
1985	--	44.5
1986	--	39.3
1987	48.9	39.5
1988	47.2	35.9
1989	45.2	36.1

Source: Wang Shaoguang, "The Role of the State in the Transition to Market Economy: The Declining State Extractive Capacity and Its Consequences in China," in Yang Gan, ed., *China after 1989* (Hong Kong: Oxford University Press, forthcoming).

3. *Extrabudgetary funds have skyrocketed.*[26]

Extrabudgetary funds are funds in the public sector that are not subject to central budgetary control. Before Deng's reform, there were two periods in which extrabudgetary funds expanded rapidly: the Great Leap Forward period (1958-1960) and the Cultural Revolution period (1966-1976). In 1978, on the eve of the reforms, the size of extrabudgetary funds was 31 percent as large as the size of total budget revenue. In the ten years between 1979 and 1988, while budget revenues grew 133 percent, extrabudgetary funds increased five-fold. Many items in today's extrabudgetary funds were previously budgetary items. What has happened is a shifting of some items from one category to the other. Once falling out of the category of budgetary revenue, funds are no longer within the reach of Beijing. By the beginning of the 1990s, almost as much public funds were circulating outside the state budget as within it. In many provinces, extrabudgetary revenues have surpassed budgetary revenues. Given their magnitude, some Chinese economists have begun to call extrabudgetary funds China's "second budget." On paper, only a small fraction of extrabudgetary funds (2 percent) is under the direct control of local governments, while most are to be managed by enterprises. But, as the discussion of *tanpai* shows, local governments have no difficulty encroaching on the resources of the enterprises under their jurisdictions.

4. Local control over banking institutions has increased.

Initially, central decision makers expected that granting some autonomy to commercial banks in their credit decisions would improve microeconomic efficiency and strengthen macroeconomic control. Neither goal has been achieved, however. Instead, bank loan decisions are still very much based on political rather than economic grounds. The only difference is that political interventions have intensified at the provincial level and below, while the central government has lost much of its macroeconomic control over credit.[27] The reason for the heavy local role in bank loans is simple. On the one hand, the interest rate of loans was often lower than the inflation rate in the second half of the 1980s, which meant that bank loans were virtually free. Demand for loans was thus understandably high. On the other hand, local bank branches have to place their immediate superiors' wishes above anyone else's. Otherwise, life for their staff could become miserable. An investigation shows that most bad bank loans were made under pressure from local governments.[28] The pressure of local governments resulted in an explosion of bank loans for capital investment in the late 1980s. Bank loans for fixed capital investment amounted only to 29 billion yuan in 1984, but rose to 127 billion in 1987, representing an average annual increase of 59 percent in each of the four years.

The above discussion of the effects of Deng's decentralization leads to two conclusions. First, decentralization has not reduced public authorities' extractive activities in general, but it has weakened the central state's extractive capacity. If funds generated outside the budget are added to budgetary funds, we would find that the ratio between resources kept in the public sector and national income has actually steadily increased since 1980. A Chinese economist estimated that in 1987 the sum total of budgetary and extrabudgetary revenues plus *tanpai* totaled 460 billion yuan, accounting for 50.3 percent of national income in that year. In comparison with other countries, this ratio was very high. But, of this 460 billion yuan, the central government controlled only 26 percent, or 120 billion.[29] Second, as local governments are amassing more resources under their direct control, their intervention in economic life has become more frequent and the range of their intervention has become wider.

In sum, while decentralization has demolished some aspects of the command economy, it has also reproduced and even strengthened other aspects of the command economy on a smaller scale. There is a real danger that China's national economy could be further fragmented, which would pose a threat not only to China's market-oriented economic reforms but also to China's national unity.

The Consequences of the State's Declining Extractive Capacity

With more resources at their disposal, local governments have become increasingly capable of pursuing goals according to their own preference orderings rather than central guidelines. By the same token, their behavior now has great impact on the macrostability of the system. Macrostability, however, is a "public good." Although it is in the common interest of all local governments to maintain macrostability, none of them would make voluntary contributions to the provision of the good. Rather, they all tend to use funds under their control to further their special local interests even at the expense of macrostability, hoping that the central government or someone else will clean up the mess they create. The central government is obligated to maintain macrostability, but it is pinched for money.[30]

Where do local governments spend their money? First of all, they tend to spend money on themselves. After 1979, administrative expenditure has grown rapidly. Before 1979, administrative expenditure usually accounted for 4 to 6 percent of total budget expenditure. For most of the 1970s, it was kept below 5 percent. After 1979, the ratio of administrative expenditure to total budgetary expenditure began a steady increase. In 1988, it reached an unprecedented 9 percent. Administrative expenditure has grown much faster than total budget expenditure or any other budget expenditure item except one--scientific research and education. The local share of the increase was higher than the center's.

In addition to money from budgetary funds, local governments also spent a growing proportion of their extrabudgetary funds on public administration. Administrative expenditure outside the formal budget increased 16.7 percent in 1984, 42.8 percent in 1985, 25.5 percent in 1986, and 32.2 percent in 1987.[31] A large amount of money was spent on luxury items such as cars, air conditioners, refrigerators, modern office equipment, nice office buildings, and the like. Extravagant local administrative expenditure runs counter to the interests of the local population as well as the interests of the central government. It demonstrates that local governments are now able to pursue their own preferences even when their preferences are divergent from the central government's preferences and local societal preferences.

When local governments' preferences are convergent with local societal preferences, it is even easier for local governments to translate their preferences into policy actions. In the 1980s, luxury hotels, state-of-the-art amusement parks, sky-high TV towers, modern overpasses, giant stadiums, and many other types of large non-productive projects sprang up like mushrooms after rain throughout China. Since local residents do not object to improving the appearance of their towns, local governments can claim that they represent local interests by spending money on such projects. But local bosses intend to kill two birds with one stone. Their other aim for investing in such projects is to build up their personal public images. No wonder many such projects are called "monument projects of so-and-so."

Of course, local governments would not invest all of their money in non-productive items. To expand the basis of their future revenues, they tend to invest as much money in productive projects as they can generate. In selecting projects for investment, local governments usually act very "rationally." They are reluctant to invest in infrastructure projects such as energy, raw materials, highways, railroads, education, and the like, because such projects generally need large amounts of investment, take a long time to finish, run a high risk, and, worst of all from the local governments' point of view, they benefit other localities too. Local governments' favorites are high-profit processing projects that employ local laborers and yield quick returns. Thus, the decade of the 1980s saw small cigarette factories, small breweries, small textile mills, and small home electronic appliance plants springing up throughout China.

Having lost control over the purse strings of local governments, central planners find it increasingly difficult to control aggregate demand for investment and consumption. In the past, expansion drives were usually initiated by ambitious central planners. Now local officials are the driving forces behind capital expansion. The problem is that while there is a self-constraining mechanism at the center, there is no constraint at local levels. Central planners may start a "great leap forward," but they cannot afford to ignore imbalances in the national economy for long. However, local governments don't have to worry about macroeconomic instability when they initiate expansions.[32] Every local government thinks that its investments are smart, rational, and absolutely imperative for local socioeconomic development. If there are problems with the national economy, other local governments or the central government are to blame. Since no region wants to cool down its own investment fever, the national economy is often overheated. Since 1982, the central government has made countless efforts to cut fixed asset investments, but that investment increased 28.6 percent in 1982, 14.5 percent in 1983, 33.4 percent in 1984, and 38.7 percent in 1985.[33] In 1986, it also increased by a big margin. In January 1987, the center convened a national conference of provincial governors, at which the governors were told that no more new projects were to be permitted. But in the first two months of that year, however, 1,105 projects broke ground, among which 88.8 percent were financed by local authorities. In March, the central government issued a strongly worded directive demanding that all new projects be stopped. And in July, Yao Yilin, then China's Vice Premier, repeated the warning. In the end, however, fixed investment went up 20.7 percent that year.[34] After 1987, except for the years 1989 and 1990, the central government has never been able to keep capital investment under control.

Central control has been deficient because the central government simply does not possess adequate tools to direct local investments. By the end of the 1980s, less than 10 percent of fixed asset investment was financed by budgetary funds, and the rest of it by bank loans, extrabudgetary funds, *tanpai*, and foreign investment. Under such circumstances, state planning becomes a chimera. The direction and magnitude of local investments are, to a large extent, out of the center's reach. The center can merely hold down its own spending, while watching local governments continue their expansion of investment.[35]

Central control over consumption levels is as loose as its control over investment. In the past, controlling the overall level of consumption only required the central government to issue an annual aggregate wage plan for lower levels of government. The latter then disaggregated the central wage plan into wage quotas for each and every individual enterprise in their jurisdictions. After the reforms, the central government still sets the ceiling of the total wage bill, but it is no longer effective at controlling the level of consumption, because local authorities have more say about bonuses which now constitute a very large proportion of people's income. In the 12 years between 1978 and 1989, while the nation's total wage bill increased by 460 percent, bonuses registered a 4,525 percent increase.[36]

As investment and consumption were constantly expanding, aggregate demand consistently exceeded supply during much of the 1980s. The cumulative result was inflation. In the first three decades after 1949, prices scarcely rose. From 1951 to 1978, the average annual inflation rate was 0.7 percent. In the first years of economic reform, inflation remained mild, rising 2.6 percent annually on average from 1979 to 1984. After 1984, the situation got worse every year. In 1988, the inflation rate rose to 18.5 percent, and in the first half of 1989, it reached 25.5 percent. The urban cost of living increased even faster. As inflation rose to levels that had been quantitatively unknown in recent years, it threw the whole nation into a panic, contributing to the emergence of the 1989 protest movement.[37]

The enormous expansion of local autonomy also resulted in growing regional inequality. During the Maoist era, as Lardy points out, the central authorities were able to reduce the large initial interregional differences in levels of development by redistributing resources from richer to poorer provinces.[38] Today, the center still tries to use differential revenue-sharing rates, with the individual provinces as a primary mechanism for redistribution.[39] But this old method is not effective any more. A World Bank study reveals an interesting phenomenon: of the ten provinces with the highest levels of per capita output, six had below-average revenue growth during the reform period. In contrast, of the ten provinces with the lowest level of per capita output, nine had above average growth in revenue collection. The difference in revenue growth does not mean that poor provinces have caught up with rich provinces. Rather, it tells us that the poor provinces tend to make a greater collection effort than their richer counterparts. Why is there such a behavioral difference? Because under the provincial contracting system of "eating in separate kitchens," rich provinces have to remit a certain proportion of the shared taxes to the central government, while poor provinces can retain all the revenue they collect. By collecting less than what is required, rich provinces can keep more resources "at home," and thus available for *tanpai*. In fact, the development gap in today's China is the largest it has been since the founding of the People's Republic in 1949, reflected in the widening of fiscal expenditure differentials between the provinces. Between 1983 and 1986, for instance, Shanghai's budgetary expenditure tripled, Guangdong's increased 138 percent, and Zhejiang's rose 132 percent; but Tibet's increased only 61 percent, Qinghai's 65 percent, Shanxi's 71 percent, and Ningxia's 73 percent. Another symptom of the central government's growing inability to direct redistribution among the provinces is the declining role of the transfer system. Take Ningxia, one of China's poorest provinces, as an example. During the Second Five-Year Plan period (1958-1962), its fiscal subsidy from Beijing increased on average 71 percent annually, and during the Fourth Five-Year Plan period (1971-1975) it still grew over 20 percent a year. But the increase in the central subsidy declined to just 14.3 annually percent during the Sixth Five-Year Plan period (1981-1985), 11.8 percent in 1986, and 8.4 percent in 1987.[40]

Budgetary incomes account for only part of the fiscal resources available to local governments. As pointed out above, extrabudgetary funds have exceeded budgetary incomes in many provinces. In comparing the growth rates of the provinces' extrabudgetary incomes, we find that the rates tend to be higher in rich provinces than in poor provinces. Between 1982 and 1985, the average annual rate of increase was 111 percent in Shandong, 86.5 percent in Liaoning, 68 percent in Zhejiang, 57 percent in Jiangsu; but only 33.9 percent in Ningxia, and 41.3 percent in Gansu. In 1985, the total extrabudgetary income of seven poor provinces (Guizhou, Yunnan, Tibet, Shaanxi, Gansu, Qinghai, and Ningxia) was less than Liaoning's alone.[41] Since extrabudgetary funds tend to be self-multiplying, the gaps are likely to be perpetuated and widened. The 11 coastal provinces, for instance, procured 55 percent of all local extrabudgetary funds in 1985. Two years later their share rose to over 70 percent.[42]

Even under the capitalist system, the central government has to master sufficient fiscal resources to serve three general policy objectives: the provision of social goods (allocation function), adjustment of the distribution of income and wealth (the distribution function), and maintenance of macroeconomic stability (the stabilization function).[43] However, Deng's decentralization has weakened China's central government's extractive capacity to the degree that it lacks adequate resources to perform these basic functions. First, there exists a substantial backlog of infrastructure needs, which is believed to be a major impediment to growth. The central government sought to allocate more resources to bottleneck sectors such as energy, transportation, and basic raw materials, but local governments' investments in the processing industries have always increased at a higher rate. As a result, the sectoral imbalance has only deteriorated.

Second, inequalities have become greater. Traditionally, the state socialist system didn't use fiscal policy to adjust the distribution of income and wealth. What was considered fair or just was generally factored into the primary income distribution through wage policy. Thus, when economic reform generates greater inequalities, China doesn't have an efficient mechanism to adjust increasingly unequal primary distribution. And the central government lacks sufficient funds for building new safety nets to replace old ones.

Third, aggregate demand has greatly exceeded available output in recent years. In such a situation, to stabilize the economy, the central government needs to adopt restrictive measures to reduce demand. However, due to Deng's fiscal decentralization, the center was no longer able to control local governments' expenditures. Although China's rate of increase in output value was impressive during the 1980s, the country suffered high inflation, low efficiency, and volatile economic fluctuations.

A modern state has to perform the functions of allocation, [re]distribution, and stabilization. Otherwise, the state will lose its legitimacy to rule. But in China, the central government's ability to extract resources is now very limited, falling far short of the level necessary for performing the three basic state functions. Unable to cut expenditures to match revenue declines, the central government did what it could: it ran up the debt. China had gone into debt before. This doesn't mean that every time it ran a deficit it was in fiscal crisis. Between 1950 and 1978, there were 12 deficit years in China, among which four occurred during the decentralized Great Leap Forward period and another four during the chaotic Cultural Revolution period. Except for those occurring during the Great Leap Forward period, the magnitude of deficits was generally small, and the government was able to eliminate them when it became worried about the red on its balance sheet. Since

1979, however, the budget has been characterized by continuously rising deficits. In the 14 years between 1979 and 1992, there has not been a single year in which the government escaped a large deficit. The deficits occurred mainly at the central level.[44] And the size of the deficits has been getting larger and larger with time. To finance its fiscal deficit, the Chinese government has issued billions of yuan of government bonds in the last decade. Beginning in 1990, China started to repay what it had borrowed in the 1980s. It is estimated that throughout the 1990s the annual repayment of principal and interest will amount, on average, to 30-40 billion yuan--equivalent to 40 percent of the central government's annual budget income in the late 1980s.[45] If the current distribution pattern of financial resources is to endure, it will be even more difficult for the central government to perform the functions of stabilization and redistribution, which are essential to securing future growth and welfare.

Donnithorne once likened the Chinese central government to a medieval king who was not able to live off his own funds and who had to rely on funds extracted by feudatories.[46] But now the "vassals" have begun to feel and act like independent lords of their soils and to detach themselves in spirit from the vassalage. They are so powerful and assertive that they can resist the fulfillment of their fiscal obligations. Here we have what Schumpeter calls "the crisis of a fiscal system: obvious, ineluctable, continuous failure due to unalterable social changes."[47]

A weak state tends to be a corrupted state. The better the quality of a ruler's information about the actual wealth, income, and property produced in the land, and the more resources in the ruler's hands to be allocated, the more effective is his control over the behaviors of government bureaucrats. Conversely, the more alternatives there are for local bureaucrats to gain access to resources, the more likely they are to become corrupted under an undemocratic system. In China, there has never been an institutional mechanism to check bureaucrats from below. After Mao's death, the mechanism to check them from above--political campaigns--was set aside. Deng's decentralization thus greatly increases opportunities for those in power to profiteer by abusing their power. The result has been widespread corruption.

A weak state cannot be a fair state. With limited extractive capacity, a weak state would have little to be redistributed, thus becoming unable to adjust the distribution of income and wealth to assure conformance with what society considers "fair" and "just." Intraregional as well as interregional disparities have been exacerbated as a result of the reforms.[48] The increasing variance and inequality spawn dangers of social polarization and political disaffection. Tremendous resentment against the "winners" has been building among the "losers" of Deng's policy of "letting some people get rich first." A 1987 survey of residents in 33 cities found that 88.7 percent of people thought that social inequalities were "great or very great." It is noteworthy that in 1980, when the group Solidarity first emerged, a public opinion poll in Poland found 85 percent of people thought that social inequalities in Poland were "great or very great." This percentage is even lower than that found in China in the late 1980s.[49]

Macroeconomic instability, skyrocketing inflation, widespread corruption, and growing economic inequality have severely shaken people's confidence in the Chinese state's ability to manage the economy, control its own bureaucratic elites, and ensure social justice. Were one to single out one factor conditioning the Chinese people's support for the current regime, it would be an expectation of protection from inequality and uncertainty by a strong welfare state. Deng Xiaoping gambled on being able to compensate Chinese people with greater prosperity in exchange for erosion of equality and security. It is still too early to say whether his experiment will succeed. Despite China's impressive record of economic growth in the last fifteen years, the government seems to have not been able to "engender and maintain the belief among its citizens that the existing political institutions are the most appropriate ones for the society."[50]

A weak state is also unlikely to be able to arrest centrifugal tendencies among local governments. Local governments' financial muscle can be easily converted into political muscle. Throughout the 1980s, local political elites in China were busy building political machines that dominated local economies and engaged in sometimes fierce competition with the center and with one another over scarce raw materials, goods, and funds. Having a stake in maintaining and expanding their control over such resources, local governments would spare no efforts to protect local industries. The local authorities in peripheral regions well endowed with natural resources tend to keep raw materials for local processing industries. They sometimes employ a police force and militia to patrol their borders in order to block local suppliers' attempt to "smuggle" raw materials out. There have been numerous media reports on interregional "silkworm wars," "wool wars," "tobacco wars," "tea wars," "cotton wars," "coal wars," and wars over other raw materials in recent years. To retaliate, core regions dependent on the import of raw materials tend to block technology transfer to resource-endowed regions. And all local governments tend to prevent the inflow of finished products from other localities in order to protect the sale of local products.[51] Local protectionism has resulted in the "balkanization" of China's economic system. A number of Chinese economists and political scientists have used the term "feudalist structure" to characterize the situation in the late 1980s. They believe that China has been split into 30 dukedoms (provinces) with some 2,000 rival principalities (counties).[52] Although "vassals" have not been bold enough to openly challenge the ultimate political authority of Beijing, the emergence of local power centers has produced deep cracks in the regime.

Conclusion

In the recent history of China, the decline of the central government's extractive capacity seems to have played an important part in regime transition. And, whenever this happened, it was not societal forces but centrifugal forces within the state that were responsible for weakening the center. Characterized by a monolithic structure, the original fiscal system of the Ming Dynasty (1368-1644) was designed to impose a unified administration over all the financial resources of the empire. The main concern of the dynasty's founders was to prevent local governments from challenging central authority through over-developing their financial potential. But fiscal practice diverged increasingly from the original design. Later on, tax collectors became more and more intrusive. However, this was not a sign of strength, but of a loss of central control. "The arbitrary and excessive demands of the tax collectors ... in part reflected this loss of control, and in part represented attempts by officialdom to compensate for its own organizational weakness." Toward the end of the dynasty, "Though the imperial government was in theory omnipotent, in practice it was often unable to act."[53]

The Qing Dynasty (1644-1911) started with an effective centralized fiscal system too.[54] But, from the late 18th century on, the central government became increasingly unable to extract sufficient resources for sustaining its rule. In the 150 years from 1750 until the early 1900s, the center suffered an enormous decline (of almost two thirds) in the real values of the revenues collected from direct taxes. The growth rate of indirect taxes did begin to accelerate in the latter part of the 19th century, but much of this increase was siphoned off by local governments.[55]

The late Republican period witnessed a similar situation: while the bureaucratic power of the central government was becoming parcelized, the fiscal foundations of local governments were actually strengthened in the process. The weakening of central control thus went hand in hand with the unprecedented expansion of state penetration in society.[56] In retrospect, one has good reason to speculate that there were direct or indirect causal links between the degeneration of the state's fiscal extractive capability and the fall of these three regimes.

Developments in the last fifteen years seems to resemble what happened to the three previous regimes on the eve of their collapse: the thickening of local statehood occurred concomitantly with the thinning of central statehood.[57] In other words, the deepening of state penetration in local society was not accompanied by a strengthening of the capacity of the state as a corporate whole. What exactly will happen to the current Chinese regime is hard to predict. But, one thing seems clear: for good or ill, the Chinese political system will undergo a fundamental change in the near future.

Notes

1. Margaret Levi, *Of Rule and Revenue* (Berkeley: University of California Press, 1988), pp. 2-3.

2. Ibid., pp. 32-33.

3. Li Xianglu, "Weishemo Shuo Fenquan Rangli Gaige Fangzhen Shi Zhengque De" (Why I Think the *Fenquan Rangli* Reform is Right), *Zhishi Fenzi* [The Chinese Intellectual].(Fall 1990).

4. Zuo Chuntai and Song Xinzhong, *Zhongguo Shehui Zhuyi Caizheng Jianshi* (The History of Chinese Socialist Public Finance) (Beijing: Chinese Financial Economics Press, 1988), p. 453.

5. Ibid., pp. 431-452.

6. David Granick, *Chinese State Enterprises: A Regional Property Rights Analysis* (Chicago: The University of Chicago Press, 1990).

7. Susan L. Shirk, "Playing to the Provinces: Deng Xiaoping's Political Strategy of Economic Reform," Paper presented at the annual Meeting of the American Political Science Association, San Francisco, September 2, 1990.

8. In fact, the 1980 fiscal decentralization was supposed to be accompanied by the return of several thousand large enterprises to direct central government subordination. But due to strong local opposition, the second part of the reform was never implemented. It also needs to be noted that right before he was purged a second time in 1976, Deng Xiaoping made a decision to recentralize financial resources, which was reversed after his fall. See Allen S. Whiting,"Domestic Politics and Foreign Trade in the PRC, 1971-1976," Michigan Papers in Chinese Studies, No. 39 (1979), Ann Arbor.

9. Christine P. W. Wong, "Fiscal Reform and Local Industrialization: The Problematic Sequencing of Reform in Post-Mao China," Unpublished paper, March 1991.

10. Yang Peixin, "Shuili Fenliu Wenti Xuyao Shenru Tantao" (It is Necessary to Discuss the Pros and Cons of the "Separating-Profits-from-Taxes Reform"), *Jingji Guanli* (Economic Management) 1 (1991): p. 60.

11. Shirk, op. cit., pp. 20-21.

12. David Bachman, "Implementing Chinese Tax Policy," in David M. Lampton (ed.), *Policy Implementation in Post-Mao China* (Berkeley: University of California Press, 1987).

13. The World Bank, *China: Revenue Mobilization and Tax Policy* (Washington, D.C., 1990), p.11. Also see Wang Yunguo, "Dui Dangqian Qiye Fudan Zhuang-

kuang De Fenxi He Jianyi [An Analysis of Burdens on State Enterprises]," *Hubei Caizheng Yanjiu* (Hubei Research Papers of Finance) 4 (1992):28.

14. Wang Shaoguang, "The Role of the State in the Transition to a Market Economy: The Declining State Extractive Capacity and Its Consequences in China," in Yang Gan (ed.), *China after 1989* (Hongkong: Oxford University Press, forthcoming).

15. Interview with an official from the Ministry of Finance.

16. Wang Shaofei, "Yao Zhongshi Jijinfeng He Jizire Dui Caizheng Fenpei Di Chongji" (Taking Seriously the Effects on Public Finance of Fund Pools), *Caizheng* (Public Finance) No.8 (1989).

17. The Enterprise Management Division of the National Planning Commission, "Zhizhi Sanluan Jianqing Qiye Fudan" (Forbid the Three *Luan* and Relieve Enterprises from Their Heavy Burdens), in the Editorial Committee (eds.), *Zhongguo Qiye Guanli Nianjian 1991* (China's Yearbook of Enterprise Management, 1991), p. 327.

18. Wang Shaofei, "Zhongyang he Difang Caizheng Guanxi de Mubiao Moshi" (An Ideal Model of Central-Local Fiscal Relations), *Caimao Jingji* (Financial Economics) 5 (1988).

19. Liang Huaping, "Jiaqiang Yushuanwai Zijin Guanli Bahao Zonghe Caili Pingheng" (Strengthen Control over Extrabudgetary Funds and Strive for a Comprehensive Fiscal Balance), *Jianghuai Luntan* (The Jianghuai Forum) 4(1989); Zhu Wei, "Zhouqian Guojia Yushuanwai Zijin de Xin Renshi" (On Comprehensive State Budget: A New Perspective on Extrabudgetary Funds), *Caijing Yanjiu* [Research in Financial Economics] 7(1990); Li Nianhua, "Shuilianjiao Huanshi Lianjiaoshui" (Reluctance to Pay Taxes or Difficulty in Collecting Taxes), *Liaowang* (Outlook), No.27 (1991).

20. Wang Wentong and Xiao Houxiong, "Guanyu 100 Hu Qiye Shuifei Fudan Qingkuang de Diaocha Baogao" (A Report on the Tax and Non-Tax Burdens of 100 Enterprises), *Hubei Caizheng Yanjiu* 1 (1992).

21. Richard A. Musgrave, *Fiscal Systems* (New Haven: Yale University Press, 1969), p. 33.

22. Ibid., p. 42. In the mid-1960s, the ratio was 76.9 percent in Czechoslovakia, 62.6 percent in Bulgaria, 54.8 percent in Poland, and 50.6 percent in the USSR.

23. The World Bank, op. cit., p. 6.

24. Ibid., p. 80.

25. Ibid., pp. 76-80.

26. Wang Shaoguang, "The Rise of the Second Budget and the Decline of State Capacity: The Case of China," in Andrew G. Walder (ed.), *The Political Consequences of Departures from Central Planning: Economics Reform and Political Change in Communist States* (Stanford, CA: Stanford University Press, forthcoming).

27. Huang Yasheng, "Web of Interests and Patterns of Behavior of Chinese Local Economic Bureaucracies and Enterprises during Reform," *China Quarterly* (1990), pp. 451-453.

28. Rongzi, "Xianshi Yunxing De Jizhi Jiqi Gaige" [Finance: The Existing System and Its Reform], *Jingji Yanjiu* (Economic Research) 11 (1987).

29. Wang Shaofei, "Zhongyang he Difang Caizheng Guanxi de Mubiao Moshi".

30. Li Qinding, Fan Yong, and Cong Yenzi, "Dangqian Caizheng Mianlin de Zhuyao Wenti ji Duice (Main Problems in Public Finance and Possible Solutions)", *Caimao Jingji* 4 (1987).

31. Cong Yezi, "Jiaqiang dui Yusuanwai Zijin de Hongguan Guanli (Strengthen Macro Control over Extrabudgetary Funds)", *Caimao Jingji* 1 (1990).

32. Chen Kang, "Enterprise Autonomy, Local Government Authority, and Central Directives: The Failure of Recentralization in China", Unpublished paper, 1990.

33. Liu Shuinian, "Kongzhi Touzi Guimo, Tiaozheng Touzi Jiegou, Baozheng Guomin Jingji Wending Fazhan (Control the Size of Investment, Adjust the Structure of Investment, Strive for Stable Economic Development)", *Zhongguo Jingji Nianjian 1986* (China's Economic Yearbook, 1986), pp. 1-9.

34. Yao Yilin, "Jianjue ba Zichou Jijian Touzi Yaxialai," (Repress Self-funded Investments), *Caizheng*, No.8 (1987).

35. Barry Naughton, "The Decline of Central Control over Investment in Post-Mao China," in Lampton (ed.), op. cit.

36. The National Statistics Bureau, *Zhongguo Tongji Nianjian 1990* (China's Statistics Yearbook 1990), (Beijing: Chinese Statistics Press, 1990), p. 132.

37. Wang Shaoguang, "Deng Xiaoping's Reform and the Chinese Workers' Participation in the Protest Movement of 1989," *Research in Political Economy*, Vol. 13 (1992).

38. Nicholas R. Lardy, *Economic Growth and Distribution in China* (Cambridge: Cambridge University Press, 1978).

39. See Huo Shitao's chapter in this volume.

40. Ningxia Statistics Bureau, *Ningxia Tongji Nianjian 1988* (Ningxia Statistics Yearbook, 1988), p. 357.

41. The Comprehensive Planning Division of the Ministry of Finance, *Zhongguo Caizheng Tongji 1950-1985* (China's Public Finance Statistics, 1950-1985), (Beijing: Chinese Financial Economics Press, 1987), pp. 144-145.

42. Deng Yingtao, et al, *Zhongguo Yushuanwai Zijin Fenxi* (An Analysis of China's Extrabudgetary Funds) (Beijing: Chinese People University Press, 1990), pp.99-103.

43. Richard A. Musgrave and Peggy B. Musgrave, *Public Finance in Theory and Practice*, third edition, (New York: McGraw-Hill, 1980), Chapter 1.

44. Yun Zhipin and Wang Hong, "Nuli Tigao Caizheng Shouru He Zhongyang Shouru di Bizhong", (Strive for Increasing the Ratio of Budgetary Revenue and the Ratio of Central Budgetary Revenue), *Qiushi* (Seeking Truth) No. 4 (1990), p.14.

45. Zhou Kai, "Jiejue Woguo Caizheng Kunnan di Shilu Xuanzhe ji Duice" (Solutions to Fiscal Difficulties of Our Country), *Xueshu Luntan* (Academic Forum) (1991), p.14.

46. Audrey Donnithorne, " Central-Provincial Economic Relations in China," A Contemporary China Paper, no. 16 (Contemporary China Center, Research School of Pacific Studies, Australian National University, 1981).

47. Joseph A. Schumpeter,"The Crisis of the Tax State," in *International Economic Papers: Translations Prepared for the International Economic Association* (New York: Macmillan, 1954), p.14.

48. Ehtisham Ahmad and Yan Wang, "Inequality and Poverty in China: Institutional Change and Public Policy, 1978-1988," Unpublished World Bank Paper, 1990. See also John P. Burns. "China's Governance: Political Reform in a Turbulent Environment," *China Quarterly*, (1990), pp. 486-491.

49. Wang Shaoguang, "Deng Xiaoping's Reform and the Chinese Workers' Participation in the Protest Movement of 1989," in Yang Gan (ed.), op. cit.

50. Seymour Martin Lipset, *Political Man: The Social Bases of Politics*, expanded edition, (Baltimore: The Johns Hopkins University Press 1981), p.64.

51. Chen Kang, "Enterprise Autonomy, Local Government Authority, and Central Directives," op. cit., p.8.

52. Xia Yang and Wang Zhigang, "Zhongguo Jingji Geju Xianxiang Chutian" (A preliminary Study of China's Economic Feudal Separatist Rule), *Liaowang* 39 (1988); "Dangdai Zhuhou Jingji Youshilu" (Feudal Separatist Rule in Contemporary China), *Renmin Ribao* (People's Daily) August 6, 1989; Shen Liren, Dai Yuanchen, "Woguo Zhuhou Jingji Di Xingcheng Jiqi Biduan He Genyuan" (The Roots, Formation, and Malpractice of Economic Separatism), *Jingji Yanjiu*, 3 (1990).

53. Ray Huang, *Taxation and Governmental Finance in Sixteenth-Century Ming China* (Cambridge: Cambridge University Press, 1974), chapter 8.

54. Peng Yuxin, "Qingmo Zhongyang Yu Gesheng Caizheng Guanxi" (Central-Provincial fiscal Relations in Late Qing), in Li Dongyi (ed.), *Zhongguo Jindaishi Luncong* (Research Papers in Modern Chinese History), Vol. 2, No. 5 (Taibei: Zhengzhong Press, 1963).

55. Prasenjit Duara, "State Involution: A Study of Local Finances in North China, 1911-1935," *Comparative Study of Society and History* (1987), pp.137-138.

56. Presenjit Duara, *Culture, Power, and the State: Rural North China, 1900-1942* (Stanford: Stanford University Press, 1988).

57. Vivienne Shue, "State Socialism and Modernization in China through Thick and Thin," Paper Presented at the 1988 Annual Meeting of the American Political Science Association.

5

Rural Reform and the Rise of Localism

Luo Xiaopeng

One of the most significant consequences of China's rural reform in the 1980s was the rise of localism. By localism, I follow the customary usage in China, referring to a process by which regional officials actually make and implement some local policies based on local interests or simply on their own interests, against the will and discipline of the central leadership. It is the main argument of this chapter that the liberalization of the Chinese rural economy has led to the rise of localism and made the trend of localism irreversible. To support this argument, this paper will explain how the political and economic processes of rural reforms prompted the rise of localism in the context of the overall reform.

The first stage of Chinese rural reform was the process of restoring family farming. The dramatic success of this peaceful revolution in rural China, which took place beginning in 1978, greatly benefitted from large interregional disparities as well as from the subtle role of provincial leaders in the post-Mao power struggle.

Combined with the general reform, the continuing liberalization of the Chinese rural economy, triggered by the emergence of the household responsibility system (HRS), created a self-enforcing dynamic between the urban and rural economies through market forces. The marketization stimulated by rural economic growth interrupted the normal "reform cycle", which in later stage often leads to recentralization in socialist economies.

Driven by market forces, especially by the freed rural economy, a number of fundamental changes have been brought to every stratum of Chinese society, and these changes have undermined the basis of central power. As China is a huge country, and central authorities have proved incapable of making universal rules for the market, interventions by local authorities have become critical to keep the market functioning and to balance conflicting interests (such as urban versus rural). So localism, particularly the rise of provincial power in shaping economic policy, has grown along with the process of marketization.

Household Responsibility System (HRS) and the Localization of Rural Policies

Rural Poverty as a Political Card in the Post-Mao Power Struggle

One of Mao Zedong's ambitions was to realize regional equality through the industrialization of traditionally agrarian areas of the country. While the strong state did succeed in mobilizing and transferring industrial resources from the coastal areas to the majority of inland provinces and reducing the gap in gross industrial output among provinces,[1] the major unintended consequence of this process was the vast rural poverty that occurred in inland areas. The famine of 1959-1960 killed more than 30 million people, most of them peasants. In addition, the industrialization process impoverished more than half of all Chinese peasants in comparison with their rising living standards in the early 1950s, after the Chinese communists took power and launched the land reform campaign.[2] The peasants in the previously less industrialized regions seemed victimized by the local industrialization policies of Mao's regime.[3]

The average income of the rural population grew slowly in the 1970s, but behind the statistics lies the reality of polarization. Some rural collectives doubled their income by developing industry, while many others fell into the vicious cycle of collective poverty as industrial inputs to agriculture increased. The process of impoverishment even extended to the areas where agricultural income had long been above average, such as the Sanjiang Plain in Heilongjiang Province and the Jian Basin in Jiangxi Province. In 1975 and 1976, hungry peasants throughout the country went to cities to beg for food. Many of them carried with them the written permission of local authorities.

The Chinese Communist leaders gradually understood the political implications of the proliferation of rural poverty in China. Even before Mao's death, some disgraced party leaders started to play the political card of rural poverty as they watched the impending showdown with the radicals.[4] After Mao's death, rural poverty became an issue of paramount importance when Deng Xiaoping and Chen Yun prepared an attack against Party Chairman Hua Guofeng, Mao's successor. A special investigation into rural poverty was carried out before the Third Plenum. The astonishing reality of the rural poverty situation not only proved to be an effective weapon for Deng and Chen in their political fight with Hua Guofeng, it also created a sense of crisis within the new leadership.[5]

The Political Dynamics of Establishing the HRS

Michel Oksenberg has studied the economic policy-making of the Chinese government after Deng and Chen took over central power. Among his findings, he identified two important trends: (1) an increasing reliance on the bureaucracy, and (2) the seeking of consensus among conflicting agencies.[6] This was true for those economic policies initiated at the top levels or in the central bureaucracies and implemented down through the hierarchy. However, the populace and the local leaders did play a crucial role in bringing about the household responsibility system (HRS), even after it was ruled out by the central leadership at the very beginning of the reforms. Because of its self-contradictory nature, socialist reform could not be undertaken without crisis, so the top-down policy-making process inevitably encountered bottom-up spontaneity from the populace and local leaders. The establishment of the HRS was a miraculous success in combining these two types of processes in the pursuit of reform objectives. Therefore, five important characteristics of the processes are worth identifying:

(1) The important role of local crisis, which made local leaders unable to find economic solutions among the policy alternatives stipulated by the central authorities. Motivated by a sense of urgency, as well as encouraged by the general political atmosphere favoring change, some spontaneous actions by local people crossed the line drawn by the central leaders. In the case of the HRS, the severe drought which took place in the fall of 1978 in Anhui Province was the trigger that stimulated the first attempt at implementing the HRS.[7]

(2) Initiatives at the grassroots gained decisive support and protection from a strong provincial leader, Wan Li, who enjoyed nationwide popularity for his moral strength and a great factional advantage in the ongoing power struggle at the top. The crucial role of Wan Li was to give peasants a chance to experiment with the HRS, without which their spontaneity would have been vulnerable to bureaucratic suppression.

(3) The great interregional disparity was successfully used to break down ideological barriers to change. Since it was not difficult to under-

stand the subversive impact of introducing the HRS into the socialist system, particularly as a means of acceding to peasants' spontaneous pressure, the reformers emphasized that the HRS was only applicable to poor areas at the early stage in its implementation. This allowed fundamental change to take place with less initial opposition.

(4) The new central leadership, then still in the process of taking power from Mao's successor Hua Guofeng and badly in need of popular support, accepted the coexistence of conflicting policies in different provinces. As the HRS achieved great success in the areas where it had been applied, the debate over the HRS among local leaders intensified.[8] Deng Xiaoping wisely took a neutral position, and allowed provincial leaders to experiment with the different reform policies they believed appropriate to their jurisdictions.[9] No matter what motives and political situation prompted Deng to make this unprecedented decision, it brought about a completely new paradigm for reform policy-making.

(5) The process by which the majority of provinces converted their basic rural policy into the HRS was not primarily propelled by political pressure from the central leadership, but rather by pressure from the populace within the context of interregional competition for economic prosperity.[10]

Apparently there were some similarities between the decollectivization of the 1979-1983 period and the collectivization that took place from 1955 to 1958. Both constituted sweeping changes with far-reaching impacts and both were carried out by local party organizations driven by a prevailing policy wind. But the difference between the two processes is also fundamental. The change of attitude of many people who originally opposed the HRS was caused by economic motives, not by political coercion as it was during collectivization.

In the less-developed areas, the main opposition to the HRS came from the rural cadres and local state employees whose family members remained in villages. Eventually, however, the practice of the HRS in other localities convinced them that they could also benefit from decollectivization, perhaps even more than other peasants. Trapped by the collective poverty game, everyone was really a loser despite the fact that some appeared better off than others. The equal distribution of land gave every household the opportunity to increase its income, because productivity under collective farming fell far short of its potential.

As for the developed areas, most ordinary peasants first took a skeptical attitude toward the HRS. They feared that they would not reap more benefits because their grain productivity was already very high. The cadres, of course, worried about the demise of the collective enterprises wherein their power and money rested. But they also realized that the HRS not only produced high yields for their formerly inferior neighbors, but also brought a great deal of freedom, which could be an immeasurable advantage for making fortunes.[11]

The Localization of Major Rural Economic Policies

The process by which the HRS, once a forbidden measure, became a dominant national policy, had a profound impact on political and economic life in China. In Mao's era, local policy initiatives has been mainly manipulated by Mao himself and his supporters. More importantly, these changes had been driven by a radical left wing ideology. The "People's Commune" movement is the most typical and tragic case. When the heterodox HRS was allowed to compete with, and finally to defeat those more ideologically restrictive policies, the foundation of centralized policy-making was undermined.[12]

The restoration of family farming without privatization of the collective land ownership opened the door to an unknown world. While Deng Xiaoping and other reform leaders were excited by the unexpectedly high agricultural growth, no one in the center had clear ideas about what to do next. As a big winner in the gamble on the HRS, Deng intended to take even greater risks with reform, but Chen Yun and some other leaders became concerned about losing central control. Nevertheless, one thing was clear to all leaders: the momentum of the rural reforms needed to be maintained in order to improve the economy, so local leaders at all levels were encouraged to promote economic growth.[13] The local authorities, therefore, enjoyed unprecedented de facto autonomy in making new policies for the local economy, and rural policies became substantially localized.

In the early stages after the establishment of the HRS, the most important economic policies which local leaders made on their own were the land policy and the private enterprise policy. These two issues naturally emerged right after the decollectivization of farming, but central authorities could not respond with an unequivocal directive because of the lack of relevant knowledge and splits in opinion among the central leadership. As a temporary measure and a political compromise as well, these issues were left to local leaders, particularly at the county level. The different economic and political constraints, as well as different strategies to maximize local economic interests, resulted in significant differences in these two policies.

When local leaders made policies concerning land distribution and transference, different weight was given to considerations of family size versus labor force. According to my own observations, which are supported by some surveys (*see* TABLE 5.1), the low-income areas tended to stress the principle of equal rights in land distribution, while high income areas favored the principle of "land to farm labor." The difference in opportunities for non-farming employment is probably the major reason for this policy divergence.

The attitudes of local leaders to land policies were closely linked with their strategy for economic development. When I was studying rural industries in China in 1986, I found out that land transactions were being actively undertaken both in some poor areas--such as in counties of north Anhui where private business was encouraged--and in the wealthy Pearl River Delta, where overseas capital was a major source of investment. However, in other areas where the legacies of the collective era were still very prevalent, local leaders tended to suppress the land market. This tendency was found in some areas of China's northeast, where farming was more mechanized, and in some areas of the southeast, such as southern Jiangsu, where collective industry was the main engine of local economic development.

The policy concerning private enterprise has been the most divergent nationwide. Some Chinese leaders such as Bo Yibo attempted to stop privatization of firms by raising an ideological debate over the hiring of labor, which the reformers knew would be difficult to defend. But reformers succeeded in prolonging the final decision of the central authorities on this issue twice with the support of Deng Xiaoping.[14] The

TABLE 5.1 China's Land Distribution Policy and Income Level During the Reform Era (Percent)

Distribution vs. Income Level	< 300	301-450	451-650	651-900	> 900	Average
Equal among entire populace	84.62	71.75	70.93	66.67	53.49	69.4
Equal among all laborers	0.00	0.00	1.16	15.56	11.63	4.37
Mixed	15.38	28.85	27.91	17.77	27.91	25.00
To work team	0.00	0.00	0.00	0.00	6.97	1.19
Sum	100.00	100.00	100.00	100.00	100.00	100.00

Source: Land Study Team of China's Agriculture Ministry. Initial report on 280 villages survey in China, written by He Daofeng, 1991.

ambiguous attitude of the central leadership actually gave no ideological guidance to local leaders on this issue.

According to my observations during the 1982-1986 period, private firms were systematically suppressed by the local governments in some areas, whereas in other areas they were regarded as the main force to bring about local prosperity.[15] At an early stage after implementation of the HRS, regional policy divergence on private business reflected the splits in ideological position of the local leaders rather than local economic interests. Later on, the situation changed. The result of competition between local leaders had once again shown that an attitude of pragmatism rather than dogmatism paid off in politics. So, as a result, ideological inclination was no longer a major factor in localized policy-making, although a substantial divergence of views on private business continued to exist.

Rural Reform, Marketization, and the Rise of Localism

The most fundamental impact on the development of localism came about through the process of marketization. The liberalization of the rural economy unleashed tremendous economic energy previously fettered by the cage of the command economy. Superficially, the pyramid-like Chinese social structure seemed unchanged, particularly the hierarchical party patron-client relationship, which remained the skeleton behind the whole construction. But, since market forces had established a great number of horizontal linkages among the various units and people, the structure of interdependence in China was substantially changed by the reform process. Localism was fostered not only by the resources generated by marketization, but also by newly-established relationships through marketization.

Breaking the "Cycle of Socialist Reform"

Some scholars believe that the "reform cycle" theory is applicable to Chinese economic reforms.[16] According to this theory, the partial reform of the socialist economic system--leaving much of the structure, prices, and incentives of the centralized command economy intact--inevitably produces economic distortions and irrationalities. These economic problems give anti-reform groups the chance to force a return to centralization. In this way, economic and political forces interact to create a "cycle of reform."

It was true that in the winter of 1980, only two years after the start of economic reforms, the central leadership faced great pressure to slow down economic reform and recentralize fiscal control.[17] Some top leaders, such as Chen Yun, did seriously attempt to correct "economic irrationality" through the strengthening of central planning. However, the unscheduled implementation of the household responsibility system (HRS) and its rapid proliferation created a new economic environment in the urban sector, and efforts at recentralization were overwhelmed by expansion of the rural market. The growth rate of the economy fell during only one year (1981) instead of the predicted three to five years. As the economy vigorously returned to a high growth rate, the conventional "cycle of reform" was broken for the first time by market forces.

How did rural reforms help the Chinese economy break out of its reform cycle, while Eastern Europe and the Soviet Union had been long trapped in that cycle? Obviously this has something to do with the structural features of the Chinese economy--its predominantly rural population and basically self-subsistent rural economy. As a matter of fact, a big part of the Chinese rural economy had never been completely integrated into the centrally-planned economy. For many rural people, the state sector existed as an alien force, sharing few reciprocal economic interests with the rural sector with the exception of extraction. In the interests of the planned economy, economic exchanges among peasants were almost eliminated and the major economic activities of the peasants were confined to meeting only their own basic needs. So the Chinese rural economy was not only being excluded from the modern sector, it was also deliberately segregated and suppressed by state restrictions on market activities. When rural reform, particularly the HRS, restored economic freedoms to the peasants, the rural economy changed from a passive, expendable sub-unit into an active, self-propelled economic system existing beside the partially-reformed planned economy. It was this re-monetized rural economy that sustained the decentralization in the planned urban economy and pushed the partial reform in the direction of further marketization instead of recentralization.[18] To support this general explanation, the major spill-over effects of rural reform on the urban reform need to be explored:

(1) On the supply side, the rural reforms, especially the HRS, improved incentives and therefore led to a sharp increase in agricultural productivity without cost to the urban population. This certainly helped the industrial reform. Real wages were increased by the more plentiful supply of food and other agricultural products. (In comparison, if this had not happened, as in the Soviet Union, the bonus incentive would soon have been dampened by the disappointing food supply). The overall supply of consumer goods also improved drastically due to the growth in agricultural production. Since the consumer industry was relatively decentralized in China before the reform, the level of central control depended largely on the center's monopoly of raw materials. Once the

supply of raw materials became sufficient, the central monopoly could no longer restrain the booming local consumer industry. In this sense, the success of the rural reforms laid a material base for the decentralization of the urban economy.

(2) On the demand side, the rapid growth in rural incomes produced an unexpected demand for industrial products and created a comfortable market environment for industrial readjustment. For most socialist economies, readjustment forced by cumulative distortions and irrationalities could hardly be conducted during an economic expansion, because without capital markets, the oversupplied sectors couldn't easily transfer capacity and resources to the shortage sectors. This was particularly true for many capital goods manufacturers, whose products were obsolete but who found it difficult to convert to production of consumer goods. For this reason, in 1981, capital goods valued at billions of yuan could not find buyers. However, this industrial crisis was not solved by recentralization measures but through expansion of the rural market from 1982 to 1984, following proliferation of the HRS. A drastic increase in the peasants' level of investment took place as a result of their rapidly rising incomes. Their relatively simple technological requirements and huge level of demand actually rescued many state firms in the auto industry and other machinery lines. The state firms even transferred used equipment valued at billions of yuan to rural industrial enterprises. The situation for consumer goods was the same--a lot of old-fashioned consumer goods found new consumers in the rural market.[19]

(3) In terms of financial resources, the success of the rural reforms supported decentralization of the urban economy through two market channels. The first was rural household savings, which exceeded peasant household investments because of the fast increase in income and the restrictions on bank credit for peasants.[20] The second was the contribution to the trade balance made by the rural economy. The increase in exports and reduction in imports of agriculture products increased foreign currency available for the state industrial sector to import more producer goods and therefore made central planning even less necessary.

Above all, the expansion of the rural market in the period 1982-1984 decreased the pressure of urban unemployment, which had posed the toughest challenge to socialist reform. Everyone profited during the early stage of marketization prompted by the success of rural reforms. This positive experience was one of the decisive reasons behind the Chinese leadership's decision to further the market-oriented reforms in 1984.

The Dichotomy between Wealth and Political Eminence

Before the reforms, there was an unwritten law in Chinese society: political inferiors were not supposed to be richer than their superiors. This law was required by the state to ensure the continuation of the single political authority at the top. The process of marketization triggered by the implementation of the HRS shook the foundations of central power by separating wealth from political eminence in the rural areas. Since the Chinese leadership had to allow private businesses to develop to alleviate the problem of underemployment, they were prepared to tolerate the fact that some peasants would become richer than the communist cadres at the grassroots levels. But when the policy was implemented, they found that another political decision had to be made--to legitimize the equal rights of rural communist cadres (along with peasants) to run businesses and to receive higher incomes than state officials. Policy investigations showed that cadres at the grassroots levels might become a major threat to rural entrepreneurs if they themselves were not allowed to participate in money-making activities.

This policy of "letting some people become rich first" had far-reaching consequences. In the rural areas, tens of thousands of peasants made windfall fortunes during the re-monetization of the rural economy, and a significant portion of these people were rural cadres. In the comparatively prosperous coastal provinces, the following became a common phenomenon in the party hierarchy: the lower the rank, the higher the income. When I was conducting some investigations in 1986 in the Pearl River Delta of Guangdong Province, I found that the average salary of cadres at the village level (formerly brigade level) was as high as the Premier of China's State Council, three times higher than that of a minister in the central government, and four to five times higher than that of a county leader.

In order to prevent local officials from becoming corrupt, some people suggested that this reverse income distribution could be corrected by setting a localized rather than a unified salary standard for all officials. This suggestion was politically unacceptable to the central leadership because they knew it would undermine the unified rank order critical to imposing central control. However, if they did not localize salary standards at the middle levels, it was bound to be more difficult for them to keep control over the local leaders at middle level who had strong economic incentives to collude with the cadres at the grassroots.

The Extension of Local Property Rights

The most important source of rising local power was local property rights, which had been greatly extended during the process of marketization.

Before the reforms, China's economy had been characterized by control of industrial assets by the local governments at various levels. This was partially a result of Mao's economic strategy, which strove for self-reliance and self-sufficiency within each region. It was also partially the inevitable consequence of incomplete economic planning, caused by frequent political upheavals. In the end, a unique, so-called "regional property rights" system emerged from Mao's era.[21]

While the existence of local property rights was noticeable in China before the reforms, they were limited by many institutional factors, of which three major ones are to be explored. First, personal income was regulated by the central authorities. Although expanding local investment would improve local interests, the criteria for promotion of local leaders was basically political rather than economic. So the local leaders' incentive to privatize local interests was weak. Second, the central authorities distributed most important industrial resources, and money did not provide access to those resources. Limited bartering was permitted only between provinces rather than between state enterprises. So local investments were highly reliant on central support. The third factor is that since private business was unlawful, state-owned assets, which were subject to central regulation, dominated local property in the non-agricultural industries. All these factors gave limited room to local leaders to pursue independent local interests with the central government.

Economic reforms eliminated all these constraints. The economy was greatly monetized through replacement of physical targets with financial targets. State enterprises were allowed to market and to price some of their own products. In the name of enterprise reform, a number of incentive schemes were established by local governments that linked financial revenue from local assets with the personal income of managers, workers, and even government officials. Finally, firms of non-state ownership, including private ownership, were permitted to develop. In short, the introduction of the market had given local governments a great deal of discretion to exercise local property rights, with the exception of firing state employees. The fiscal reform which decentralized fiscal responsibility to the local governments certainly strengthened the incentive to maximize local interests through exercising of local property rights.

Three major consequences of this change fundamentally undermined the ability of the central government to recentralize economic, social, and political control, therefore making possible the rise of localism. Rural reforms significantly contributed to this development.

The first consequence was the fast expansion of local industrial assets. This development progressed so far that if the central government really tried to recentralize the economy, it would have caused a severe recession, which may have proved politically more dangerous than giving more power to the local leaders. Both the direct and indirect contribution of rural reforms to the expansion and diversification of local assets was decisive. The peasants had created 15 million new enterprises from 1983 to 1989.[22] As a result, rural industrial enterprises made up 90 percent of total industrial enterprises. In 1981, the investment of peasants amounted to about 37 percent of that of the state sector; for 1988, this number had increased to 48 percent.[23]

The second consequence of the extension of local property rights was that local governments became very important in making rules for the local economy. When China's economy was heading toward marketization, there was no an adequate institutional base to support and regulate market activities. The central policies were too general and often inconsistent; the definitions of property rights were also incomplete and unclear. In particular, there were substantial contradictions between the rules of the state sector and that of the growing non-state sector. Under these circumstances, local governments had to make local rules which could provide incentives for market activities and, at same time, balance the interests of different sectors within the jurisdictions.

The Chinese people are institutionally stratified by their work units, which are ranked in accordance with their ownership type, intermediate supervision level, and so on. State enterprises are viewed as superior to collective ones, and state workers are regarded as superior to the workers in collective firms, for instance. The same relationship holds true between the collective sector and the private one. Within each sector, there is also a clear rank order among the sub-sectors. According to this principle, rural enterprises lie at the bottom of the hierarchy. However, even rural enterprises are formally stratified as township collectives, village collectives, and three other lower statuses. Under the planned economy, enterprises of higher status could expect more resources from the planning authority, and their employees could expect more economic benefits or higher security than employees in enterprises with lower status. Therefore, social status was linked with work place, which was not freely chosen by individuals. Although the rank order is unified across the country, the compositions of those enterprises varies with the localities because of different historical and environmental backgrounds. A very important phenomenon of the Chinese economic reforms was that the Chinese leadership tried to preserve the highly institutionalized social stratification despite continuing marketization in resource allocations. Because of great inter-regional disparities, the balance between vested interests in the established social hierarchy and incentives for market activities could only be realized by giving more discretion to the local authorities. Without local rules and local government intervention, marketization could not go along with the stability of the existing status hierarchy, which is vital for the regime.

The development of rural enterprises was one of the major factors raising the need for local rules. First, rural enterprises are all non-state-owned enterprises and even before the reforms their rules for income distribution were quite localized within the framework of collective farming. After implementation of the HRS, when private business became a competitive alternative for capable people in collective enterprises, the local governments had to find a way to make collective enterprises compatible with local private businesses, or simply to place restrictions on the private sector. Second, there was systemic discrimination by the state sector against the collective sector, as well as by the collective sector against private firms. The important function of local rule was to balance the conflicting rights of all these sectors.

However, in making local rules, local authorities must confront the existing central rules because of the fundamental inconsistency of these rules. But in what way the local rules conflict with the central rules was determined by the judgement of local leaders, referring to the specific economic and political situation of their jurisdictions.

The third major consequence of extension of local property rights was commercialization of the local leadership. As Deng Xiaoping's gamble to prompt economic growth through decentralization paid off, the ideas of local leaders began to change. Ideologically, as a result of commercialization of their daily life, local leaders no longer favored the planned economy. Many of them realized the importance of property rights and became skeptical of the dominance of public ownership. Economically, local leaders could not help but form a conspiracy against central control and its extraction from the local people. There are several indicators of the significant contribution to local powers made by the rural sector. Since the establishment of the HRS, the rural labor force employed in township and village enterprises tripled, while the number of employees in the state sector increased by only 30 percent. Employees in township and village enterprises increased from 30 million in 1982 to more than 90 million in 1990, while employees in the state sector increased from 86.3 million in 1982 to about 110 million in 1990. Thus, rural enterprises created 50 percent more jobs than the state sector in this period.[24] Although the average income of the peasants had been only about 40-50 percent of that of urban residents, the incentive for savings and investment in rural areas was much higher than it was in urban areas. On the average, urban households saved only 3 to 8 percent of their income, while the peasants saved 25 to 30 percent of their income.[25] In this context, the share of rural industry in total industrial output increased from 11 percent in 1982 to about 30 percent in 1990. Even deliberate efforts to suppress rural industries made by conservative Chinese leaders after the political events of 1989 could not reverse the growth of rural industries, which continued to surpass that of state industries. In many provinces, rural industries became the main source of incremental government revenue and foreign currency. A recent report from China indicates that in 1990, for the first time, the output of rural industry exceeded 50 percent of the total industrial output of Jiangsu Province, one of the largest industrialized provinces in China. The Chinese leadership realizes that the day when the non-state industrial sector becomes the mainstream of Chinese industry is close at hand, so they are now preparing for this change rather than continuing the hopeless fight against non-state owned industries.[26]

The Growth of Provincial Power

Chinese history shows that localism can never be significant as long as provincial leaders are loyal agents of the central authorities. One of the important impacts of rural reforms was that it broke the inter-provincial economic balance and thus boosted the behavior of localism at provincial levels. Since these actions became an important part of a new equilibrium in China, the central authorities had no choice but to tolerate them, even if they conflicted with central policy and discipline. Provincial power thus increased.

The most powerful driving force behind the rise of provincial power was the uneven development of rural non-agricultural industries.[27] The uneven development of rural industries threatened the balance between urban and rural income. The measures to keep the balance, both in developed and less-developed provinces, had led to provincial blockades of agricultural trade. The conflict between Guangdong and its neighboring provinces, Jiangxi and Hunan, is typical. Concerned about the political consequences of free trade, the central government actually legitimized the interprovincial agricultural trade blockade, despite the government's repeatedly announced position against trade blockades.

Second, the uneven development of rural industry under the restrictions on labor mobility forced less developed areas to undertake industrial protectionism. Since the developed areas quickly achieved full employment and turned to developing more capital-intensive industries, the opportunity to expand employment in less developed areas was threatened by the advantages of the already developed areas in competing for industrial resources. So it was in the interest of poor areas to prevent capital goods from flowing out and manufactured goods from flowing in.

Third, uneven development increased the number of migrant workers and the illegal migration from poor areas to rich areas. Since there was no institutional basis to support free migration within China, the central government had to let provincial governments handle the problem on both a unilateral and bilateral basis. Despite the restrictions on migration, the mobility of rural labor continued to increase both in terms of size and distance from native villages. Up to 1985, the "floating population" (liudong renkou)--the special term in China for those not working in the place where they are registered as residents--was estimated to be about 50 million; by 1987 the estimate was 70 million. As *Time* magazine commented, this was one of the largest moves of population in human history, similar to the great migration that took place during the industrialization of Europe in the eighteenth century.[28]

There is no doubt that migrant laborers greatly contributed to the prosperity achieved during the period of reform. But, in terms of integration, Alan P.L. Liu points out that the migrants seemed to be more of a threat than a blessing.[29] What the communist leaders hoped when they started to relax controls on migration in 1983 was that the surplus labor force would be absorbed by local small towns and cities. This shows that they still intended to maintain social control and stability by restricting physical mobility. However, after 1987, the increasing social and economic pressure created by the flood of job-seekers from the remote countryside attracted a great deal of attention from the government and from Chinese intellectuals. Many people regarded this as an ominous sign of a looming crisis stemming form the overpopulation of China.

There is no adequate social or physical infrastructure upon which the regime can meet the challenge of free migration. So, as market forces continued to grow, the central government had no choice but to tolerate more illegal migration. On the other hand, it also had to tolerate more localism measures, by which local governments attempted to mitigate social pressure, at least on a temporary basis.

Given the cellular nature of the Chinese economy, the behavior of economic localism--including trade blockades, local financial intervention, and discriminatory local labor policy against migrant workers--could be found at all levels, from township to provincial government. However, the process of marketization tends to make the provincial government play a central role in localism.

Economically, the economy of scale tends to put the local power at a higher level instead of at a lower level. The economic legacy of Mao's strategy, which attempted to establish an independent industrial foundation for most provinces, also generated strong incentives for provincial protectionism. As marketization made the economy more complex and diversified, central authorities became less capable of performing two fundamental functions: (1) balancing urban and rural economic interests; and (2) balancing inter-regional economic interests, particularly coastal versus inland interests. Economic realities then forced the central leadership first to decentralize the function of coordinating urban-rural development and second, to encourage bilateral and multilateral economic cooperation among provinces.

Nevertheless, the central leadership knew that the increasing power at the provincial level could be a potential political danger. Zhao Ziyang, the former Premier, tried to avoid the danger by promoting the autonomy of municipal governments. While Zhao's strategy did increase the autonomy of municipal governments, it could not stop the confrontation between provincial powers and central control.

The basic reason for the increase of provincial power was that decentralization and marketization in China increased the difficulties of central control, but never reduced the need for authoritarian intervention. There was no institutionalized check from the populace on low-level local authorities; there was no institutionalized procedure to balance conflicting individual interests, including conflicts between the localities. So, with reluctance, the central government had to allow provincial leaders to take more responsibility rather than letting the situation get out of control. Of course, there were also other factors working in favor of greater provincial autonomy, including the tradition of strong provincial identity among the Chinese people.

During the last decade, the evidence of increasing local power is conspicuous. However, the best test of the strength of localism was when the conservatives in the central leadership were victorious in Beijing after the 1989 Tiananmen incident. In order to restore the central planning system, Chinese conservative leaders attempted to revoke some of the most important economic reform policies, including the household responsibility system (HRS), the local fiscal responsibility system, the dual pricing system, and the contractual management responsibility system for state enterprises. Politically, they planned to replace the provincial leaders who threatened central power, such as Ye Xuanping, the governor of Guangdong Province, and Shen Zulun, the governor of Zhejiang Province.

The battle lasted more than one year. On the issue of economic reform policy, the result was a fiasco for the conservatives. They had to reaffirm the HRS only two months after hinting at their intention to recollectivize in October, 1989. They attacked rural industries and private businesses through financial extractions and administrative pressures. But, in the spring of 1990, the central government changed its harsh attitude, partly because it realized that rural industries helped increase exports. The contractual management responsibility system was reaffirmed with some modification in the summer of 1990. In November 1990, at the Seventh Plenum of the Central Committee of the Communist Party, the conservatives failed to revoke the local fiscal responsibility system, which they regarded as a fatal threat to central power. It was a surprise to many Chinese officials that even the leaders from the provinces subsidized by the central government opposed this recentralization. The strategy of the provincial leaders was to ask the central government to take all responsibility resulting from fiscal recentralization, including the payment of foreign debts.

Based on these facts, it is possible to conclude that the central-local relationship in China has entered a new era. The central authorities can still remove local leaders, but they cannot change the policies which have made the local authorities increasingly powerful.

Conclusion

Criticism against localism, which means localized policy- and rule-making, rose not long after the reforms gained momentum, particularly when the HRS liberated the entire rural economy. As marketization progressed, criticism of localism escalated, and local governments were blamed for almost all the negative aspects of the reforms. Those who attacked localism were not just the opponents of a market economy. Some well-known academics who claimed they supported the market-oriented reforms also stood in the forefront of the criticism against increasing local power. However, most critics of localism overlooked the basic fact that the rise of localism at this time in China was accompanied by an unprecedented growth of wealth and, more meaningfully, it was also associated with the freeing of hundreds of millions of peasants from forced collective labor. For many of these peasants, this period was a golden age which they had never dreamed would occur.

The peasants in China were essentially slaves of the command economy before the reforms. It was not a coincidence that after the HRS freed the peasants from collective labor, local power grew along with marketization. Although the decentralization of rule-making was partly a result of the strategy of reform leaders to circumvent the anti-reform forces, it also indicates that a more decentralized power structure in China's central-local relations goes along with the freedom of the people and the market economy.

Since the overall institutional base for the market economy was far from adequate, localized rule-making and the competition among local governments provided a substitute framework to keep the market functioning. In many areas, the localized definition and protection of property rights seem to have generated incentives for rural entrepreneurs to capture the opportunities brought by marketization, as well as by sustained savings and investment in the rural economy.

How far will China be able to continue along its current path? Localism is particularism-oriented, so it will not lead to institutionalization of the market economy. However, given the size of the population and the firmly entrenched political culture of particularism, there is little possibility that China could impose a set of unified rules for a market economy by a top-down legislation process. In the foreseeable future it is unrealistic to allow free migration without limitations, so significant differences in social and economic rights will continue to exist in various regions.

A reasonable way to institutionalize the market economy in China would be to let the provinces have greater legislative autonomy. However, this implies a revolutionary change in the central-local power structure which would be extremely difficult for Chinese leaders and even the majority of Chinese intellectuals to accept. Based on this judgement, it is not difficult to predict that the current pattern of central-local relations--in which highly uninstitutionalized local powers play a crucial role in economic regulation--will continue as long as the social cost of marketization is not high enough to cause a general crisis.

Notes

1. Nicholas Lardy: *Agriculture in China's Modern Economic Development* (1983).

2. Chen Yizi: *China: Ten Years Reform and the Pro-Democracy Movement in 1989* (1991), pp. 26-7.

3. My judgment is mainly based on information provided by peasants and local officials during my trips to many provinces in the last twenty years. This judgment seems supported by the recently released national income statistics of the provinces, on which a systematic analysis reveals that inequality actually increased during Mao's era despite the radical egalitarian policies. See Kai Yuen Tsui: "China's Regional Inequality, 1952-1985," *Journal of Comparative Economics* (1991) 15, pp.1-21.

4. In 1975, Li Jingquan, the former head of the Southwestern region, wrote a letter to the State Council which was then led by Deng Xiaoping. Li asked for permission to cut the mandatory amount of grain deliveries to the state, because he feared a severe shortage of grain in the countryside. Ironically, Li was one of the main supporters of Mao's radical Great Leap Forward and, to a great extent, he was responsible for the death of millions of people during the famine in Sichuan Province. For Li's letter, see Zao Fasheng and others: *Dandai Zhongguo de Liangshi Gongzuo* (Administration of Grain Distribution in Contemporary China), (Beijing: Chinese Social Sciences Press, 1988).

5. Chen Yun, *Chen Yun Wenxuan* (Collection of Chen Yun's Works), 1986, p. 212 and p. 232.

6. Michel Oksenberg, "Economic Policy-Making in China: Summer 1981," *China Quarterly*, No. 90, 1982.

7. Chen Yizi, op. cit., pp. 26-27.

8. According to my own involvement with reform policy-making in China, including direct contact with Wan Li and Zhao Ziyang, I believe that the central government's highly sympathetic attitude to the peasants should not be explained only by the needs of the central power struggle. One of the important characteristics of the socialist reformers in high positions is that they are less opportunistic than many other party leaders and hold more universal humanitarian values. In this regard, Wan's support for the HRS was not merely an act of compliance with the will of his political patron Deng Xiaoping. It also constituted an effort to take advantage of Deng's unconsolidated position to push for the more radical change which Wan favored. Wan's contribution to rural reforms, especially to the decollectivization, was more significant than Zhao Ziyang's because Wan was more willing to take risks. He also had closer personal ties with Deng which allowed him to be relatively controversial. The origin of the HRS in Chuxian prefecture, Anhui province was recorded by the local party classified files. See *Thirty Years in the Countryside*, by Wang Gengjin, Yang Xun, and others, pp. 385-409.

9. The differences among provincial leaders were publicized in some dramatic ways. It is interesting to read editorials from the 1980-1982 period in the provincial newspapers, which conveyed different ideas from those of provincial leaders regarding the HRS. And along the border between Jiangsu and Anhui Province, some huge posters were put up by the Jiangsu local government, facing Anhui, with slogans opposing the HRS.

10. From September 14-22 1980, all the first secretaries of party provincial committees were called to Beijing for a meeting on rural policy. The provincial leaders could not reach a consensus on the HRS, but a compromise was reached which legitimized the HRS in poor areas. At that moment, Deng Xiaoping had already privately expressed his support for the HRS in Anhui, but he did not use his influence during the debate. On November 5th, 1980, the *People's Daily* published an article entitled "The Broadway and the Single-Plank Bridge" written by Wu Xiang, an assistant to Wan Li. The article conveyed the message that the top leadership had allowed the HRS to coexist with other forms of the responsibility system, therefore encouraging peasants and local leaders who supported the HRS.

11. In some regions, including Beijing and Jiangsu, the pressure for the HRS at the grassroots level was not as strong as in other provinces. However, in most provinces, the internal pressure for change was more important than pressure from the central government.

12. Despite its significance, the changing attitude to the HRS in those provinces originally opposed to the HRS was never publicized, to avoid political embarrassment. Several case studies provide some clue as to the motives and impact of such a change. See Yang Guansan, "Why the advanced collectives adopted the HRS" in *Countryside, Economy, Society 1981*, by the Research Group of Rural Development of China. See also Luo Xiaopeng, "Ownership and Status Stratification," in Byrd and Lin ed. *China's Rural Industry* (Oxford: Oxford University Press, 1990).

13. In the period 1981-1982, as more localities were attracted by the success of the HRS, the leaders in the provinces which originally opposed the HRS were split. The debate over the HRS took place from the provincial level on down to the prefecture and county levels. The HRS became the major political issue in provincial politics. Many low-level local leaders converted to the HRS by rebelling against provincial leaders or with the support of a patron at the provincial level.

14. According to my information, Hu Yaobang, the party general secretary at the time, was most typical of this position, which ignored the importance of institutionalization and systematic efforts at reform. During his travels all over China, he even encouraged local leaders to defy policy directives from the center if they believed that the central policy was hindering their efforts to make local people rich quickly. One well-known case of his support of local leaders vis-a-vis the central bureaucracies was his support for peasant mining industries. Because these industries were unsafe and damaging to the environment, and sometimes the peasants even tried to increase their incomes at the expense of the state mines, the central bureaucracy had been trying impose restrictions on mining--but Hu's support prevented this.

15. In 1983, provincial leaders asked central leaders to clarify the policy on private firms--particularly those that hired more than eight workers, because according to Marx, this was regarded as exploitation. Hu Yaobang and Zhao Ziyang declared that it was too early to make such a decision. In 1985, Bo Yibo, who was then in charge of Communist Party rectification, raised the question again by forbidding rural party members from hiring labor in a draft policy document on purifying rural party organizations. With support from Deng Xiaoping, Hu and Zhao dropped that issue from the document, after a delicate discussion at a meeting of the Secretariat.

16. On the divergence of local policies, particularly industrial policies, see *China's Rural Industry*, Byrd and Lin, ed., op. cit.

17. Susan L. Shirk:"The Politics of Industrial Reform," in Elizabeth Perry and Christine Wong eds., *The Political Economy of Reform in Post-Mao China* (Cambridge, Mass.: The Council on East Asian Studies/Harvard University, 1985), p. 195.

18. Chen Yun, 1980.

19. A partially reformed socialist economy could never be really efficient, but this doesn't mean that it could not be sustained for a relatively long period. The

Yugoslav economy is a relevant case. Before the collapse of Eastern Europe, it managed to survive without returning to central planning for more than two decades. The most vital factor in keeping this economy running was its integration with western market economies.

20. The state realized the great market opportunity created by the success of rural reforms in 1982. In order to promote industrial goods on the rural market, the State Council made an important policy decision in June 1982 to break the institutional urban-rural segregation in wholesale businesses. See Wang Jiye and Zhu.

21. World Bank: *China: Finance and Investment*, 1988.

21. David Granick, 1990.

22. World Bank, 1991.

23. State Statistical Bureau of China: *National Yearbooks*, 1988 and 1989.

24. World Bank: *China, Rural Enterprise, Rural Industry, 1986-1990* (draft), and *Statistics of The Chinese Rural Economy 1949-1986* (Beijing: Agriculture Press, 1989).

25. The World Bank, 1988, op. cit.

26. This message was brought by a Chinese visitor from Jiangsu Province who participated in a provincial conference on rural industry in May, 1991. It was an important political event in Jiangsu Province because the provincial leadership approved a new policy for rural industry from Beijing. The central leadership had changed their policy of curtailing the development of rural enterprises and had resumed support of these industries, even though this meant that non-state enterprises would eventually replace state enterprises as the main force in Chinese industry.

27. The uneven development of rural industry has been one of the most striking facts in China's economy, particularly considering the strong commitment of the communist leadership to special equity. In 1988, seven provincial-level units--Beijing, Tianjin, Liaoning, Shanghai, Jiangsu, Zhejiang, and Guangdong--collected 54.7 percent of total revenue from rural non-agricultural industries, while the share of the rural labor force in these provinces was only 21 percent. The importance of rural industry in causing spatial inequality was proved by two recent studies using newly-released statistics. Using the data reported by 2,340 counties, John Knight and Lina Song measured income inequality in rural China and found: (1) There is a great range of income by province. A decomposition analysis showed more than two-thirds of rural inequality (Gini coefficient no less than 0.25) arising among rather than within provinces. (2) The greater the share of non-agricultural output in total output in a county, the higher its income per capita; rural industrialization thus appears to be important in raising incomes. (3) It would seem that the forces for disequalization were strong and grew stronger during the 1980s, because rural industrialization is not significantly related to the initial level of agricultural output nor to its growth, but strongly, positively, related to previous industrialization. (See John Knight and Lina Song:"The Spatial Contribution to Income Inequality in Rural China" (draft), IES, University of Oxford) With the newly-published provincial national income data, Kai Yuen Tsui also studied the issue of China's regional inequality. His findings support J. Knight's results. Kai Yuen Tsui found: (1) The non-agricultural sector is the main source of regional inequality. (2) The rapid growth of collective enterprises

generated more extrabudgetary funds in the more industrialized coastal provinces. This appeared to be one of the major explanations for increasing regional inequality. See Kai Yuen Tsui: "China's Regional Inequality, 1952-1985," *Journal of Comparative Economics* (1991) 15, 1-21.

28. *Economic Daily* (Jingji Ribao), Sept.15, 1990.

29. Alan P.L. Liu, "Economic Reform, Mobility Strategies, and National Integration In China," *Asian Survey*, Vol. XXXI, No. 5, May 1991, pp.393-408.

6

Central-Local Relations From the Perspective of State and Non-State Industries

Xiao Geng

When China adopted the Soviet model of central planning for its industrialization program in the early 1950s, the central government was the most important actor in the economy. Large industrial plants were built and controlled directly through the ministries in charge of various sectors. The central government also set up national committees to coordinate national plans and the flow of resources across sectors and regions. However, because of the sheer size of the Chinese economy, the central government also relied on the provincial governments to carry out its industrial plans and policies.

During the late 1950s and the Cultural Revolution period (1966-76), several waves of decentralization shifted administrative control of enterprises away from the national ministries to provincial governments. However, this administrative decentralization did not encourage any significant move toward a market economy. There was little managerial autonomy for the industrial enterprises. The managers and workers played very limited and passive roles in a fragmented but planned economy. The central and local governments, as the dominant players, directed industrial investment and production.[1]

Economic reform since 1978 has also been characterized by decentralization of economic control from the central government to local governments as well as enterprises. But, the recent reform clearly encouraged shifts of the economy from a planned to a market system. Two facts have emerged during this period of reform to arouse enormous debates on the economic role of the central and local governments: First, the central government's budgetary revenue has declined rapidly; second, large gaps in regional industrial productivity have emerged.

It has been suggested that the higher productivity in the coastal region of China is a result of higher local government autonomy, granted by the central government during the recent reform period. According to this theory, more local autonomy in other regions may improve their productivity as well. Changing central-local relations have often been seen as a result of political games among central and provincial leaders of various factions.[2] The central government and its ministries have sometimes been identified with the conservative forces favoring central planning while the local governments of the coastal regions have been regarded as leaders of market-oriented reforms. The rapid growth of the coastal regions has given rise to many bold suggestions on reforming central-local relations. Some suggest that local governments may initiate more appropriate reform measures than the central government because of the large gaps in regional industrial development.

In contrast, others argue that the recent decentralization has weakened the economic capacity of the central government and may hinder future economic development of the nation. Some scholars also warn that the increasing regional gaps and the expanding economic power of local governments may lead to local protectionism and other regional conflicts, which may also endanger economic and political stability in China.

This chapter addresses the above debates by examining the sources of China's regional productivity gaps and the root of the decline of central government budgetary revenue. It brings enterprise behavior into a study of the economic role of the central and local governments in post-Mao China. Most recent research has not examined closely the behavior of Chinese enterprises and its effects on the role of central and local governments. During the period of economic reform since 1978, Chinese enterprises acquired significant managerial autonomy and controlled more economic resources. The behavior of the managers and workers in the state and non-state enterprises has created important constraints and opportunities for both the central and local governments. As central planning becomes less important, the role of central and local governments needs to be changed from primary initiators and managers of industrial projects to regulators of markets and enterprises. When exploring the role of governments, it is crucial to study the impact of specific government regulations and policies on the performance of enterprises. If the sources of rapid industrial growth in the coastal regions come from the non-state sector (private, semi-private and foreign joint-venture enterprises), then the policy of encouraging private enterprises should be supported. Increasing the power of local governments may or may not facilitate economic growth and development. This chapter emphasizes economic incentives and their effects on the behavior of enterprises and of the central and local governments. In particular, it uses results from an on-going study of the institutions of profit-sharing, managerial autonomy, and fringe benefits provisions in post-Mao Chinese industrial enterprises. The effects of this new incentive structure on performance and behavior of state and collective enterprises are examined briefly. The pattern of enterprise behavior described in this chapter provides an important base for discussion of the new economic role of the central and local governments.

I will first briefly analyze the property rights issue with regard to the Contract Responsibility System (CRS) in Chinese industrial enterprises. Some empirical findings about the performance of state and collective enterprises during the reform period will then be presented, followed by an examination of the sources of provincial productivity gaps. After discussing the challenge of state enterprise reform to the financial strength of central and local governments, opportunities provided by the rapid development of the non-state sector will then be pointed out. The final section summarizes the whole chapter.

A Property Rights Analysis of Chinese Enterprises

Since 1978 the Chinese government has transferred some important dimensions of property rights from the State to managers and workers. It has allowed both the state and collective enterprises to retain a portion of their profits for bonuses, welfare benefits such as housing, and industrial investment. The new structure of property rights can be summarized as follows:[3]

First, the profit-sharing arrangements set up between the government and the enterprises explicitly define the formal and contractual ownership structure of enterprises. The right to profits is the most important property right of Chinese enterprises. This right is widely recognized by the central and local governments, enterprises, and scholars.

Second, fringe benefits are informally controlled and "owned" by managers and workers. The amount and even the kind of fringe benefits are usually unspecified and may vary among enterprises. That is, they are not determined by explicit agreements but, instead, are a "consensual" sharing of enterprise resources. These fringe benefits can not be written into a contract and can not be unbundled and traded with other benefits because of the government ownership of non-industrial fixed capital, which is used to provide fringe benefits services. Moreover, some of the fringe benefits, such as residential housing, involve large amounts of fixed capital investment, and become an important channel for employees to accumulate quasi-private property, since it is practically impossible for enterprises to take back apartments that have been distributed to their employees, even though the apartments are officially state property. The implicitly-recognized claim to fringe benefits is largely ignored by scholars in China and abroad.[4]

Third, price-controls, wage-ceilings, production-quotas, and other administrative regulations specifically define restrictions on the managerial autonomy of enterprises. Although these administrative regulations may create some distortions and inefficiency, their role in Chinese industrial activities is declining. At the margin, more and more inputs and outputs are allocated according to market prices. Some of the regulations exist for reasons relating to revenue distribution across industries. Also, these regulations often involve very specific products, such as steel, coal, and electricity, and are implemented more effectively than the regulations on fringe benefits.

Finally, while the central and local governments still influence enterprises through arrangement of loans, subsidies, and appointments, significant control over resources in the enterprises has been implicitly and non-contractually delegated to the managers. As the Chinese economy becomes more decentralized, and as economic resources are controlled to a greater extent by enterprise managers, it becomes important to study the behavior of managers under the new institutional context.

This author formalizes a new structure of property rights described above in a dynamic model of the Contract Responsibility System.[5] Several important theoretical results are derived:

The Contract Responsibility System, which consists mainly of profit-sharing between the government and enterprises, managerial autonomy, and the provision of in-kind fringe benefits, is more efficient than the pre-reform planning institution, but less efficient than the private property institution. Under the Contract Responsibility System, managers and workers receive full marginal return from fringe benefits production but only a fraction of marginal return from industrial production. Since it is costly for the government to monitor effort, regulate fringe benefits, and distinguish industrial and non-industrial investment, the new system creates incentives for Chinese enterprises to divert effort and capital away from industrial to fringe benefits production. The enterprises, behaving rationally, equate private returns on the margin, but this leaves social marginal returns from production of industrial profits unequal.

Greater government claims lead to reduced use of resources in industrial production and to inefficiency. Hence, state enterprises are less productive industrially than collective enterprises.

Performance of State and Collective Enterprises

Using firm and city-level data for the 1980-1987 period and econometric techniques, the behavior and performance of Chinese state and collective enterprises has been examined empirically.[6] The evidence shows forcefully that the post-Mao Chinese industrial reform has successfully stimulated individual incentives and started a promising process of evolution toward a private market economy. This section summarizes some major findings in the study and their implications.[7]

Economic reform in the 1980s increased productivity of both the state and collective enterprises. But the growth rate of productivity in collective enterprises is much higher than that in state enterprises. During 1980-1985, the estimated annual total factor productivity growth from the firm sample of this study is 3.9 percent for state enterprises and 8.8 percent for collective enterprises. According to the city-level data from 1985-1987, the state sector has stagnant productivity growth in the later period of the decade-long reforms. The collective sector maintained high productivity growth of 4.4 percent per year in the 1985-1987 period. These findings confirm the analysis in the last section.

Although the productivity gap between state and collective enterprises decreases when non-industrial activities are taken into account properly, the decreased gap is still significant. State enterprises are less efficient than collective enterprises in using labor and capital. The estimated gaps in total factor productivity between the two sectors after controlling for economies of scale are 23.7 percent in 1985 and 34.8 percent in 1987 according to city-level data. From the firm sample, the measured gap of total factor productivity between the state and collective enterprises is about 60 percent during 1980-85, if fringe benefits are ignored. However, the gap decreases to about 30 percent if the fringe benefits services are counted as output. The evidence shows clearly the effects of the ownership structure on productivity. State enterprises have much higher fringe benefits than collective enterprises. The level of fringe benefits is positively correlated with the level of government investment in Chinese enterprises.

According to the firm sample, during the 1980-1985 period, controlling for industrial capital and other variables, fringe benefits capital has grown about 30 percent for state enterprises and about 80 percent for collective enterprises. The more rapid growth of fringe benefits capital in collective enterprises does not change the basic pattern of fringe benefits capital stock. In the firm sample, controlling for industrial capital and other variables, state enterprises have about 100 percent more fringe benefits capital than collective enterprises in 1980. This gap narrows to about 50 percent in 1985. It is found that fringe benefits capital is positively correlated with industrial capital. So capital-intensive firms have significantly higher levels of fringe benefits capital for their workers, in addition to higher wages, than the labor-intensive firms. One explanation for this pattern is that Chinese managers and workers are able to divert more industrial capital to non-industrial uses when they control more government property. Hence, the managers and workers in large state enterprises have captured some of the monopoly rents which would have gone to the government in the pre-reform system.

Sources of Regional Productivity Gaps

According to the theoretical and empirical analyses in last two sections, Chinese industrial reform in the post-Mao era has increased the productivity of both state and collective enterprises through changes in incentive structure and property rights. It is also shown that collective enterprises are more efficient than state enterprises. This section examines the impact of the non-state sector on the productivity of a region and the sources of regional productivity gaps.

Industrial productivity during the reform period has been uneven across the regions. From city-level industrial data, the total factor productivity (TFP) index for Chinese provinces has been estimated.

The eastern (or coastal) provinces have achieved the highest level of productivity and the western provinces the lowest. The average TFP indexes for the eastern, inland, and western regions are 114.5, 94.2, and 87.4 respectively. These indexes mean that given a certain amount of input such as capital and labor, if the western region produces $87.4 in output, the inland and eastern regions would produce $94.2 and $114.5 respectively.

There are many reasons for these productivity gaps. Historically, industrialization started in coastal cities such as Shanghai and Tianjin. Recent reforms and the opening policy also largely benefit the coastal provinces such as Guangdong and Fujian, which have close business contacts with Hong Kong and Taiwan.

The exceptionally rapid development of the eastern region has also been accompanied by a rise in local government autonomy during the reform period. Guangdong, Fujian, and Jiangsu, where productivity

TABLE 6.1 China's Regional and Provincial Productivity Index

Province	Region Classification	Non-state Sector Share of Gross Value of Industrial Output	Total Factor Productivity Index	Provincial Share of National Gross Value of Industrial Output
ALL PROVINCES		40.3%	100	100.0%
Provinces with 15%-23% Non-State Sector Share of GVIO			86	9.9%
GANSU	West	15.3%	85	1.2%
QINGHAI	West	16.6%	85	0.2%
XINJIANG	West	17.1%	92	0.8%
HEILONGJIANG	Inland	19.4%	84	4.1%
NEI MENGGU	Inland	20.8%	75	1.1%
GUIZHOU	West	21.1%	83	0.9%
XIZANG	West	21.8%	85	0.01%
NINGXIA	West	22.2%	85	0.2%
YUNNAN	West	22.8%	97	1.3%
Provinces with 25%-41% Non-State Sector Share of GVIO			100	51.9%
GUANGXI	East	25.5%	99	1.5%
SHANGHAI (city)	East	25.9%	123	7.7%
JILIN	Inland	28.2%	100	2.6%
SHAANXI	West	28.3%	84	1.9%
JIANGXI	Inland	28.9%	104	1.9%
BEIJING (city)	East	30.0%	108	3.2%
TIANJIN (city)	East	30.6%	108	2.9%
SICHUAN	West	32.5%	91	5.2%
HUBEI	Inland	34.0%	91	4.8%
HUNAN	Inland	34.6%	103	3.3%
SHANXI	Inland	35.1%	79	2.2%
LIAONING	East	36.0%	99	7.6%
ANHUI	Inland	38.7%	110	2.9%
HENAN	Inland	40.9%	102	4.3%
Provinces with 45%-67% Non-State Sector Share of GVIO			120	38.2%
HEBEI	East	46.8%	108	4.6%
FUJIAN	East	47.5%	119	1.9%
SHANDONG	East	49.5%	107	7.5%
GUANGDONG	East	50.6%	126	6.5%
JIANGSU	East	63.4%	123	11.5%
ZHEJIANG	East	66.7%	139	6.2%

Sources: Total Factor Productivity Index from Xiao Geng (1991); others from *Statistical Yearbook of China*.

exceeds the national average by 26 percent, 19 percent, and 23 percent respectively, also enjoy very favorable profit-sharing arrangements between the central and local governments. The Special Economic Zones developed during the post-1978 reforms are all located in coastal regions. Hence, it is suggested that higher productivity in the coastal region may reflect the higher local government autonomy in those regions. And it follows that the central government should give more autonomy to local governments since they are better able to initiate reform measures for their own regions.

Recent decentralization of economic control from the central to provincial and lower levels of governments may have contributed positively to productivity growth. However, local governments do not always produce good economic policies. In addition to local protectionism, provincial governments potentially have all the weakness the central government has. Hence, it is important to identify specific local policies that contributed to better local economic development.

The last two sections suggest that collective enterprises are more efficient than state enterprises. Hence, if a region has more collective or non-state enterprises, it should have higher regional productivity. In addition to its own high productivity, the non-state sector competes directly with the state sector. As a result of competitive pressure, the state enterprises in that region should also have higher productivity than those in the other regions.

The above analyses are all consistent with the general pattern of regional productivity discrepancies, which rank the coastal regions at the top and the western provinces at the bottom. In this section, a regression analysis is used to determine which factor is most important in explaining the productivity gaps.

The regression analysis is based on the data in TABLE 6.1. In the table, the provinces are grouped into three regions with different concentrations of the non-state sector. The region where 15 percent to 23 percent of the Gross Value of Industrial Output (GVIO) comes from the non-state sector has a TFP index 14 percent lower than the national average, while the region where 45 percent to 67 percent of GVIO comes from the non-state sector has a TFP 20 percent higher than the average. Clearly, productivity is positively correlated with the concentration of non-state enterprises in a region.

This pattern is shown in FIGURE 6.1. The significantly positive correlation between the provincial TFP index and the share of non-state industrial output is illustrated by the closeness of sample points to a regression line.

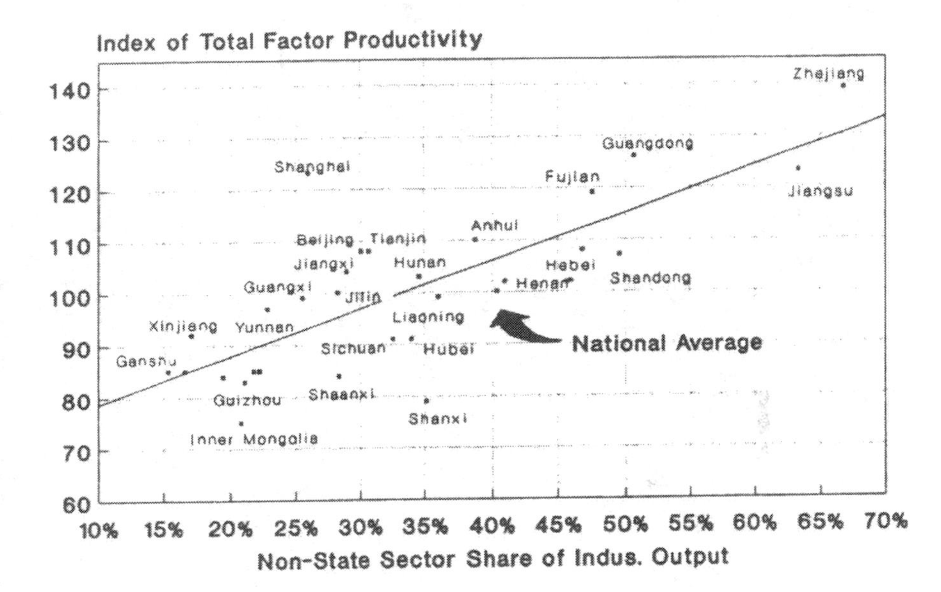

FIGURE 6.1 Impact of the Non-State Sector on China's Regional Productivity Gaps, 1985-1987

Source: See TABLE 6.1.

In TABLE 6.2, weighted OLS regressions are used to explain total factor productivity gaps across the provinces. The explanatory variables are the Non-State Share of GVIO in the provinces and dummy variables for the Western Provinces, Eastern Provinces, and Cities under the direct control of the central government.

Shown also in FIGURE 6.1, Shanghai has exceptionally higher productivity with its low share of non-state industrial output. Beijing and Tianjin also have low shares of non-state industrial output. Since these three cities are controlled directly and tightly by the central government, it is natural to use a City dummy to separate out their special circumstances.

Regression (2) in TABLE 6.2 shows that the TFP correlates positively with the Non-State Sector Share of GVIO. Regression (3) confirms that the TFP also correlates with the dummy variable for the coastal (eastern) provinces. Regression (1), however, is used to find out whether the TFP

TABLE 6.2 Regressions Explaining Regional Productivity Gaps in China

Regression	Sample and Number of Observations	R-Square (Adjusted R-Square)	Coefficients for each variable (t-statistics)				
			Constant	Non-State Sector Share of GVIO	Western Province Dummy	Eastern Province Dummy	City Dummy
(1)	29 provinces	0.774	66.97	88.28	-1.29	3.85	20.98
(2)	29 provinces	0.516 (0.498)	75.82 (12.03)	78.96 (5.36)			
(3)	29 provinces	0.525	95.32		-6.16	21.42	-0.37
(4)	11 eastern provinces	0.621 (0.526)	67.66 (4.87)	94.35 (3.62)			22.44 (2.53)
(5)	9 inland provinces	0.360 (0.268)	67.54 (4.71)	67.54 (4.71)			
(6)	9 western provinces	0.06 (-0.08)	84.83 (12.62)	16.30 (0.66)			

Note: Dependent variables for all regressions are TFP. All regressions are Weighted OLS with Provincial Share of National Gross Value of Industrial Output as weights.

Source: See TABLE 6.1

is still significantly correlated with regional variables after controlling for the concentration of non-state enterprises. According to Regression (1) in TABLE 6.2, the regional dummy variables are not statistically significant except for the City dummy. Hence, if the impact of the non-state sector were separated out and removed, the eastern provinces would not have performed significantly better, while the western provinces would not have had significantly lower productivity than the inland provinces during the 1985-87 period.

It should be emphasized that this surprising result does not contradict the theory that increased local government power in the coastal regions may contribute to productivity growth through policies encouraging the development of private, semi-private, and foreign businesses in those regions. In that case, the degree of local autonomy correlates with the concentration of non-state enterprises. Hence, the explanatory variable of Non-State Sector Share of GVIO may pick up the effects of both local autonomy and the non-state sector on productivity.

The above evidence shows forcefully that other than the concentration of the non-state sector, geographic location does not seem to have an important impact on regional productivity gaps (Shanghai, Beijing and Tianjin are the exceptions). Regressions (4) to (6) explore further the impact of the non-state sector on provincial productivity gaps by dividing the national sample into three regional samples. It shows that the correlation between productivity and the non-state sector share of GVIO is significant within the coastal or inland region, but is not significant within the western region. This can be illustrated by examples from FIGURE 6.1. Both Zhejiang and Guangdong are coastal provinces. The productivity of Zhejiang is higher than that of Guangdong since Zhejiang has a higher concentration of non-state enterprises.

It should be noted that the regression analysis only reveals a pattern of relations between productivity and ownership structure of the provincial economies. In particular, it does not prove that ownership structure is the only important factor in determining productivity. Other factors, such as local government autonomy, may also contribute to the productivity gaps. However, the pattern presented here does suggest that ownership factors cannot be excluded from a serious analysis of regional productivity gaps in China.

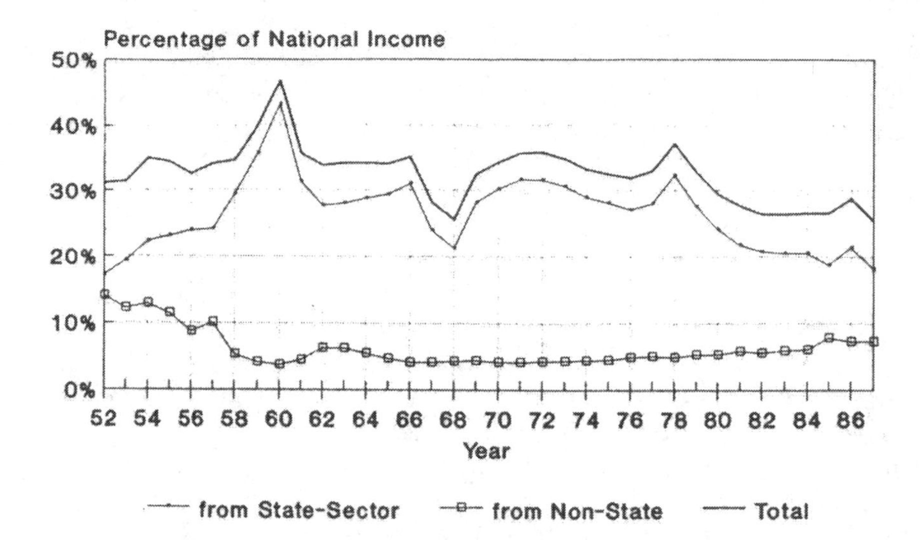

FIGURE 6.2 Contributions to Budgetary Revenue by State and Non-State Sectors, 1952-1986

Sources: *Statistical Yearbook of China*, 1992, pp. 32, 217, and 228.

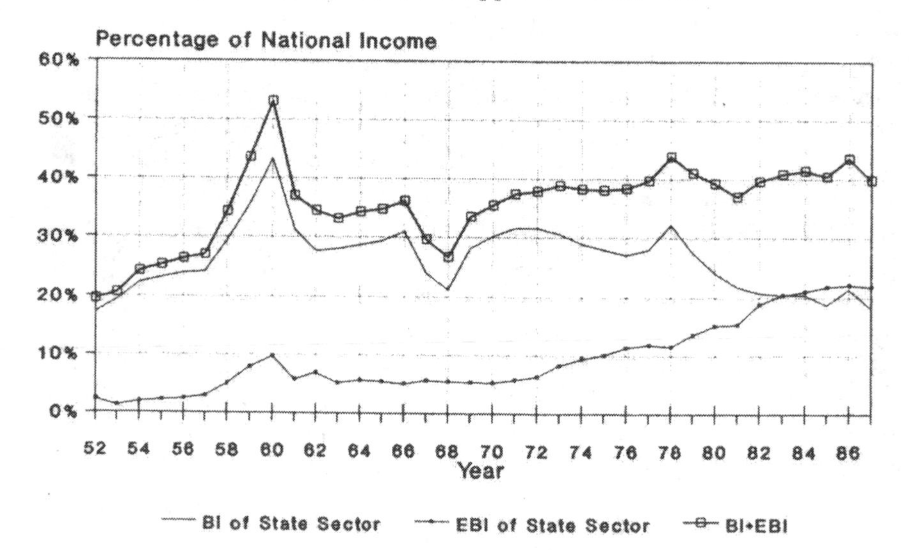

FIGURE 6.3 Budgetary and Extra-Budgetary Revenues of the State Sector, 1952-1986

Sources: *Statistical Yearbook of China*, 1992, pp. 32 and 228.

Decline of Budgetary Revenue: Roots, Consequences, and Solutions

In the last section, we examined the contribution of the non-state sector to industrial productivity and explored the sources of regional productivity gaps. However, most industrial reforms in the last decade were aimed at the state sector. The central and local governments have delegated much economic control to managers and workers in state enterprises. As discussed early in this chapter, increased enterprise autonomy has improved productivity in the state enterprises. However, the budgetary revenues of the central government have not increased as a result of this increased productivity.

FIGURE 6.2 shows the contributions of the state and non-state sector to the central government's budgetary revenue from 1952 to 1987. It is clear that the contribution of the non-state sector has been stable and increasing, although the non-state sector provided budgetary revenues at a level less than 10 percent of the national income throughout the recent reform period. The decline of central government budgetary revenue is primarily due to the fall in budgetary revenues originating from the state sector. In 1978, the state sector contribution to budgetary revenue was more than 30 percent of national revenue, but this contribution declined to less than 20 percent by 1987.

However, as shown in FIGURE 6.3, the fall of budgetary revenue has been accompanied by an increase in extra-budgetary revenue in the state sector. In 1978, budgetary revenue exceeded extra-budgetary revenue by about 20 percent of national income. In 1986, extra-budgetary revenue exceeded budgetary revenue by a few percentage points of the national income, while the sum of budgetary and extra-budgetary revenue held quite stable at about 40 percent of national revenue from 1978 to 1986.

Hence, the decline of government budgetary revenue during the reform era has been characterized by decentralization of control over revenues and profits away from the central government. Nevertheless, local governments did not increase their extra-budgetary revenue very much. This can be seen from FIGURE 6.4, which presents the division of extra-budgetary revenue among the local governments, administrative units, and enterprises in the state sector. The extra-budgetary revenue of local governments as a percentage of national income has actually been declining since 1978. Most of the increases in extra-budgetary revenue went to enterprises and administrative work units.

The above pattern of decentralization is closely related to enterprise reform or the Contract Responsibility System. As discussed in the first two sections, the profit-sharing, managerial autonomy, and fringe benefits provision, key elements of the Contract Responsibility System, provided incentives for enterprises to use resources more efficiently. However, because of the limitation of state ownership and information costs, this increased efficiency has not contributed to budgetary revenue.

The sources of budgetary revenue (taxes and profit remittances) are from sales of industrial products. However, Chinese state enterprises produce not only industrial products but also non-industrial services or fringe benefits within the enterprises. The fringe benefits raise the real income of the managers and workers in the state enterprises but do not contribute to government budgetary revenue. As the enterprises control more resources, they tend to bias investment toward non-industrial projects since the government (not the employees of enterprises) would claim most of the industrial profits from the state enterprises.

A trend toward decentralization has characterized Chinese economic reform since 1978. However, the central government rarely initiated this decentralization. More often, the farmers, enterprises, or local governments first demanded "policies" which gave them some autonomy, and the central government then yielded to them. After more than ten years

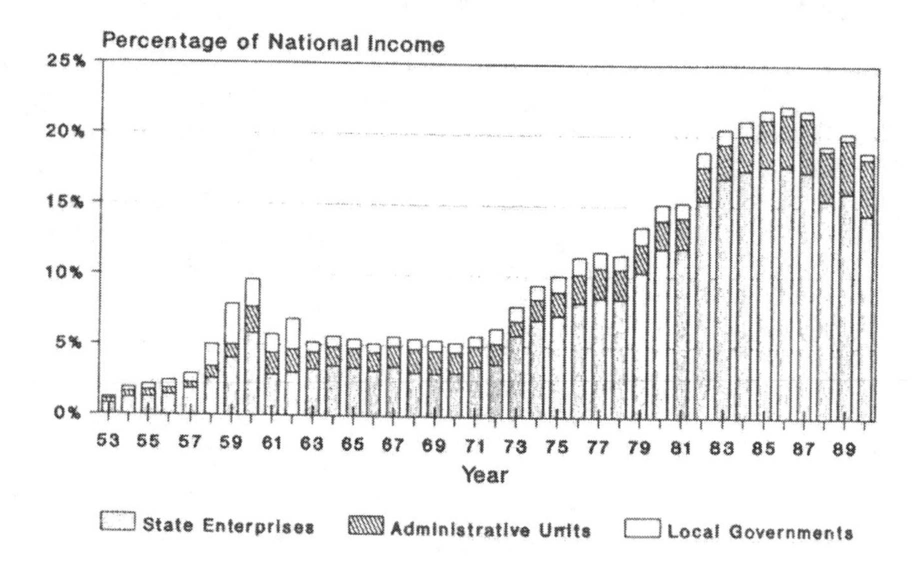

FIGURE 6.4 Size and Distribution of Extra-Budgetary Revenue, 1953-1989

Sources: *Statistical Yearbook of China*, 1992, pp. 32 and 228.

of reforms, the central government now controls less economic resources and has become weaker financially. On the other hand, private business, rural enterprises, and urban collective enterprises have grown rapidly, competing with the state enterprises. The state enterprises, though less efficient than the non-state enterprises, have also improved their productivity. However, the state enterprises have failed to provide enough revenue for the government, not simply because of lower industrial productivity but also because of an expansion of fringe benefits. Even the state enterprises operating at a loss have not given up efforts to continue the expansion of fringe benefits projects.

Reforms in the state sector have produced a dilemma for the central government. If it continues the current decentralization reform, state enterprises may maintain their productivity and fringe benefits expansion but contribute little to budgetary revenue. Recentralization, however, may lower productivity and yield no profits for the central government.

The solution lies in privatization and changes in the economic role of the government. The rapid development of the non-state sector provides the government with new opportunities. Private firms not only have high productivity but are also potential sources of tax revenue. There are significant economies of scale for Chinese enterprises.[8] These economies of scale are currently unavailable to private firms because of their limited size. Large private firms should be able to reap benefits from both the economies of scale and the efficiency of private ownership. The Chinese government is used to the concept that the government invests in state enterprises and so shares some of the profits as budgetary revenue. As the central government invests less in state enterprises, it seems necessary for the government to tap new sources of tax revenue. It is true that it is difficult to collect taxes from small private business. But that situation is also true in other countries. If the property rights of large private firms or corporations are effectively protected by the Chinese government, they may be more than happy to pay taxes and still retain adequate profits for themselves.

At present, however, government regulations do not protect the growth of private enterprises and in many cases discriminate against them. The future uncertainty over government policy toward private business severely restricts the type and size of private firms. Since it is only efficient for government to monitor business accounts and tax files of large firms, the financial benefits of promoting private business for the government will come when large private and semi-private firms have earned significant profits.

In FIGURE 6.5, the state and non-state sectoral shares of budgetary revenue are related to the sectoral share of the gross value of industrial output. During the post-1978 reforms, the non-state sector's share of budgetary revenue has been increasing, with its share of the gross value of industrial output as the leader. Since the non-state sector share of GVIO may continue to increase in the future, the central and local governments should be able to benefit from the rise of non-state industrial enterprises.

To tap budgetary revenue from the private sector, the economic role of the central and local governments has to change. It is not necessary for the government to initiate investment projects, since private firms have incentives to do that if societies demand those projects. However, it is important for the central government to enforce free contracting and protect private property rights. The central government has a monopoly on making and enforcing laws and regulations about markets and economic organizations. If these laws and regulations are effective in facilitating efficient production and exchange, there are tremendous economies of scales for the central government to provide those public services.

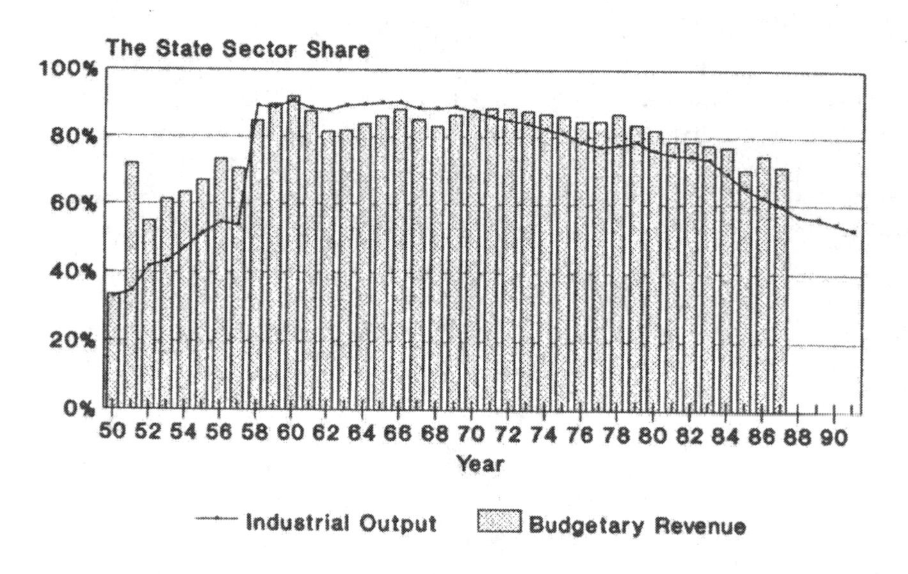

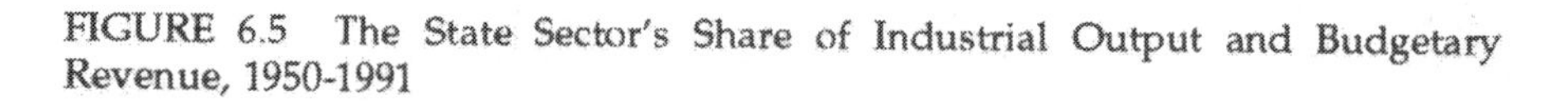

FIGURE 6.5 The State Sector's Share of Industrial Output and Budgetary Revenue, 1950-1991

Sources: *Statistical Yearbook of China*, 1992, pp. 408, 215, and 217.

Since private businesses do not provide extensive fringe benefits such as housing, medical care, public transportation, and education, it is important for local governments to organize these community services to attract profitable businesses into their regions. The central government does not have enough information or the capacity to provide these public goods. In some places such as Wenzhou, the private sector has very sophisticated transportation services. But in most of China, local governments have to take over some of the responsibilities which have fallen to enterprise management in the state sector. The new economic role of the central and local governments should be to serve the growth of the private sector. The growth of the private sector should be able, in turn, to provide the necessary budgetary revenue for better functioning of the central and local governments.

Conclusions

Since 1978, the Chinese government has devolved significant economic control to local governments and enterprises. Two facts have emerged during this time that aroused enormous debates on the economic role of the central and local governments: first, there was a rapid decline in the central government's budgetary revenue; second, there were large discrepancies in regional productivity.

It has been suggested that the higher productivity of China's coastal region may be a result of greater local government autonomy. Hence, more local autonomy in other regions may improve their productivity as well. On the other hand, it has also been argued that the recent decentralization has weakened the economic capacity of the central government and may hinder future economic development in China.

This chapter addresses these debates by examining the sources of China's regional productivity gaps and the root of the decline of the central government budgetary revenue. It finds that the ownership structure of China's regional economies correlates strongly with regional industrial productivity. The impact of the non-state sector on regional productivity was so important that there would have been no significant differences in productivity among the coastal, inland, and western provinces if the contribution of the non-state sector to provincial productivity gaps had been separated out.

Also, the decline of central government budgetary revenue largely resulted from rising extra-budgetary revenue, which was primarily controlled by state-owned enterprises. The state-owned enterprises were able to use extra-budgetary revenue to carry out both industrial and non-industrial projects. The latter would not yield future revenue for the government but nevertheless represented rational investment from the perspective of the managers and workers of the enterprises.

The author therefore argues that the decline of the central government's budgetary revenue was not due to the problems of central-local relations. The root of the decline in budgetary revenue lay in the decline of state enterprise profits. A policy of encouraging development of the non-state sector may be more important than a policy of reforming central-local relations. Both the central and local governments will be better off shifting their attention to new challenges and opportunities arising from the rapid growth of the non-state sector. And an encouraging sign is that both the share and the size of the budgetary revenue originating in the non-state sector has been increasing throughout the period of China's economic reform.

Notes

1. Nicholas R. Lardy:"Economic Planning in China's Central-Provincial Fiscal Relations," in Joint Economic Committee, U.S. Congress, *China: A Reassessment of the Economy* (Washington D.C.: U.S. Government Printing Office, 1975), pp. 94-115.

2. Susan L. Shirk:"Playing to the Provinces: Deng Xiaoping's Political Strategy of Economic Reform," mimeo, Department of Political Science, University of California at San Diego, 1991.

3. Xiao Geng, "Managerial Autonomy, Fringe Benefits and Ownership Structure," *China Economic Review*, 2(1), 47-73, Spring 1991; also Xiao Geng, "The Impact of Property Rights on Productivity and Equity in Post-Mao Chinese Industrial Enterprises," Ph.D. Dissertation, University of California at Los Angeles, June 1991.

4. Ibid., this author reveals the importance of incorporating fringe benefits into the formal analysis of Chinese enterprise behavior.

5. Xiao Geng, Ph.D. Dissertation, op. cit.

6. Xiao Geng, *China Economic Review*, op. cit.

7. Xiao Geng, *China Economic Review*, op. cit.

8. Xiao Geng, Ph.D. Dissertation, op. cit.

7

Foreign Trade Decentralization and Its Impact on Central-Local Relations

Zhang Amei and Zou Gang

Since 1978 the unmistakable trend in China has been the delegation of authority by the center to the provinces and cities, and the erosion of the highly centralized structure of decision-making. The new decentralized structure has had a significant impact on central-local relations. This chapter focuses on decentralization reform in the foreign trade sector and its impact on the relationship between the center and localities. It also analyzes the process of decision-making and implementation of related policies. The main argument is that the nature of the central-local relationship has changed from one of paternalism to either a rivalry or partnership through the process of bargaining during the reform era.

The first section of this chapter classifies three distinct phases of reform and points out that the development of foreign trade during the third phase was the most significant and successful. The second section attributes this success in foreign trade to decentralization, and analyzes the decision-making and implementation of decentralization as a bargaining process between the center and the localities during the third phase. The third section discusses the real nature of the center and localities by testing the following two hypotheses: (1) when the center and localities are rivals, local government and enterprises become allies; and (2) when the center and localities are partners, both of them as well as enterprises form a triple-alliance. Finally, the fourth section discusses the implications of foreign trade decentralization.

TABLE 7.1 Indexes of China's Foreign Trade Growth, 1978-1992

Year	Export	Import
1978	53.81	54.40
1979	75.39	78.27
1980	100.00	100.00
1981	121.47	109.99
1982	123.18	96.35
1983	122.68	106.84
1984	144.26	136.91
1985	150.94	211.04
1986	170.75	214.29
1987	217.66	215.88
1988	262.25	276.12
1989	289.96	295.40
1990	342.66	266.48
1991	396.52	318.58
1992	469.09	402.70

Sources: Indexes are calculated according to *Zhongguo Tongji Nianjian 1991* (Chinese Statistics Yearbook 1991), p. 615; and "A Buoyant New Era for Trade and Investment," in *China Daily*, January 8, 1993, p. 1.

The Phases of the Reforms

As a result of the implementation of reform and the opening policy since 1979, foreign trade has played a much more important role in the growth of the national economy in China than it did before the reforms. This can be seen by examining the following two indicators. First is the growth index of the gross value of imports and exports, compared to the level of 1980 (1980=100). The data contained in TABLE 7.1 shows this growing trend.

The second indicator concerns the changing policies of foreign trade system reform, as shown in TABLE 7.2.

By putting together these two sets of indicators, the results suggest that trade development and reform took place in three phases: the first took place from 1979-1983, the second from 1984-1987, and the third from 1988-1992.

Before 1979, the level and pattern of trade was arranged on the principle of importing only what China could not produce and exporting whatever China could produce in surplus, in order to finance imports. During the first phase of foreign trade reform (1979-1983), this pattern began to change. Trade grew at a relatively high rate, and the center decentralized the right to import and export to a few provinces and municipalities such as Guangdong, Fujian, Beijing, Shanghai, and Tianjin.

During this period, however, some fundamental foreign trade problems were not resolved, and no obvious progress was made in systemic reform. For example, the nation's centralized mandatory planning of foreign trade still controlled the objectives, range, and aims of foreign economic activities. Administrative intervention was still a major means of guaranteeing that the central mandatory foreign trade

TABLE 7.2 Policy Changes in Foreign Trade

Phase	Year	Policies
	Pre-1979	- Balanced trade policy. - The center monopolized trade.
I	1979-83	- A very limited number of provincial governments (Guangdong, Fujian) and some non-MOFERT companies allowed to import and export. - Adoption of the internal settlement rate, and adjustment of the RMB exchange rate.
II	1984-87	- The trade agency system adopted. - The foreign trade plan simplified. - The system of foreign exchange retention implemented.
III	1988-92	- The local and enterprise contract responsibility system adopted. - An increasing number of independent units allowed to participate in foreign trade. - Foreign exchange rate further devalued and the exchange rate mechanism reformed. - Fiscal subsidies removed. - The foreign exchange retention system unified.

Source: Compiled by the authors.

plan was carried out and fulfilled. Fiscal subsidies from the center to cover losses for import and export formed a base on which foreign trade had been dependent. In addition, central decision-making through the Ministry of Foreign Trade remained largely unchanged. The localities, industries, and enterprises were generally not permitted to participate in international trade directly. To a large extent, reform of the foreign trade system lagged behind reform in other sectors for several years.

In the second phase (1984-1987), foreign trade increased faster but fluctuated more than in the first phase. In September 1984, trade system reform was carried out throughout the whole country. The core of the reform included liberalizing trade, merging trade and production enterprises based on free association, separating economic administration from policies by granting much greater autonomy to basic economic units, and streamlining by reducing the number of administrative layers.[1] The most important change was the introduction of the trade agency system (*waimao daili zhi*), in which trading corporations simply served as agents for productive or commercial enterprises who offered exports or required imports in the conduct of trade.[2] This system shifted the financial responsibility from the center to the localities and enterprises. In this phase, the role of highly centralized state trading monopolies was reduced, while some industrial ministries were allowed to set up their own export-import corporations, and some privileges were extended to the provincial and lower-level authorities. As a result, all provincial governments were encouraged to make parallel efforts to expand their trade, especially in the coastal areas.

This new system, however, created several serious problems. One of these can be called "trade-off-deficits," which is defined as a negative relationship between fiscal and trade deficits. This means that the higher the fiscal deficit, the lower the trade deficit, and vice versa, as a result of fiscal subsidies supporting foreign trade. This definition is the opposite of "twin deficits", defined as a positive relationship between fiscal and trade deficits (illustrated by the cases of the U.S. and Japan). The trade-off relationship between fiscal and trade deficits in China was a direct result of distortionary domestic policy with the following features: (1) the central government was responsible for profits and losses in the foreign trade sector, which discouraged firms from seeking to maximize profits and minimize losses, and (2) the central government directly intervened in the operation of trade enterprises and production firms through raw materials allocation and foreign exchange allocation. Empirical study provides evidence that trade-off-deficits are a common phenomenon in large, less-developed countries because of the often close relationship between the ministry of finance and the ministry of foreign trade.[3] Such countries--India, Pakistan, Kenya, and China--face the same policy choice

TABLE 7.3 China's Average Annual Growth Rate of Trade, 1979-1992 (percent)

Phase	Total	Exports	Imports
I	8.3	10.2	6.4
II	11.5	10.8	12.1
III	10.0	12.3	7.8

Sources: *Zhongguo Tongji Nianjian 1991* (Chinese Statistics Yearbook, 1991), p. 615; and "A Buoyant New Era for Trade and Investment," in *China Daily*, January 8, 1993, p. 1.

between growth of foreign exchange supported by large fiscal subsidies and a rapid reduction of the fiscal deficit at the cost of a large trade imbalance. China also faced another foreign trade problem during the second phase. This was the conflict between international and domestic markets, shown in the following relationships: first, for a very large amount of primary goods and resource-intensive manufactures, demand exceeded supply in the domestic market, but supply exceeded demand in the world market. The domestic price was getting higher and higher as shortages increased, but the selling price in the world market was dropping due to shrinking world consumption. When the purchasing price was higher on the domestic market and the selling price was lower on the world market, the gap had to be covered by the state budget. Second, prices on the world market went up or down according to changes between demand and supply, but the prices of some products in the domestic market were still set by the state plan instead of the market. Third, enterprises whose products entered world markets had to bear the risk of price fluctuations, but they could get stable and increasing profits in the domestic market, where price fluctuations were much less and continued price increases were normally anticipated.

In the third phase (1988-1992), foreign trade rose dramatically. During the whole period of reform between 1979 and 1992, the average annual increase in foreign trade was 13.9 percent.[4]

As TABLE 7.3 shows, the annual growth rate of export was 10.2 percent in the first phase of foreign trade reform, 10.8 percent in the second phase, and 12.3 percent in the third phase. The gross value of exports rose from $30.9 billion in 1986 to $39.4 billion in 1987, $47.5 billion in 1988, $52.5 billion in 1989, $62.1 billion in 1990, $71.9 billion in 1991, and $85 billion in 1992.[5] At the same time, budget subsidies went down. Export subsidies amounted to $6.7 billion in 1986, $7.6 billion in

1987, \$6.0 billion in 1988, \$6.1 billion in 1989, and \$4.2 billion in 1990.[6] These subsidies were removed altogether effective January 1, 1991,[7] and the exchange rate was further devalued. In short, the trade-off-deficit situation improved, and the conflict between international and domestic markets lessened during the third phase.

What accounted for all of these trends? Incentives for local governments and enterprises to export induced by deepening reform of the foreign trade system played a very significant role in the third phase. During this period, a series of important steps were taken to reduce overcentralization of the foreign trade sector.

First, the local contract responsibility system was introduced, accompanied by the coastal development strategy. Under the local contract responsibility system, provinces, municipalities, and autonomous regions began to sign export contracts with the Ministry of Foreign Economic Relations and Trade (MOFERT). The contracts include export volumes, the amount of foreign exchange earnings, and allowable losses. If the contractors over-fulfill the targets, they can keep a certain proportion of the extra income. As a result of this local contract responsibility system, the mechanism of central control over foreign trade was replaced by multi-tiered control--that is, by the center, the provinces and cities, and their affiliated enterprises.

Second, the structure of the trade system changed significantly. Numerous new foreign trade enterprises and companies were set up, including provincially-run enterprises, city-run enterprises, and collective enterprises. While by December 1987 only around 800 enterprises were permitted to import and export, this figure skyrocketed to around 5,000 thousand in early 1988.[8] This indicates that the monopolistic position of MOFERT had been replaced by a new organizational framework. Except for certain commodities, such as coal, oil, food grains, and steel, which are still exported by enterprises under the direct control of MOFERT, all other commodities can be exported by enterprises under other ministries or by trading companies established under the jurisdiction of provincial governments.

Third, fiscal decentralization took place. This introduced another local contract responsibility system, in which all foreign trade enterprises and production firms, particularly those affiliated with MOFERT, have been forced to accept financial responsibility for their own profits and losses--including their foreign exchange needs for short-term financing or long-term capital expansion.

It is illuminating to observe the course of the third phase. At the beginning, MOFERT-owned enterprises still received preferential access to imports and exports with the help of overt or hidden central budget subsidies. According to a survey by the Chinese Economic System

Reform Institute conducted in Shenzhen city in March 1988, foreign trade companies affiliated with MOFERT continued to receive a multitude of subsidies. These included subsidies for price, quality, production levels, new equipment, advance delivery, special technology, high-priced raw materials, transportation costs, and interest paid for credit. In addition, the difference between the official exchange rate and the internal settlement rate gave more advantages to MOFERT's firms than others.[9] Thus, these MOFERT enterprises and companies still had numerous advantages, even though MOFERT's power had been weakened and its inferior companies' advantages were reduced.

These problems intensified in the period of economic adjustment that began in early 1989, characterized by a recentralization of control over foreign trade. In mid-1989, the Eighth Five-Year Plan emphasized centralization in order to increase macro control and adjustment of the center.[10] It was even announced that economic system reform would follow a new path in order to centralize a number of important powers.[11] For instance, the central government adopted policies of constraining the economy through tightening credit, slowing the rate of growth, and recentralizing control over resources and the right to make decisions that had previously been delegated to provincial governments. It was also stressed that the adjustment of the foreign trade system would enhance necessary administrative management.[12]

But will these actions reverse the decentralization process described above? The failure of attempts at recentralization suggests it is not likely to happen. Local governments, having already gained control over vast amounts of resources, are in a powerful position to push reforms along the lines of further decentralization and resist efforts to reassert central control. For example, after the 1989 Tiananmen event, the provincial governors were called to Beijing on September 13-19, 1990 to discuss the proposed Eighth Five-Year Plan, which attempted to reverse some of the decentralization reforms made in the 1980s. The governors were generally against recentralization, and demanded that "the center not take regional interests away." Zhao Zhihao, the governor of Shandong Province, said that the center should not counter regionalism by weakening the powers of local governments; instead, it should seek to differentiate responsibilities between the center and the localities.[13] As a result, the central government's attempts to recentralize were not effectively implemented and ultimately failed. This outcome was unanticipated by the center and shows that, as the strength of the local governments grows, their active participation in both local and national economic and political affairs becomes irreversible.

In addition to domestic factors, there were also external influences on China's foreign trade development. International economic sanctions taken by Western countries in response to the 1989 Tiananmen event had a negative impact on China's foreign trade. Nevertheless, it seems that the foreign trade sector was less affected by these sanctions than the domestic economy. Instead, the former showed greater flexibility in dealing with external crises than did the latter. There were a number of reasons for this flexibility. First of all, the foreign trade sector benefitted from its relatively decentralized organizational structure, which directly resulted from decentralization reforms. Second, price reform had brought more market forces to bear on this sector than on others. According to the official *China Daily*, by 1992, 95 percent of the prices of foreign trade products were being determined by the market, while 85 percent of the domestic prices of farm produce and by-products and 70 percent of the prices of means of production were determined by the market.[14] Third, the foreign exchange rate system reform has contributed to the success of the foreign trade sector. As TABLE 7.4 shows, the exchange rate of the Renminbi steadily declined relative to the U.S. dollar between 1979 and

TABLE 7.4 China's Official Foreign Exchange Rate, 1979-1993

(Yuan Per US Dollar)

Year	Exchange Rate
1979	1.50
1980	1.53
1981	1.75
1982	1.92
1983	1.98
1984	2.80
1985	3.20
1986	3.72
1987	3.72
1988	3.72
1989	4.72
1990	5.22
1991	5.43
1992	5.73
1993*	5.77

* Estimate

Sources: For data from 1979 to 1991 see *International Financial Statistics Yearbook, 1992*, p. 279, published by International Monetary Fund, 1992; 1992 data is from *China Daily*, December 31, 1992 and the 1993 data is from *Shijie Ribao* (World Journal), February 6, 1993, p. 35.

1992.[15] The above three phases of foreign trade reform illustrate the progression of foreign trade decentralization. The third phase was the most important and buoyant, because it made the real breakthrough of undermining the monopoly of MOFERT. As a result, provincial and lower-level governments began to play an important role in expanding foreign trade, thus fundamentally changing the relationship between the central and local governments. The roles played by local governments during this phase, and the way in which these roles fundamentally changed compared to previous periods, are the focus of the next two sections.

The Bargaining Process

As foreign trade decentralization deepened during the third reform phase (1988-1992), the power of local governments increased, while that of the center decreased. Such a change was reflected in the process of decision-making on foreign trade policy, as central-local bargaining replaced the central directive as the primary means of decision-making. We will now examine the process of bargaining in foreign trade decentralization. This process can be divided into two phases: decision-making and implementation. Bargaining in the decision-making phase usually occurs in the CCP's Politburo Standing Committee, while bargaining in the implementation phase occurs in many arenas.

Who Bargained?

Let us first examine the process of China's foreign trade decision-making in late 1987 and early 1988 with regard to deepening the nation's foreign trade reform and economic development strategy. The Politburo Standing Committee held several meetings on this subject with Zhao Ziyang, Li Peng, Yao Yilin, Hu Qili, and Tian Jiyun in attendance. In addition, Du Runsheng (Director of CCP's Research Office for Rural Policy), Deng Tuobin (MOFERT Minister), and Li Lanqing (Vice Minister of MOFERT) were also present. These policy-makers were divided into two different groups, those who endorsed decentralization and those who were more skeptical. Zhao Ziyang, the primary advocate of decentralization, proposed that MOFERT enter into contracts of responsibility with provinces, a number of selected cities, and autonomous regions. This would reduce the scope of import and export mandatory plans and the distribution of foreign exchange. It would also allow a greater number of companies and corporations to enter the market, thus increasing competition.

Coupled with this proposal for foreign trade system reform, Zhao Ziyang also attempted to implement a new strategy to develop the coastal economy after he made a tour to the region at the end of 1987. Such a strategy, it was assumed, could be implemented under the local contractual responsibility system.

Both the local contractual responsibility system and the coastal developmental strategy were approved by the Politburo Standing Committee. Zhao's apparent aim was to make a real breakthrough in foreign trade system reform and export development, although there might have been another intention, as Susan Shirk argues--that of "keeping the provinces satisfied and on board the reform drive"[16]--an important consideration for the reformist decision-maker. However, Zhao was criticized later for attempting merely "to prove his own ability and reaffirm his political leadership within the Party and to regain economic policy-making power."[17] The proposals and decisions were endorsed by Deng Xiaoping, since he believed an important step in promoting the reform and opening-up policies was to accelerate the opening of the coastal areas to the outside world.[18]

While much literature about this debate emphasized the development of foreign trade, few people noticed the implications of intensifying reform, particularly the breaking up of MOFERT's monopolistic power in foreign trade activities. In this sense, Yu-shan Wu's analysis underestimates the significance of this decentralization reform and coastal development strategy aiming at achieving export-led growth like that of the four East Asian tigers.[19] Wu claimed that this export-led growth strategy was merely an improvement on the old opening policy, because no material interests were immediately threatened by it (unlike marketization), nor was it ideologically or politically risky (unlike privatization).[20] Our study provides evidence that MOFERT's material interests were directly threatened by this decentralizing reform, and accordingly MOFERT had resisted such measures ever since reform of the foreign trade system began in the early 1980s. Moreover, while foreign trade reform did not directly concern fundamental issues such as property rights, a look at political and economic implications have shown that it involved a structural change instead of a mere policy shift.[21]

In contrast to the above pro-decentralization school, other high-ranking leaders questioned the merit of deepening the reform process and the related trade strategy. According to Yu Yulin, Li Peng stood aloof from this strategy by pointing out that the strategy for developing the coastal areas was proposed by Zhao Ziyang. Meanwhile, Yao Yilin emphasized stable rather than accelerated growth. Yao urged that the strategy should be promoted in a systematic way with a view to enhancing the economic stability of the whole country,[22] and stressed the necessity for renewed centralized controls over the economy.[23] As a matter of fact, both Li and Yao wanted to change the decentralization process to put more funds at the disposal of the center.[24] In addition, some participants referred to these reforms in a more directly negative way, accusing them of creating a colonial economy, economic aggression, capitalism, and dependence on the outside world generally and on some foreign countries in particular.[25]

We now turn to the process of policy implementation, in which local governments have played increasingly important roles. The central government' policy implementation has been through one-on-one, informal and non-institutionalized bargaining with the localities, mainly through the following channels: (1) provincial officials going to Beijing to negotiate directly with the center concerning certain issues, characterized by one-on-one negotiations; (2) central officials travelling to the provinces to inspect development and reform, meeting with provincial officials who report on their work and to present their demands for money or privileges; and (3) provincial officials negotiating with the center during the annual governors' working conference in Beijing. Finally, reformers and local officials also found advocates among officials, consultants, professors, or members of think tanks from Beijing. During the decade-long reform era, it was not uncommon for policy suggestions initially presented by the above "consulting groups" (in a general sense), who were concerned by or actually investigated those particular issues, to be adopted by the center. In this regard, the coastal development strategy proposed in late 1987 constitutes a good example.

What Were the Motivations of Bargainers?

As an influential factor within the bargaining game, pressure from the top decision-maker was maintained during the whole bargaining process. Zhao Ziyang firmly claimed that a multi-power structure is better than a one-power structure in terms of decision-making, and this became an initial goal of the pro-decentralization school.[26]

Yet MOFERT wanted to prevent a weakening of its power. MOFERT's opposition to decentralization stemmed from its aversion to the following factors: (1) a net reduction in the amount, types, and scope of resources under its control, and (2) a decrease in the importance of its functions relative to local governments and enterprises. Susan Shirk goes further, noting that MOFERT's monopolistic power over foreign trade was destroyed by local governments and industrial ministries who established their own trading companies.[27]

Localities, intending to come out on top, were pursuing their own interests within their borders. Were their actions rational? Many assume that localities are egoistic, rational, utility maximizers. In other words, local governments have certain specific characteristics, including a set of tastes or preference orderings, a capacity to make rational decisions, and the ability to choose the most efficient resolution when they face choice dilemmas.[28] By using a rational choice approach, one can clarify the choices facing a decision-maker (individual or institutional) in deciding how best to achieve specific goals as efficiently as possible.[29]

In reality, however, a locality cannot be expected to go beyond the logic of protecting its own interests in order to consider the national interest. Only within its boundary will local choices be generally rational. One cannot imagine the mayor of Shanghai taking into account the interests of other provinces or cities, let alone the whole nation, in decision-making. It is ideal that the behavior of localities is constrained by the rules of the game, which should be set up, complied with and carried out by all players. Yet, with China having no sound legal system and being ruled by man instead of by law, it is inevitable that localities would attempt to achieve their goals as efficiently possible based on their own regional interests. For example, with cigarette tax revenues accounting for some 30 percent of Henan's total revenue income under the present fiscal system, the province has a very strong incentive to fight to retain more tobacco for local processing,[30] and even to adopt a protective industrial policy.[31] The same incentive applies, to an even greater extent, to foreign trade activities, because localities pursue strategies aimed at maximizing their share of earned foreign exchange. For instance, local governments would encourage firms under their jurisdiction to offer lower prices (sometimes over-competing) in response to international market signals, and to increase the price of products with the potential to be exported from other provinces.

Bargaining usually took place over the distribution of existing resources rather than increases in resources. This is because participants in the process of bargaining generally have a common interest in expanding the "size of the pie," but have conflicting interest in dividing it--i.e., the "prisoners' dilemma."[32]

What Did the Center and the Localities Bargain about?

The Ministry of Foreign Economic Relation and Trade (MOFERT) was the representative of the center. Compared to other central ministries, MOFERT had more monopolistic resources before the reform, including (1) financial resources, such as subsidies, (2) material resources, such as raw materials, semi-finished products, and finished products, and (3) policy resources, such as the power to issue licenses, the power to import and export, the power to exchange foreign currency, the power to negotiate directly with foreigners, and so on. Local governments had little autonomy in using these resources because the central government used largely administrative intervention rather than market regulation to promote foreign trade. Beginning in 1980, the monopolistic resources of the center have declined as greater autonomy (allocating material resources and directly running foreign economic activities) has been granted to local governments, while the scope of centrally-planned products and policy resources have been reduced. Nevertheless, during the first and second phases of foreign trade reform, MOFERT retained its special power to allocate budget subsidies, which were only granted to MOFERT-owned enterprises. But during the third phase of decentralization, local governments under the local contract responsibility system became responsible for a part of subsidies. As for material resources,[33] which were generally dominated by MOFERT through the center's foreign trade plan before reform, the amount, type, and scope of MOFERT's control have been considerably reduced after years of reform. For example, the number of planned export commodities decreased from 3000 before the reform to just 112 in 1988.[34] As for policy resources, MOFERT's monopoly has been altered as well. New policy resources have given autonomy to localities and many enterprises in terms of importing and exporting, issuing licenses, trading foreign exchange, and so on.

Whether the negotiations were successful between localities and the center depended on how much bargaining power a province possessed, in addition to its political position and geographic location in the nation. Generally speaking, the more resources a province owned, the more powerful was its bargaining position. Guangdong province, for instance, is a well-known powerful bargainer with the center. As a pioneer of reform experimentation, the province has strengthened its economic and political position, and has had an increasingly important influence on the center. From the very beginning of reform, the province's leadership asked for financial resources and policy privileges and complained that the center had provided little material support for its development during the decades from 1949 to the beginning of the reform, due to the fact that Guangdong is geographically close to the hostile Taiwan. But as the central government gave similar policy privileges to the neighboring province of Fujian, Guangdong would ask for more special treatment. In early 1988, accompanying the further opening of coastal areas and implementation of the local contract responsibility system, Guangdong bargained with the center and gained much broader policy privileges in 10 spheres, including financing, banking, issuing bonds, setting up a foreign exchange adjustment center, pricing, absorbing foreign investment, and managing real estate.[35] Moreover, Guangdong was allowed to take the lead in political structural reform at the same time, including introducing a state civil service system, implementing an administrative lawsuit system, and dissolving party groups in government departments.[36] The case of Fujian province is similar to that of Guangdong. In April of 1988, the center approved a proposal by Fujian regarding comprehensive experimentation with reform and opening. Fujian was granted broader policy privileges in eleven areas including finance, economic and trading cooperation with Taiwan, economic planning, prices, fiscal policy, personnel and wages, real estate, rural and enterprise reform, technology and education, and administrative agency reform.[37]

Shanghai's case seemed different. Shanghai had been backward in terms of economic development and systemic reform during the period from 1979 to 1988. For example, Shanghai' revenue had been decreasing for several years, from 26.4 billion in 1985, to 25.8 billion in 1986, to 24.1 billion yuan in 1987.[38] In some important areas, such as national income, Shanghai had lagged behind Jiangsu, Shandong, Sichuan, and Guangdong since 1983; Shanghai's exports were also overshadowed by Guangdong.[39] Some important reasons for this were: (1) several successive mayors of Shanghai were very concerned with their prospects for promotion to the center, making them less bold in negotiating with the center; (2) the center restricted Shanghai's bargaining capability on the grounds that Shanghai's products and corresponding revenues belonged to the whole country as Shanghai had been using resources from the latter; and (3) Shanghai relied heavily on allocations from the center in the form of cheap, centrally-subsidized raw materials. Meanwhile, the center actually relied on collecting close to one-fourth of its fiscal revenues from Shanghai.

This mutually dependent relationship between the center and Shanghai under centralized planning lasted until the end of 1987. Shanghai, complaining about its deteriorating economic situation and infrastructure, took an opportunity to demand greater support from the center when Deng Xiaoping inspected the poorest area of Shanghai at the beginning of 1988. Thereafter, Shanghai received 1.5 billion yuan from the center for infrastructure development.[40] Although Shanghai had lost several chances to get on the "express train" of reform previously, it finally climbed aboard in 1988. Under its new contract responsibility system with the center, Shanghai got perhaps the best deal of the various provinces, probably even better than that of Guangdong. For instance, a new financial contract system was implemented, under which Shanghai would hand over only 10.5 billion yuan annually, for the next five years, to the central government. The city would split 50/50 with the center any additional revenues exceeding 16.5 billion by 1991. This contract system was described by Zhu Rongji, then the mayor of Shanghai, as "most favorable for the city to solve its economic difficulties."[41] As a result of these reforms, Shanghai's foreign trade developed at a very quick pace. The annual growth index of gross exports was 3.9 percent annually in the first phase of foreign trade reform, 3.8 percent in the second, and 4.9 percent in the third phase.[42]

The Shenzhen Special Economic Zone provides another example of the deepening of reform in the third phase. At the beginning of 1988, faced with the further opening of coastal areas--particularly Guangdong's comprehensive experimentation and Hainan Island's new open policy that was unique among the special zones--Shenzhen felt threatened. It hoped to get more autonomy to grant foreign trade licenses, to make laws, etc. Shenzhen officials invited the Economic System Reform Institute to diagnose its entire development and reform situation and to report Shenzhen's demands to the center. It thought that this would be a good way to strengthen its bargaining power. At the same time, Beijing, Tianjin, Jiangsu, Hubei and other localities also took the opportunity to present the center with their own proposals in an attempt to gain more policy-making autonomy.

As a result of the above bargaining process, a fundamental change in terms of the nature of the relationship between the center and the localities had taken place.

The Changing Nature of Central-Local Relations

David Lampton argues that the Chinese polity is a bargaining rather than a "command" system due to several structural features: (1) decision-makers at all levels must decide how to allocate exceedingly scarce resources with few, or no, market signals; (2) a small market sector uneasily coexists with the rigidities of the still dominant administered economy; and (3) trade-offs are involved in decision-making due to the complexity of many decisions.[43]

This chapter takes this argument further. It suggests that the nature of bargaining in China's pre-reform era was characterized by paternalism, i.e., a high degree of local dependence on the center and dependence of firms on the government. Janos Kornai described the relationship between a state socialist country and enterprises as similar to the relationship between father and son, since "the state budget is responsible for compensating some firms for losses, keeping some prices at a low level by covering part of the costs, and subsidizing some unprofitable foreign trade transactions..."[44] The reason for this paternalism was that the center monopolized resources through a highly centralized planning system that penetrated all aspects of economic life. The localities had no right to use these resources freely--they depended on allocations from the center. All foreign exchange earnings of localities and enterprises had to be handed over to the center, and any demands for local use of foreign exchange had to be approved by the center. All foreign trade activities were run by the center, and profits and losses were borne by the center. In short, localities had to depend on the center in all foreign trade activities.

We would argue that the decentralization reforms, however, changed the localities' dependent relationship with the center by altering the nature of bargaining from a form of paternalism to a rivalry or partnership. As a result, (1) when the center and localities are rivals, local government and enterprises become allies; and (2) when the center and localities are partners, both of them and enterprises form a triple-alliance.

Central-Local Rivalry

As rivals, when both the center and localities insist on their own interests, bargaining has to take place. For instance, localities and the center confronted each other over the issue of what kind of enterprises would have the right to import and export on their own. In December 1987, MOFERT proposed to the CCP Politburo that enterprises earning up to $100 million in foreign currency each year be able to import and export directly. Opponents of this proposal argued that although it was necessary to decide who could import and export according to how much foreign currency they earned, this $100 million entry barrier was too high for most enterprises. In fact, it was likely to strengthen the monopoly of the specialized corporations under MOFERT, since the higher the entry barrier, the less likely enterprises would be to challenge the dominant position of MOFERT. For instance, the entire projected foreign currency earnings for the city of Guangzhou in 1988 were $640 million, $230 million for Dalian, $190 million for Chongqing, $180 million for Qingdao, $110 million for Harbin, $100 million for Shenyang, and $40 million for Xian.[45] Thus, under MOFERT's proposal, even Guangzhou--China's largest city in terms of generating foreign exchange--would have only three to five enterprises qualified to apply for the right to import and export. And, not surprisingly, virtually all of these enterprises were affiliated with MOFERT. Thus opponents of MOFERT's proposal demanded that the entry barrier be lowered so that more local foreign trade enterprises could compete in the international market, and earn more foreign exchange revenue. Eventually, MOFERT made a concession under pressure from China's reformist leadership and lowered the level of earnings required.

Localities have tried to capture more resources from the center in the following ways: First, local governments have made flexible interpretations of central policy to realize and promote their own interests. Li Xianglu observes that localities were willing to implement policies compatible with their interests. If not, they interpreted policies in the way they preferred, which was probably the opposite of the center's intention.[46] Zhao Suisheng notes that the center lacked effective monitoring tools to control policy implementation by the localities. This made it possible for local governments to ignore central policies that ran against local their interests, or to deviate from the central policies in ways which favored local interests.[47] Likewise, Dorothy Solinger says that provinces are now freer to use local resources for their own self-determined ends.[48]

Second, localities have been able to increase their bargaining power by hiding benefits at the enterprise level. Jiangsu Province, for instance, did not collect all enterprise profits that should have been handed over to the center. Instead, it set a reduced tax rate and granted ad-hoc tax relief to enterprises. It was estimated that in 1988, 10 billion yuan of national taxes were reduced in this way.[49] An unintended outcome of this, as Wang Xiaoqiang argues, is that the more benefit goes to local enterprises, the more powerful enterprises become in bargaining with local governments.[50]

Third, some provinces even boldly confronted the center on the policies of mobilizing resources and other specific issues. For example, at the beginning of 1985, the central government tried to propose a "tax for profit" policy, but failed to put it into effect because provinces disliked the proposal's constraints on their power. Jilin provincial officials told enterprises that although the center had made this proposal, they could ignore it and continue the profit-contracting system.[51] Another example is the Pudong development zone. The center had approved only one such development zone in Shanghai. However, Jiangsu, Zhejiang, Shandong, Anhui, and even Xinjiang and Inner Mongolia, all developed Pudong-type development zones without the center's approval.[52] The center now regards localities as greater rivals because decision-making power at the enterprise-level was taken over by the localities. This is the major reason that opponents of decentralization criticized this policy. Localities have even used the center's own reform slogans, such as "enlivening the economy," to fight any attempts at recentralization.[53] These flexible explanations of the central policy and bold confrontations have produced a policy bias in the course of implementation. As Zhao Suisheng puts it, the policies of the center have seldom been implemented as the central government originally intended.[54]

A big change in the distribution of policy resources in "open" cities confirms the hypothesis about the rivalry between the center and localities. Let us take the distribution of import and export licenses as an example, using results of a Guangdong survey conducted by the authors.

The authority to issue import and export licenses had been decentralized to the provincial governments. In Guangdong province, 87 products required export licenses in 1985, 127 in 1986, 217 in 1987, and 257 in 1988. Of these 257 products in 1988, 35 were issued licenses by MOFERT, 56 by special agencies of MOFERT, and 166 by the provincial Economic and Trading Commission. In this case, the localities already held an advantage on the quantitative distribution of licenses, yet they demanded further decentralization of license approval procedures and license management. The center, however, still controlled the right to license a number of important products with high-prices, low-costs, and large profit margins, and MOFERT often distributed these licenses administratively to its own foreign trade companies or enterprises. Arguing that allowing local governments to issue more licenses would disrupt the foreign trade order, MOFERT was reluctant to give up further rights to issue licenses for import and export.

On the other side of the coin, when localities and the center confronted each other, localities and their enterprises often became allies in the process. A large body of research confirms that local governments were unable to ignore the will of enterprises. Huang Yasheng argues that the economic reforms of the last ten years produced a hybrid system under which local economic bureaucrats and enterprise managers came to share some crucial economic decision-making power without clearly defined rules or well-specified divisions of labor.[55] Similarly, Susan Shirk suggests that the economic incentives offered to local officials under the current reforms make them more solicitous of enterprise managers and more willing to defer to the latter's judgments. Meanwhile, some local officials have themselves become executives of local holding companies whose interests are closely allied with those of the company managers.[56] Li Xianglu notes that localities took over some powers that the center had intended to hand over to the enterprises or lower administrative units while, on the other hand, the localities often then handed these powers over to enterprises in their own way.[57]

Let us take fiscal subsidies as an example. The decentralization of 1987 was carried out in order to eliminate the fiscal deficits of the center. But localities were not willing to bear the share of the deficit caused by loss-making enterprises, and thus preferred to give up control over those enterprises. Furthermore, a number of local governments even granted special benefits to the firms and enterprises under their jurisdiction. To encourage these foreign trade firms and enterprises producing export goods and to be responsible for their own profits and losses, localities returned a part of or all of the foreign exchange earnings that these firms and enterprises had turned over to the local governments.[58]

Why should localities want to grant such benefits to the enterprises? One explanation is that localities do not only seek to guarantee production of important goods and maintain the level of local employment, but also to use appropriated enterprise revenue for their own uses. These uses include financing the renovation of enterprise staff housing, building a staff hospital, purchasing consumer durable goods, and paying bonuses.[59] Yet this is only part of the reason. In fact, the mutual dependence of localities and enterprises has a profound institutional basis. Local governments have dual administrative and economic functions, while Chinese firms are not only production units but also administrative ones characterized by a sense of community. This feature makes it very difficult for firms to be independent of local government, since the latter not only controls their economic affairs, but also their political and social affairs. In the allocation of foreign exchange, localities rely heavily on the foreign exchange earnings of enterprises, and thus have an incentive to take good care of enterprises. For both, the more foreign exchange earned, the better. This common interest encourages both sides to strengthen their coalition. For example, Guangdong province's joint industrial-commercial foreign trade enterprises benefitted from a special arrangement in which 20 percent of the firm's foreign exchange earnings were sent to Beijing, and 30 percent to the provincial or metropolitan level. This left 50 percent of these earnings as the firm's entitlement.[60] In this case, the larger the basic amount of foreign exchange earned, the more both local governments and firms receive.

Central-Local Partnership

The center and localities do not always have a confrontational relationship. Sometimes they cooperate as partners. Successful cooperation takes place when participants face an increase in the size of the "pie" and share a common interest. Specifically, it is easier to reach a consensus when both the center and the localities expect foreign trade to develop quickly, which is a basic premise underlying the decentralization of foreign trade. They all realize that vigorous foreign trading enterprises with more autonomy are crucial to expanding exports, so neither the center nor the local government can afford to ignore the will of firms and enterprises.

In such cases, localities may induce their local enterprises to accept the center's rules of the game in order to achieve their mutual goal of expanding exports. For instance, in the case of trade, if the goal is to build export bases for raw material production, both sides would work together to set up a joint venture. In such cases, the relationship between the center and the localities is reciprocal and mutually dependent. In many cases, firms also join this sort of project. There are at least two patterns generally followed. First, three parties put a certain percentage of funds into the construction of a raw material base, or two sides put funds in while the third contributes technicians. Second, ministries, localities and enterprises sometimes make a spontaneous joint effort to resist a certain policy. Take the general issue of "tax for profit" as an example. In the mid-1980s, top decision-makers tried to implement a "unified tax" system to replace the contract system. This proposal was not only resisted by localities--due to its intent to reduce the influence of local governments--but also resisted by ministries and enterprises.[61] Facing this "triple alliance," the central decision-makers finally backed away from the proposed plan.

Implications of Foreign Trade Decentralization

Under the foreign trade decentralization reform, the highly centralized structure of decision-making is being replaced by a more pluralist one. Within the new framework, the governments of thirty provincial-level units, more than ten *jihua danlie* core cities (on a "core city separate list" in the national planning system),[62] and numerous enterprises, play an increasingly important role in China's political economy. This is reflected in the fact that more efficient and effective foreign trade policies have been emerging from decentralized bargaining than from the central government's direction. Since an increasing number of local players have been granted a certain degree of autonomy in trade decisions by being allowed to establish their own trade organizations to compete with MOFERT, the inefficiency of the monopolistic foreign trade system prior to the reforms has been reduced. In this sense, decentralization is helping change China's foreign trade system from the center-monopolistic type to a market-oriented one. This is true not only because the number of firms and companies that can directly compete in the foreign trade market has vastly increased, but also because the scope of the centralized foreign trade plan has been reduced and the exchange rate has gradually drawn closer to the market rate.

Most importantly, both the bilateral alliances between localities and enterprises and the "triple alliances" formed among the center, localities and enterprises, suggest that the bargaining power of localities vis-a-vis the center has been increasing. This implies an expanding local autonomy, in which the local governments' ability to pursue and sustain their own interests and policy objectives is enhanced by their growing ability to make import and export decisions, to introduce foreign investment, and even to issue government bonds abroad. This increase in local bargaining power has challenged the existing authority of the center, and undermined the monopolistic position of MOFERT. The weakening of the center's ability to control foreign trade resources throughout the period of reform parallels the trends of economic reform in other areas such as the fiscal system, and agricultural and industrial management systems.

All the above changes suggest that it is likely that an autonomous society capable of competing with the state monopoly in various economic spheres will finally appear in China. This likelihood has improved since Deng Xiaoping's tour of southern China at the beginning of 1992. In particular, more private businesses have been encouraged to get involved in the export-oriented economy. Currently, the center plans to further remove the unreasonable caps that have hindered the development of the private economy[63] and to return more rights to the state enterprises.[64]

China's foreign trade system was mainly characterized by the center-monopoly model in the pre-reform era. After 1978, under the influence of foreign trade decentralization and the open-door policy over more than a dozen years, the center's monopolistic position was largely undermined. The period from 1988 to 1992 witnessed a real breakthrough, with indications that the center will no longer be able to rollback the decentralization process. During this phase, localities and firms have played an increasingly important role, gaining a large portion of decision-making power and control over resources. Meanwhile the relationship between the center and local governments has shifted from one of paternalism to one of either rivalry or partnership. These new relations will help further China's foreign trade and intensify the nation's economic reform in other areas.

Notes

1. S. K. Tsang and T. O. Woo, "The Post-1979 Trade Liberalization in China: Ideas, Policy and Reality," Joseph Chai and Chi-heung Leung eds., *China's Economic Reform* (Hong Kong: University of Hong Kong, 1987), p. 408.

2. Ibid., 409.

3. We examined the data of several countries, including India, Pakistan, Kenya and other less developed countries, made graphs and found that there was a common trend in the relationship between trade deficits and fiscal deficits in these countries. The results appeared in a term paper titled "Two-gap Model and the Choice of Policy in China," done at Yale University in 1989.

4. Calculated according to *Zhongguo tongji nianjian 1991* (Chinese Statistics Yearbook, 1991) (Beijing: Zhongguo Tongji Chubanshe, 1991), p. 615; and "A Buoyant New Era for Trade and Investment," *China Daily*, January 8, 1993, p. 1.

5. Ibid.

6. Zhang Yuxian, "Zhongguo duiwai maoyi bixu shixian sanda zhuanbian" (China's Foreign Trade Must Have Three Changes), *Jingji Daobao* (Economic Reporter, hereafter *JJDB*), October 21, 1991, p. 10.

7. Li Lanqing, "Zhongguo waimao xingshi he fazhan quxiang" (The Situation and Trend of Chinese Foreign Trade Development) in *JJDB*, October 12, 1992, p. 23; and "Wuyi tan waimao tizhi gaige" (Wuyi on Foreign Trade System Reform), *JJDB*, October 19, 1992, p. 21.

8. Zhu Ang, "Zhongguo waimao tizhi gaige jiang maichu xinbu"(Chinese Foreign Trade System Reform will Take a New Step), *JJDB*, December 21, 1987, p. 9.

9. According to a survey concerning setting up a new system in Shenzhen conducted by the Economic System Reform Institute of China in March 1988. See Zhang Amei, "Guanyu Shenzhen waimao de fazhan yu gaige," (On the Development and Reform of Shenzhen's Foreign Trade), *Shenzhen xintizhi yanjiu* (The Research on the New System in Shenzhen), edited by Zhonggong Shenzhen shiwei zhengce yanjiushi (Policy Research Division of the CCP's Shenzhen Municipal Commission), 1988, pp. 172-187.

10. Yulue, "Zhixing shidang jizhong yuanze de kunnan" (Difficulties in Carrying out Appropriate Centralization), *JJDB*, October 8, 1990, p. 15.

11. See *JJDB*, November 19, 1990, p. 11.

12. Zhou Wei, "Jingji fazhan qushi yu zhongguo gaige" (The Economic Development and Reform of China), *JJDB*, October 1, 1990, p. 9.

13. *Zhongguo zhichun* (China Spring) (January 1991), pp. 22-23.

14. See "Market plays a dominant role," *China Daily*, January 4, 1993, p. 2.

15. Nicholas Lardy has a good description of the sources of trade expansion. He explains China's trade growth as the result of three critical developments: decentralization of decision-making in foreign trade, reform of the prices of traded goods, and devaluation of the Renminbi. See "Chinese Foreign Trade," in *The China Quarterly* (hereafter CQ), No. 131, (September 1992), pp. 695-710.

16. Yu Yulin, "Why should Zhao Reemphasize Coastal Economic Development?" *Issues and Studies*, Vol. 24, No. 12 (December 1988), p. 2.

17. Susan Shirk, *The Political Logic of Economic Reform in China*, Chapter 4, "Playing to the Provinces," Manuscript, August 1990, p. 25.

18. Yu Yulin, "A Heated Debate on the Coastal Areas' Development Strategy," in *Issues & Studies*, Vol. 24, No. 6 (June 1988), pp. 1-2.

19. Yu-shan Wu, "Reforming the Revolution: Industrial Policy in China," *The Pacific Review* (Oxford University Press), No. 3, 1990, p. 249.

20. Ibid., 255.

21. Yu-shan Wu borrows the distinction between economic reform and policy changes from Ed A. Hewett. According to him, economic reform refers to changes in the institutional arrangements constituting the system by which the resources are allocated. They change the way economic decisions are made and deal with fundamental causes of performance problems. Policy changes, on the other hand, use the existing system to implement new policies designed to improve performance. Policy changes are generally an ineffective substitute for genuine reform. See Ibid., 255.

22. Yu Yulin, "A Heated Debate on the Coastal Areas' Development Strategy," op. cit., p. 3.

23. Y.Y. Kueh believes that the need "for restrengthening economic controls is most clearly spelled out by none other than Yao Yilin," *The Australian Journal of Chinese Affairs*, No. 24 (July 1990), p. 93.

24. Susan Shirk, "The Politics of Industrial Reform," in Elizabeth Perry and Christine Wong eds., *The Political Economy of Reform in Post-Mao China* (Cambridge, Mass.: The Council on East Asian Studies/Harvard University, 1985), p. 48.

25. Yu Yulin, "A Heated Debate on the Coastal Areas' Development Strategy," op. cit., p. 3.

26. Some American scholars express a similar view about this Chinese reform issue. For example, Christine Wong suggests that adjustments necessary to correct the economic problems could be better handled in a decentralized way by localities and enterprises. See Christine Wong, "Material Allocation and Decentralization," p. 276.

27. Susan Shirk, "The Politics of Industrial Reform," in Perry and Wong, eds. *The Political Economy of Reform in Post-Mao China*, p. 217.

28. This is borrowed from Martin Staniland, *What is Political Economy? A Study of Social Theory and Underdevelopment* (New Haven and London: Yale University Press, 1985), p. 36.

29. Ibid., p. 39.

30. Christine Wong, "Material Allocation and Decentralization: Impact of the Local Sector on Industrial Reform," Elizabeth Perry and Christine Wong eds., *The Political Economy of Reform in Post-Mao China* (Cambridge, Mass.: The Council on East Asian Studies/ Harvard University, 1985), p. 274.

31. Sometimes, local governments also adopt policies to protect infant industries.

32. Beth Yarbrough and Robert Yarbrough, "International Institutions and the New Economics of Organization," *International Organization*, Vol. 44, No. 2 (Spring 1990), p. 238.

33. China's production materials were divided into categories under the Soviet material allocation system in the pre-reform era as follows: Category I comprises the widely used, key materials directly allocated by the State Planning Commission (*tongguan*). Specialized key materials under Category II are allocated by central ministries, or *buguan*. Category III materials are under local allocation, or *diguan*. Local foreign companies and corporations could not use foreign materials that were *buguan*. See Christine Wong, "Material Allocation and Decentralization: Impact of the Local Sector on Industrial Reform," in Elizabeth Perry and Christine Wong eds., *The Political Economy of Reform in Post-Mao China* (Cambridge, Mass.: The Council on East Asian Studies/Harvard University, 1985), p. 257.

34. Lardy, "Chinese Foreign Trade," op. cit., p. 702.

35. FBIS-CHI-88-052, March 17, 1988, p. 41.

36. FBIS-CHI-88-012, January 20, 1988, p. 49.

37. Gao Jieguang, "Zhonghe gaige shiyan jiang gai Fujian kaifang chu xinhuoli" (A Comprehensive Reform Experiment Will Revive Fujian Again), *JJDB*, June 6, 1988, p. 14.

38. *Shanghai tongji nianjian 1991* (Shanghai Statistics Yearbook, 1991), p. 53.

39. Chen Yonghao, "Zhongguo dalu de disanci kaifang langchao" (The Third Opening Wave in China), *JJDB*, May 30, 1988, p. 7.

40. The sources of the material are from a field survey done by the authors in 1985 and a workshop regarding the relationship between the central government and local governments during the reform era, organized by the Chinese Scholars of Political Science & International Studies, Inc. in Washington D.C., March 1991.

41. FBIS-CHI-88-078, 22 April 1988, p. 33.

42. Calculated according to *Shanghai tongji nianjian 1991* (Shanghai Statistics Yearbook, 1991), p. 326.

43. David Lampton, "Chinese Politics: The Bargaining Treadmill," *Issues & Studies*, Vol. 23, No. 3 (March 1987), pp. 12-15.

44. Janos Kornai, *Economics of Shortage* (Amsterdam, New York: North-Holland Press, 1980), p. 592.

45. According to Guangdong investigations conducted by he Economic System Reform Institute of China in 1987 and 1988.

46. Li Xianglu, "Weishenmo shuo fenquan gaige fangzhen shi zhengque de" (Why is the Policy of the Decentralization Reform Correct?). *Zhishi fenzi* (The Chinese Intellectual) (March 1990), pp. 1-4.

47. Zhao Suisheng, "The Feeble Political Capacity of Strong One-Party Regimes --An Institutional Approach Toward the Formulation and Implementation of Economic Policy in Post-Mao Mainland China (Part One)," *Issues & Studies*, Vol. 26, No. 1 (January 1990), p. 48.

48. Dorothy Solinger reviews *Center and Province in the People's Republic of China: Sichuan and Guizhou 1955-1965* by David Goodman (Cambridge: Cambridge University Press, 1986), in *The Pacific Review*, Vol. 1 (1988), p. 104.

49. Wang Shaoguang, "From Revolution to Involution: State Capacity, Local Power, and (Un)governability in China," manuscript, p. 37.

50. Li Xianglu, "Shinian gaigezhong de fenquan qingxiang" (The Trend of Decentralization during the Ten Years Reform), *Zhongguo zhichun* (China Spring) (October, 1990), p. 32.

51. Ibid.

52. *Zhongguo jingji yuebao* (Chinese Economy Monthly), Vol. 20 (December 1990), p. 32.

53. According to the interview by Susan Shirk, see her "*The Political Logic of Economic Reform in China*, Chapter 4, "Playing to the Provinces," p. 47.

54. Zhao Suisheng, "The Feeble Political Capacity of Strong One-Party Regimes --An Institutional Approach Toward the Formulation and Implementation of Economic Policy in Post-Mao Mainland China (Part One)," op. cit., p. 48.

55. Huang Yasheng, "Web of Interests and Patterns of Behavior of Chinese Local Economic Bureaucracies and Enterprises during Reforms," *China Quarterly*, No. 9 (1990), pp. 432-433.

56. Susan Shirk, "The Politics of Industrial Reform," p. 219.

57. Li Xianglu, "Shinian gaigezhong de fenquan qingxiang" (The Trend of Decentralization during the Ten Year Reform), op. cit., p. 32; and "Weishenmo shuo fenquan gaige fangzhen shi zhengque de" (Why Is the Policy of the Decentralization Reform Correct?), op. cit., p. 4.

58. Zhou Guofang, "Zhongguo waimao tizhi gaige ruhe jinxing" (How to Take Action about China's Foreign Trade System Reform), *JJDB*, October 1, 1991, p. 18.

59. Huang Yasheng, "Web of Interests and Patterns of Behavior of Chinese Local Economic Bureaucracies and Enterprises During Reforms," p. 451, and footnote No. 65.

60. Ezra Vogel, *One Step Ahead in China: Guangdong under Reform* (Cambridge, Mass.: Harvard University Press, 1989), p. 390.

61. Li Xianglu, "Weishenmo shuo fenquan gaige fangzhen shi zhengque de" (Why Is the Policy of the Decentralization Reform Correct?), p. 4.

62. It indicates some cities which have the same rights as provinces since the reform.

63. See "Controls on private sector to be loosened," *China Daily*, January 4, 1993, p. 2.

64. Yuan Baohua, the director of China's Enterprises Management Association, spoke about this in a 1992 meeting attended by directors and managers of factories, see *JJDB*, September 14, 1992, p. 25.

PART THREE

Regional Differentiation and Case Studies

8

Regional Inequality Variations and Central Government Policy, 1978-1988

Huo Shitao

The transformation of central-local relations constitutes one of the most fascinating aspects of the Chinese reform process since the late 1970s. Control over some major resources has shifted from the center to the provinces and the various local entities; central control over policy-making and implementation has been replaced by greater regional and sectoral policy diversity; and, finally, more actors have entered the picture between the central and lower levels of government.

As one of the salient outcomes of the changing relationship between the central and local governments, regional inequality is generally believed to have been greatly exacerbated due to reformist policies that favored the relatively advanced coastal regions of China.[1] However, my statistical research on regional income inequality since 1980 has shown contrary results. My research on regional income inequalities reveals that the "coastal policy" has, in fact, not been responsible for this inequality. This striking result raises several problems associated with previous research on this issue. First, many of these studies arrive at their conclusions with little calculation of the factors that influence regional variations in inequality. Second, as a corollary to the first problem, these studies place less attention on the sources that induce the regional variations, especially central management policy, which plays a decisive role in causing regional inequality variations. Third, the misinterpretation of indicators also creates confusion. For example, one aspect of inequality may be interpreted as the comprehensive inequality between regions. Or relative inequality may be considered as equivalent to the absolute inequality.

My purpose here is to analyze the issue of regional inequality in terms of per capita income by provinces, and discuss the policy responses of the central government to these regional variations. To understand certain policies and their outcomes, one must explore the dynamics of socioeconomic structure and its underlying philosophy. Similarly, a brief review of the geographic distribution of China's center and periphery, and its impact on regional differences and regional development policy since 1949, provides additional insight into this issue. An approach that considers the changing reform process and its outcomes is also necessary. Therefore, this study will survey policy debates on the issues of decentralization and regional inequality, as well as some of the underlying theories. An institutional policy approach is used to study variations in regional inequality and management policy.

Decentralization and Regional Inequality

Even though the Third Plenum of the Chinese Communist Party (CCP) at the end of 1978 provided the basic outline for economic structural reform, the debate over a market-oriented versus planning-oriented economy has never ended. As a matter of fact, the debate became much more intense and controversial in 1980 when the problem of regional inequality emerged as a serious issue. In addition to the mechanisms of market versus planning, the issue of decentralization and its impact on regional inequality has also been hotly contested.

The term "decentralization" is commonly defined as a mechanism associated with decision-making powers, in which the responsible organ of government has some discretion over how the central government directives are to be interpreted and implemented. With decentralization of policy, even rule-making powers will be more spatially diffused.[2] Before 1978, China's centrally-planned economic bureaucracy exercised mandatory power over both rule-making and interpreting of economic directives. The market mechanism that has been brought into play since 1978, on the other hand, tends to disperse any administrative or artificial power of control, and is necessarily related to the idea of decentralization. The debate over market versus planning mechanisms has continuously been associated with both the concept of decentralization and the regional development strategy and policy.

Three major arguments have emerged since 1980 during this long-running debate. Among the most predominant positions is that represented by China's well-known economic planner Chen Yun. As one of the highest economic advisors to Mao, Chen inherited the principal legacy of a centrally-planned economy, although he seemed also willing to introduce some market mechanisms after Mao's death. However, in Chen's vision, a fully market-oriented economy is fundamentally incompatible with Chinese-style socialism, and should therefore not been assigned a distinctly dominant economic role. Chen believes the Chinese economy must preserve its basic equilibrium: balance between government revenues and expenditures, balance between exports and imports, and balance between supply and demand for major commodities.[3]

The central-planning argument in the post-1978 period lay the theoretical and practical foundations for a balanced regional development policy. Two years of experimental reform in the agriculture and state enterprise sectors (1978-1980) caused an economic development imbalance at the national and regional levels. Facing such problems, Chen Yun initiated a proposal, accepted by a central work conference at the end of 1980, for a period of retrenchment and readjustment to remedy these imbalances.

Acceptance of Chen's approach has been based on the claim that a central-planned economy and balanced regional development strategy can (1) more effectively distribute limited resources through state mechanisms, (2) avoid regional competition and separation, and (3) ensure the common welfare of the people of the whole country.

In contrast to this approach, another group of party leaders had been struggling hard to introduce market mechanisms into China's economy. This group, which consisted of party leaders like Zhao Ziyang, Hu Yaobang, and Hu Qili, believed that the market should be paramount, with the mechanisms of the planned economy of secondary importance.[4] They proposed more economic autonomy for both provincial governments and enterprises to improve economic efficiency.

As for regional policy, two different approaches had been debated under the decentralization-oriented idea of economic development. The first approach emphasized the interests and discretion of the provincial level. Scholars such as Yu Guanyuan believed that the existing industrial and economic structures should be used to speed up reform and development in the coastal areas, which would be both a more rational and realistic strategy, as well as a means to improve the national economy and the conditions of interior areas.[5] The regional economy and its growth under the management of provincial governments, though generating a certain degree of regional inequality, conflict, and separation, was still believed to be an indispensable stage in the economic development process.[6] The second approach shared the belief in a market economy and a decentralized regional development strategy. However, it focused on reform of the private enterprise system, granting more discretion to grass-roots units, trying to allow private enterprises to make their own decisions according to market mechanisms.[7] This group has also actively argued for radical reform of property ownership, thinking that such a step would lead to fundamental change of the entire system.

Each of these approaches to economic development and regional strategy carried its own advantages and problems. The traditional approach, emphasizing a centrally-planned economy and a balanced regional policy, sought to avoid extreme regionalism, while maintaining balanced growth and social welfare for the whole society. This approach presented problems, however, such as a less dynamic and efficient economy, egalitarianism at a low standard of living, and a relatively easy mechanism for the consolidation of political autocracy. In particular, since this philosophy still dominates the Chinese Communist Party's economic policy and regional development strategy, it represents the next cycle in the policy dilemma that swings back and forth between planning and growth, although such cycles have also been greatly restrained by the new dynamics of reform.

The vision which attempts to transform the economic structure from below is a most courageous idea, and the least feasible policy option under China's' current conditions. The lack of a unified domestic market is a primary problem confronting this reform design. Decentralization at the enterprise level could definitely contribute to the task of establishing a unified market-based economy. Yet, under current conditions, such a reform plan will not work because enterprise reform is ultimately a reform of property ownership. But property reform still faces a series of difficulties before it can be implemented, such as different levels of market development, diversified financial systems, and finally and most difficult, the division of public property and the principles that guide such property division. Such reform will probably have to rely on provincial or local governments to deal with all these difficulties.

Decentralization on the provincial level currently enjoys good conditions in China due to both the substantial autonomy that provinces have experienced and to the fact that different interests have become more economically and politically acceptable. First of all, decentralization has actually allowed local economic initiatives that have eased the economic burden of the central government. Second, given the unprecedented flexibility in fiscal, foreign trade, and investment policy, more incentives now exist to facilitate rapid growth. Finally, regional development within the confines of various comparative advantages has given rise to competition among regions, which might stimulate the whole economy. On the other hand, as has been repeatedly pointed out, the increase in provincial power also tends to encourage the narrow interests of a particular region and to cause regionalism and conflict.

These seemingly tough and unresolvable difficulties raise several theoretical questions. What is the relationship between modernization and decentralization? What is the thrust of the problem during the process of decentralization in China? How should the issue of economic inequality be tackled during the process of modernization? These questions need to be addressed in order to pave the way for exploring the issue of regional differences and government management policy.

It seems clear that the reform process is actually a modernization process. Generally speaking, the goal of the "Four Modernizations"[8] has enjoyed a national consensus in China. Real modernization, however, implies a socioeconomic transformation that includes several dimensions of social life. First, it indicates economic modernization that is sometimes called "industrialization." Economic modernization may be the most important aspect of the modernization characterized by modern science and technology, highly organized markets, high levels of consumption and so on. Second, it involves political modernization. As pointed out by Sammul Huntington, such a process would produce a modern bureaucracy, and relatively democratic, pluralist, and participatory polities. Third, as suggested by Inkeles and Smith, modernization has been necessarily connected to tremendous psychological change. New values arise that break away from the old traditions and challenge the new style of life. People are more open to new experiences, more ready for social change, and more willing to entertain new opinions.[9] In sum, I would call modernization simply economic industrialization, political democratization, and social transformation.

This classification of modernization will allow us to understand the relationship between modernization and decentralization. Decentralization, as mentioned above, refers to the diffusion of rule-making and rule-interpreting power from the center of the state. Modernization logically requires highly organized markets operating on a pluralistic and participatory basis. Therefore, decentralization here relates to a democratic polity and distribution of power.

Early theories tended to treat the state as part of the "extraction-coercion cycle," in that it is the prime function of governments to maintain law and order by controlling military and policy forces. Contemporary theories now view the state as a regulator or service supplier. This has led to state intervention in the social economic structure to counterbalance the inequalities created by a market system. David Easton describes the state's function in a political system as "authoritatively allocating values."[10] This implies rewards or subsidies that the state uses to meet the interests of either individuals or groups within society.

On the other hand, state power within a political system is also subject to distribution. Robert Dahl posits that one of the important measures of democratized politics is whether or not power is dispersed so that control is exercised democratically.[11] Based on this assumption, we may ask who governs and where power is located. The question of where power is located feeds into the problem of central-local relations and regional and local autonomy.

In recognizing the relationship between modernization and decentralization, we can posit that decentralization is supposed to be coordinated with democratization. In light of this assumption, another theoretical assumption is that democratization is based upon a pluralistic and free economic system. As Charles Lindblom pointed out, although not all market-oriented economies are paired with democratic political systems, all political democracies have market-oriented economies.[12] Under existing state socialist countries, decentralization challenges the centrally-planned economy and political autocracy through the growing free economic appeal and democratic values. Decentralization should be based on the prerequisites of enterprise autonomy and a market economy. Therefore, the diffusion and distribution of power between the central and provincial governments should not necessarily be perceived as the transfer of political management of the economy from the central to provincial level. Instead, the transformed relationship between national and provincial governments can be significant only to the extent that it allows provincial governments to enjoy more autonomy to facilitate the development of a market-oriented economy rather than a centrally-planned economy or a provincial government-controlled economy. With such autonomy, the central government would be left with the responsibility of helping to establish a unified domestic market. The central government would also assist and intervene in regional competition and rule-making to mitigate regional tensions.

As the economy is decentralized, regional inequality would probably become an unavoidable problem for China's less developed areas, such as its deep hinterland and border areas. The rationality of a regional development policy lies in its recognition of such an imbalance in the early period of development and its expectation that such inequality should be gradually reduced as the economy becomes developed.[13]

The purpose of the above theoretical analysis is to show that (l) once the route of modernization has been chosen by a state and society, the perceptions and behavior of this state and society are all subject to examination in line with the norms of modernization; (2) decentralization is a logical process for realizing modernization; (3) the market economy is a necessary condition that could facilitate growth and greatly mitigate the tensions among regions; (4) inequality is probably a "necessary evil" that can be reduced only after achieving a developed economy rather than by attempts to artificially eliminate it at an early stage. Next I will examine regional inequality and the central government's relevant management policies based on a comparison of these theoretical assumptions.

Regional Differences and the Pattern of China's Regional Development Policy after 1949

Patterns of regional development in China have been related to the geographic relationship between the center and periphery. In order to understand the changing policies in the 1980s reform process, a brief review of geographic patterns prior to 1949 is necessary.

Prior to the onset of the modern era in China, a distinct pattern developed in China between the center and periphery. In the Zhou Dynasty (1066-256 B.C.), China's city culture emerged, centered around the Yellow River of Northern China. Economic centers developed and shifted to the Yangzi River and Southern China around the time of the separation between the Northern and Southern kingdoms (420-589 A.D.). During the Tang (618-907 A.D.) and Sung Dynasties (960-1279 A.D.), China experienced the most prosperous period in its history, during which cities grew rapidly in the areas south of the Yangzi River, where there was a highly developed commercial economy. The most important economic center that finally emerged was Shanghai, which became the largest port city in China and all of Asia after the Opium War in 1840.

While such a geographic distribution of economic center and peripheries in China developed gradually, different attempts were made to divide the economic areas. Even so, three divisions have always been of basic importance: the coastal region, the deep interior and border areas of the minority provinces, and the interior regions between the coastal and border areas.[14]

Each of these different regions has their own geographic and economic advantages and disadvantages. The coastal area has long been known for its industries, and its relatively convenient transportation and communications facilities. It occupies a relatively small area with a significant proportion of the country's overall population. It lacks many natural resources, with the exception of oil and iron. The situation in the border areas is just the opposite. While most of these border areas have been endowed with a rich quantity of natural resources, the population is extremely sparse and scattered, and very little effort had been made to modernize the area. Other interior provinces contain a large proportion of population as well as rich natural resources, but the level of industrial development is between that of the coastal and border areas.[15]

By the time the People's Republic was established in 1949, China was characterized by two economies. While there was a relatively modern sector engaged primarily in the management of foreign trade and the manufacturing of cotton textiles and certain heavy industrial products, China also had a traditional indigenous sector. This economic division can be traced according to a rough geographic demarcation. The modern economic sector existed in the seven coastal provinces--Liaoning, Hebei, Shandong, Jiangsu, Zhejiang, Fujian, and Guangdong. The traditional economic sector, in contrast, existed in the rest of the provinces of interior China. The second relevant economic characteristic is the high concentration of economic activity and population in the coastal region. Eight coastal cities (Beijing, Tianjin, Shanghai, Shenyang, Anshan, Luda, Fushun, and Benxi) produced 55 percent of the total gross value of output for the coast region in the 1970s.[16] By 1950, around 42 percent of railway transportation was located in the coastal region.[17] The immediate effect of such a two-tier economic structure has been economic inequalities between the coastal areas and other regions.

These economic inequalities have been a constant concern for the Chinese government. With regard to economic policy, efforts were made to overcome the fact that the nation's industrial center was located far from the sources of raw materials. In addition to such economic considerations, post-1949 policies were also influenced by several political factors. Many Chinese leaders were greatly concerned about those interior areas from which they had come. In terms of strategic policy, the Maoist leadership also wanted to avoid the vulnerability of industrial centers in the coastal areas, which could be damaged in the event of war with the United States or the Soviet Union. Finally, a goal of social policy was to equalize standards of living to the extent possible.[18]

With these economic and political concerns in mind, the Chinese government worked hard to reduce regional disparity and to balance economic development. Beijing's experience since 1949 has been one of painstaking effort with little impact on its policy goals. At the same time, this process has proved to be a cyclical oscillation between growth and equality, or between a focus on coastal areas and interior regions, due to many economic constraints. Five major stages of such oscillatory regional development policy can be identified since 1949.

The first stage started in 1949 and lasted until the end of First Five-Year Plan (FFYP) in 1957. The major policy goal during this period was post-war economic restoration. However, the FFYP also stressed the shift of industrial activity to the interior. For example, more than two-thirds of the 694 major projects started between 1953 and 1957 were located in the inland areas.

In the second stage, from 1958 to 1966, the central government reevaluated its industrial policy. Mao, who still believed that 90 percent or more of the nation's heavy industrial projects should be located in the interior, indicated that industrialization of the interior regions could be quickened by initially allocating more resources to the coastal area. As a result, development of coastal industries was emphasized. After the Great Leap Forward of 1958, industrial development was also considered a major priority as a means of supporting agriculture.

The initiation of the Cultural Revolution in 1966 ushered in the third stage, which lasted until 1976. Economic chaos was the major feature of this period. The emphasis on economic efficiency and the old industrial bases was rejected, and less than half of the projects completed between 1967 and 1970 were located in the coastal regions.

The end of the Cultural Revolution in 1976 and the beginning of economic reforms in 1978 started yet another round of coastal industrial development. More economic resources from at home and abroad have been put into almost all the major cities of China's east coast. The industrial output of some coastal areas has become fifteen to twenty times higher than some of the interior areas.[19]

Finally, developments in China since 1989 do not yet present a clear picture of any significant shift in resource allocation. Therefore, the short-lived attempt to reassert a centrally planned economy in some sectors in 1989-1990 seemed to imply a new round of oscillation.

The scrutiny of patterns in regional developmental policy since 1949 demonstrates that such policy has been like a pendulum swinging back and forth between the coastal and interior regions. These shifts in policy have been the result of constant central government concern over economic, political, strategic, and social policy-making, which obviously reflects the underlying problems of politicization and irrationality in a centralized and planned economy.

The reforms initiated after 1978 have been viable and their impact has been far-reaching. Several significant features of the policy pattern since 1980 can be identified. First, regional policy since 1980 has basically been developed within the whole orientation of structural reform. Second, such orientation has been worked out mainly by the top political elite, who are influenced in part by their bitter long-term learning process (particularly during the Cultural Revolution), by domestic pressures at different levels, and by the political and economic pressures of the international arena. Third, given the above conditions, pressures that have facilitated structural reform could be translated into dynamics either to promote the reform process or to restrain the attempt to reverse policies. The policy pattern within the different socioeconomic conditions needs particular attention. An institutional policy analysis can explain the changing features of policy-making in the reform context.

Institutional Policy Analysis of Regional Development since 1980

An institutional policy analysis can help explain variations through the investigation of (1) the dynamics of institutional reform, (2) the administrative mandate for a new structure of rules and routines in regional development policy, (3) the process of implementing institutional reform, and (4) the consequences of such reform.

The study of institutional policy requires attention to the changeable aspects of governance.[20] Policy change is usually rooted in past structures and experiences. The ten years of the Cultural Revolution destroyed the normal order of production and prevented many projects from being constructed in the coastal areas. At the Third Plenum of the Eleventh Central Committee of the CCP in December 1978, the Chinese government took steps to rectify this problem. The explicit goals of economic modernization have helped allow new perspectives to prevail.

Among these new perspectives on economic reform, some were directly related to the institutional problems of economic management. Decentralization was seen as a remedy for the inefficiencies caused by over-centralization, bureaucratization, and inappropriate local policies. Decentralization, it was argued, would emphasize greater autonomy for each local enterprise, and would improve policy-making and efficiency. Similarly, regionalization was seen as both a corollary for greater enterprise autonomy and an alternative to the systemic problems of the command economy. As these perspectives developed, the separation of economic management from state administration was tried, with the goal of protecting local economic autonomy.[21]

An important implication of these new perspectives was greater respect and protection for the economic autonomy of local enterprises. Furthermore, the management of production began to be increasingly based on economic, rather than political factors. Besides challenging the rationale for a command economy, these perspectives also promoted an "uneven development" theory and challenged the pre-1978 Maoist policy of regional equality. The country's largest official newspaper, *People's Daily* (Renmin Ribao), argued that uneven development is both an objective law of economic development and a proven economic strategy in both capitalist and socialist countries. The Sixth Five-Year Plan, while still adhering to the pre-1978 goal of assisting underdeveloped areas, emphasized a program focusing on large and medium cities in the coastal regions.[22]

Since 1978, we have seen the administrative mandate for a new structure of rules and routines in regional development policy. The official theory of uneven development and its corresponding policies were, in part, practical results of the post-1978 perspectives, suggesting that these perspectives and policies demonstrate the government's promotion of institutional reform. Since 1979, a variety of policies, laws, and executive mandates have been issued to stimulate regional development, such as the 1979 trade decentralization measures, the 1980 fiscal reform, micro-economic reforms expanding enterprise autonomy, introduction of enterprise profit retention rates, and changing sectoral priorities.[23] Overall, such changes produced by laws, by executive fiat, and by legislative committee mandate are actually, as March and Olsen suggest, the reform of political institutions.[24] Since this is an extensive and intensive reform of economic structures, tremendous repercussions have been reported on the process of policy implementation.

There have been three types of local responses to the process of policy implementation. The first response comes from the developed coastal regions, which had been subjected to heavy revenue sharing with the central government, and which have turned out to be more receptive to the new regional policy. Having contributed a great part of their economic prosperity to the interior regions, these coastal regions have kept only a minimum of revenues to expend on their own area and people. These mandatory sacrifices were the major cause of resentment in the eastern coastal provinces. Thus these regions felt quite happy about the reforms of resource allocation and fiscal policy, which have reduced revenue sharing and allow for the discretionary retention of a higher percentage of revenues. In Shanghai, for example, the government has increased its share of retained income from 10 percent to 25 percent of output, in contrast to the pre-1978 level of extraction of 90 percent of output.[25]

The second type of response is from those areas between the developed and underdeveloped regions. Since reform has generally been implemented within a national economic planning system, some allocation of resources is still mandatory. Therefore, local resistance to central constraints in the course of economic "readjustment" is quite strong. Sichuan province, for example, was dissatisfied with the order to shift emphasis from heavy industry to light industry. The province's government, having received benefits from heavy industry for many years, argued that it must not totally readjust its industrial structure from heavy to light industry. Fujian province, a relatively underdeveloped coastal province, expressed dissatisfaction with the central government's idea that it should focus on production of tea, sugar, and stone carvings. Located in a warm temporal climate, Fujian claims the need for key industrial development, including oil refineries, chemical engineering, hydroelectric power, airports, railroads, and light industries.[26] Since many provinces seek to protect their own regional advantages, the centralized and unified plans of the state are often ignored. Such resistance has frustrated China's central government leadership, even the pro-coastal former premier Zhao Ziyang. Such impediments to the reform process even led the *People's Daily* to call for recentralizing economic control in 1982.[27]

The third type of response comes from many of the interior regions calling for more state assistance. The intensity of their response focuses on the "readjustment plan" of the state. On the one hand, the national emphasis is to shift to the "key" and coastal cities. A corollary of this policy is the tendency to decrease annual investment in interior areas. The alternative of continuing state subsidies to the interior stressed more of an inter-regional technological cooperation between interior and coastal areas. On the other hand, a major development focus is planned for the interior in the 2lst century. Because of these changes, many interior areas, including Inner Mongolia, Yunnan, Guizhou, Ningxia, Xinjiang, and Shanxi, have complained about the decrease in state subsidies and the deferment of development projects. Almost every one of these provinces has called for the state to place greater attention on their development, stressing their strengths and regional advantages. At the same time, the backwardness of the area has become the best argument for more state support.[28]

To fully examine the consequences of the major policy devices of the government requires much more analysis. This is because regional inequality in terms of the major indicator--income per capita--has been a controversial issue. Some studies have declared that such inequality has been greatly aggravated.[29] Others argue that it has been reduced.[30] Rather than dismissing this issue as unresolvable, this paper will use scientific methods to examine this sensitive issue. In the next two sections, this chapter will investigate China's regional policy outcomes through some data-based calculations.

Variations in Regional Inequality

Previous studies of regional inequality either lack a convincing data-based calculation or, for those data- based studies, usually apply only a single measure. Moreover, these studies tend to lose their accuracy by not defining the notion of "difference". For example, the regional difference study by P. Aguigniey uses the indicators of industrial structure (i.e. light industry and heavy industry) and industrial growth rate, but does not present detailed data or take into account the correlation between growth rate and regional differences in terms of income.[31] The research by Chinese scholars Zen Chunjiu and Jin Yongsheng, while taking for granted that there is a comprehensive regional difference between the east and west of China, does not provide any statistical data.[32] American scholar David Denny's research paper claims that provincial economic differences diminished in the years of reform. While his data-based findings are more convincing than those of others, his study is compromised by several problems. First, readers of this study may be confused by the interchangeable use of the notions of "diminished" difference and "narrowed" difference, and "production" difference and "income" difference. Second, a single measure of "net material product" has been used, which not only simplifies the complex economic-social performance, but also excludes the important factor of service economies in the coastal cities. Third, his analysis of the impact of the "open door" policy on regional economic inequality is neither quantitative nor convincing.[33]

This study tries to examine the regional difference issue by using a multi-measurement, data-based method, with a limited notion of regional difference defined in terms of income per capita. For the policy outcomes, especially the aggravation or reduction of regional income inequalities, two basic measurements are used: Standard deviation and Lorenz Curve with Gini Coefficient (both cross-sectional).

1. Standard Deviation (Cross-Section)

$$\sigma_x = \frac{\dfrac{\sqrt{\Sigma(x-\bar{x})^2}}{N}}{\bar{x}}$$

σ_x = standard deviation
Σ = sum
x = indicator[34]
$\bar{x}$ = mean

This measurement examines and shows the variation of dispersion about the mean in order to categorize the distribution of values among provinces.

2. Lorenz Curve with Gini Coefficient (Cross-Section)

(a) The Lorenz Curve examines the differences between the distributions in the form of deviations away from the diagonal line.

(b) Gini Coefficient

$$D_s = \frac{\Sigma |X_i - Y_i|}{2}$$

D_s= gini
Σ = sum of $|X_i - Y_i|$
X_i= individual indicator X[35]
Y_i= individual indicator Y[36]

Another set of three measurements is used to examine some of the major sources of policy results. In other words, a coordinated management policy of the national government is investigated by examining:

(1) Financial revenue/national income by province (all in per capita income); This provides insight into the level of revenue-sharing or fiscal subsidies between central and local governments.

(2) Property investment/financial revenue by province (all in per capita income); this looks at the differences in the ratios between investment by the state and revenue-sharing by each province.

(3) Property investment/national income by province (all in per capita income); this looks into the differences between provinces in terms of the ratio of state investment and revenue-sharing by each province.

TABLE 8.1 Standard Deviation, 1980-1988

Year	X[38]	$\bar{X}$[a]	$(X-\bar{X})^2$	Σ_x
1980	12420	460	5296458	0.9630
1981	13076	484	5379988	0.9215
1982	13993.7	518	5292264	0.8552
1983	15134.9	561	5392621	0.7968
1984	17609.6	652	6499247	0.7531
1985	21083	781	9236571	0.7490
1986	23231	860	9868487	0.7035
1987	26593	985	11951318	0.6751
1988	32560	1206	16182840	0.6418

[a]$\bar{X}$ here is real average income, which is slightly different from $\bar{X}$ of national average income.

Sources: Converted data from Statistical Yearbook of China, 1980-1989, and the Statistical Yearbooks of each province and municipality, 1980-1989

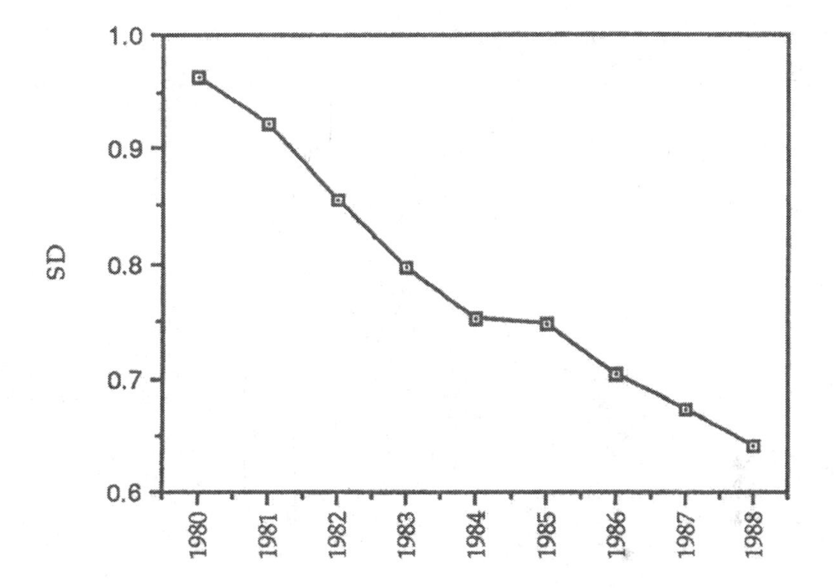

FIGURE 8.1 Standard Deviation (SD): 27 Provinces and Municipalities, 1980-1988
Source: See TABLE 8.1

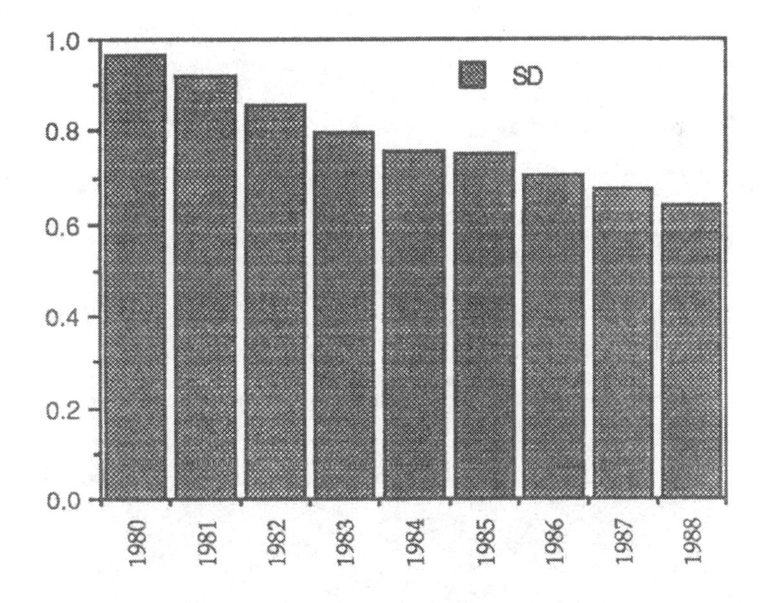

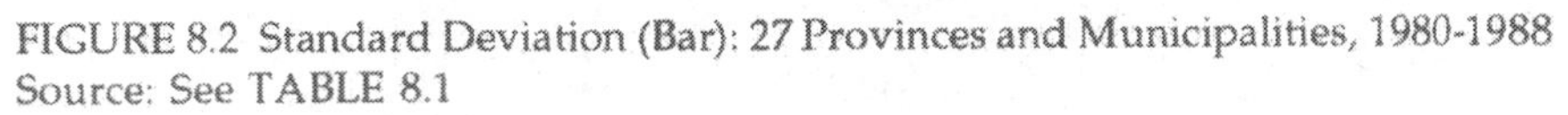

FIGURE 8.2 Standard Deviation (Bar): 27 Provinces and Municipalities, 1980-1988
Source: See TABLE 8.1

In this part of study, I begin by examining the policy outcomes. Therefore, the measurement formulas include standard deviation and Lorenz curve with Gini coefficient.[37]

1. Standard Deviation (σ_x time series--TABLE 8.1 and its graph--FIGURE 8.1 and 8.2). The results of the standard deviation show that per capita income inequality dropped between 1980 and 1987. This striking outcome is corroborated in our second measurement.

2. Lorenz Curve with Gini coefficient

(a) Lorenz Curve

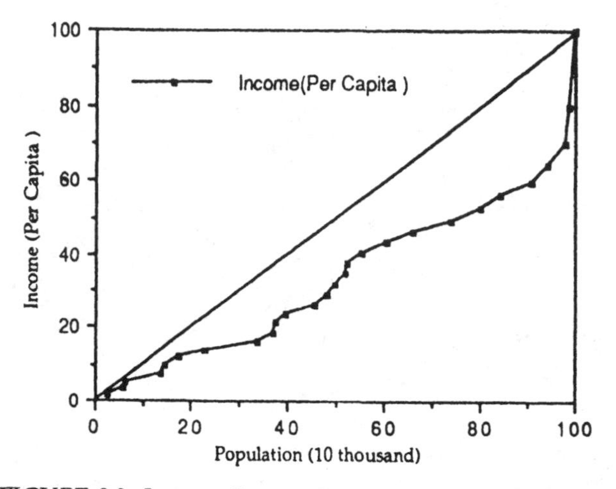

FIGURE 8.3 Lorenz Curve (Cross-Section): 27 Provinces, 1980
Source: See TABLE 8.1

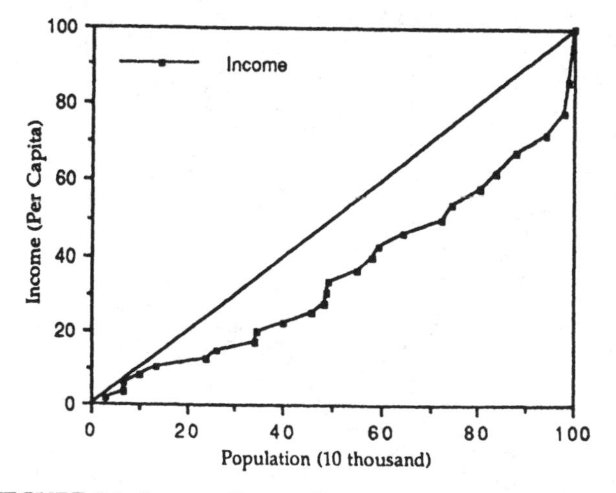

FIGURE 8.4 Lorenz Curve (Cross-Section): 27 Provinces, 1987
Source: See TABLE 8.1

The visible figure of the curves shows that the deviation away from the diagonal line of 1987 has been apparently reduced compared to that of 1980 (FIGURE 8.3 and FIGURE 8.4).

(b) Gini Coefficient

Moreover, the Gini (D_s) of the eight years from 1980 to 1987 further prove the results shown by the curves (TABLE 8.2 & FIGURE 8.5).

TABLE 8.2 Lorenz Curve (Gini Coefficient): 1980-1987

Year	Σ	D_s
1980	83.40	41.70
1981	82.30	41.15
1982	79.90	39.35
1983	78.20	39.10
1984	77.50	38.75
1985	76.40	38.20
1986	75.30	37.65
1987	73.50	36.75

Source: See TABLE 8.1

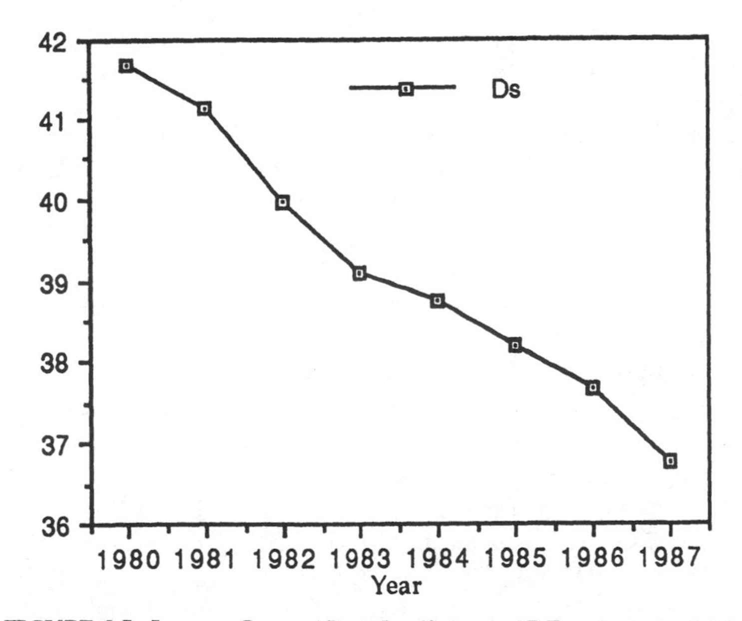

FIGURE 8.5 Lorenz Curve (Gini Coefficient): 27 Provinces and Municipalities, 1980-1987
Source: See TABLE 8.1

The measurement of standard deviation and the Lorenz Curve both lead to the same conclusion: that there was a reduction in regional income inequality in the years from 1980 until 1987.

Such results naturally raise questions about a coastally-biased regional development policy. What was the logic behind such a diametrically opposed cause and effect? Was there any parallel policy that was less obvious but highly effective in offsetting the unequalizing tendencies of the coastal policy? What were the mechanisms that contributed to such unexpected results? The next section will answer these questions.

Management Policy of the Central Government

Having gone through the relevant data, it appears that a tremendous government effort, although not evident directly from the yearly statistical data, had kept pace with the decentralized regional policy that favored the coastal areas. This effort had reduced regional income inequality. The mechanism depended largely on particular tax/revenue policies and investment policies, which drew less from or even subsidized many interior and border regions, and put many times more capital investment back every year into these areas. This "equalizing policy" can be seen in both fiscal and investment policies.

In terms of fiscal policy, we can start with a table of revenue sharing between the central and local governments:

TABLE 8.3 shows four types of situations. First, within the provinces and municipalities that share their revenues with the center, all coastal provinces or municipalities retain less than fifty percent of their revenue. The more developed an area, the less revenue it is allowed to retain. Second, four of the interior provinces retain all their revenues. Third, the deep interior and border provinces not only retain all revenue, but also receive increasing subsidies from the center. Finally, two coastal provinces retain their revenue but return funds to the center on the basis of a contract with the central government.

In order to understand how disproportionate these ratios are, we can look at FIGURE 8.6.[39] Coastal areas are defined as Region I, interior areas as Region II, and deep interior and border area as Region III (with each containing seven Provinces).

FIGURE 8.6 shows a results similar to TABLE 8.3, and tells us at least two things. First, Region III was supposed to enjoy a much lower level of revenue-sharing than Region I; second, such a tendency changed little after 1984, when Region I's sharing went down and Region III's subsidies were reduced to the level of 1980.

TABLE 8.3 Revenue Sharing between the Center and Local Governments, 1985[a]

	Province and Regions	Percent Retained	Amount to Provinces from Center (+) or Transferred to Center from Provinces (-) (million yuan)
1. Fixed percentage of total revenue retained by province, remainder remitted to center (15 provinces)	Beijing	48.2	
	Tianjin	33.5	
	Hebei	69.0	
	Shanxi	97.5	
	Liaoning	51.5	
	Heilongjiang	96.0	
	Jiangsu	39.0	
	Shanghai	26.0	
	Zhejiang	55.0	
	Anhui	80.1	
	Shandong	59.0	
	Henan	81.0	
	Hubei	66.5	
	Hunan	88.0	
	Sichuan	89.0	
2. Province retains all its own revenue and receives fixed amount from the center (4 provinces)	Jilin		397
	Jiangxi		239
	Shaanxi		270
	Gansu		246
3. Same as 2, but amount from center increased by 10 percent annually (8 provinces)	Inner Mongolia		1,783[b]
	Guangxi		716
	Guizhou		743
	Yunnan		637
	Tibet		750
	Qinghai		611
	Ningxia		494
	Xinjiang		1,450
4. Province retains its own revenue and pays fixed amount to the center (2 provinces)	Fujian		-235
	Guangdong		-772

[a] These arrangements were to govern revenue sharing between the central and local governments for five years beginning in 1985.

[b] These are base-year figures for 1985 and would be increased each year by 10 percent for each of the 8 provinces in this group.

Source: A World Bank Country Study, *China: Finance and Investment*, 1988, Table 11.6, p. 441. Reprinted by permission.

Now let us look into the central government's investment policy. The same method of dividing regions is used here.

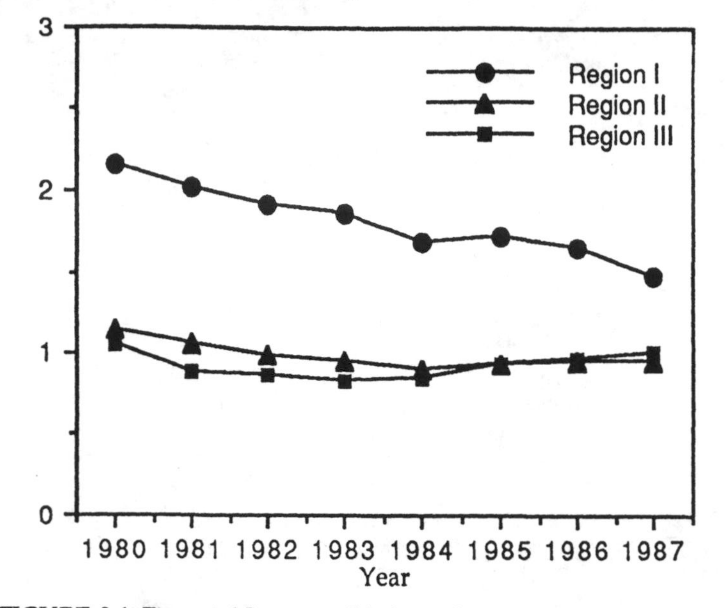

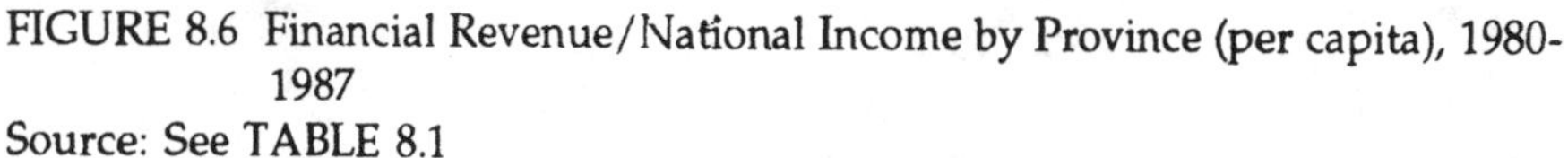

FIGURE 8.6 Financial Revenue/National Income by Province (per capita), 1980-1987

Source: See TABLE 8.1

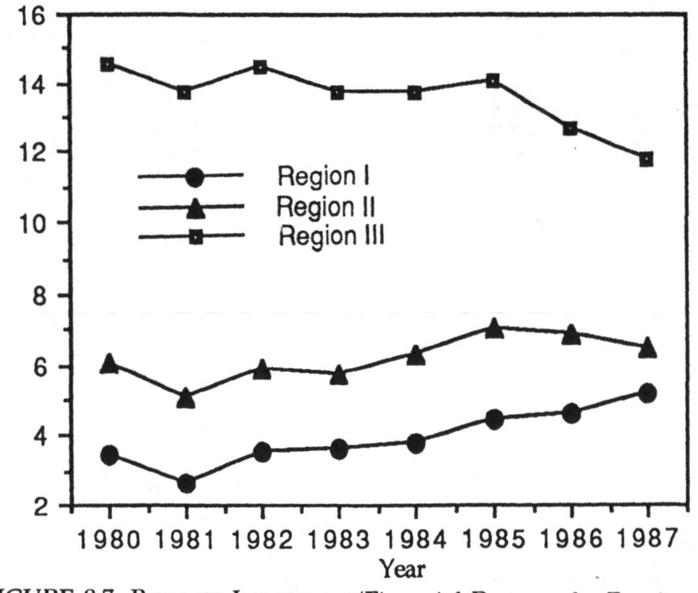

FIGURE 8.7 Property Investment/Financial Revenue by Province (per capita), 1980-1987

Source: See TABLE 8.1

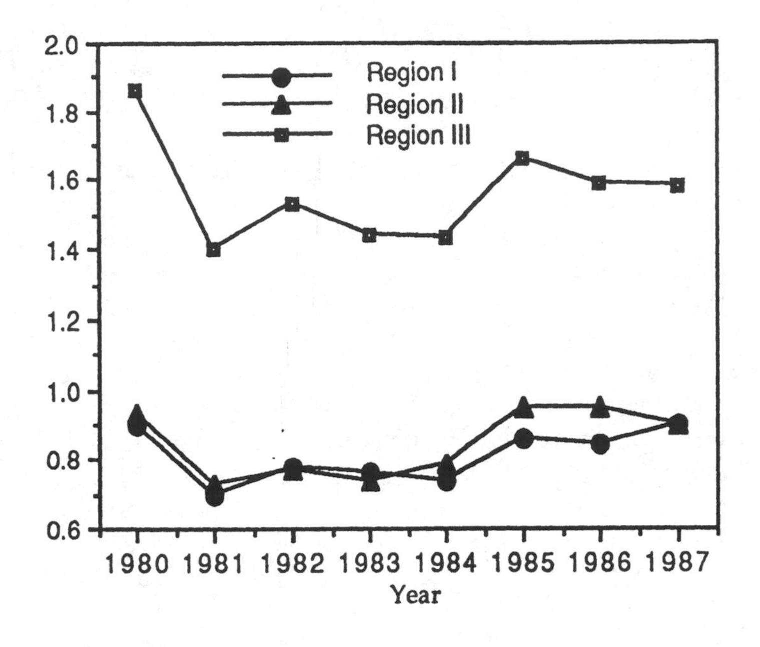

FIGURE 8.8 Property Investment/National Income by Province (per capita), 1980-1987

Source: See TABLE 8.1

FIGURE 8.7 shows that the less developed an area, the more investment resources it was given. Moreover, Region III received many times more assistance than both Region I and Region II. Finally, the investment direction had never been decided by the quantity of revenue-sharing that took place; rather, it had rested upon the principle of a "balanced development strategy." In other words, the importance of economic efficiency had given way to political influence and social welfare concerns. FIGURE 8.8 provides a similar picture by showing the ratio between investment and per capita income.

Several general conclusions can be inferred from these charts. First, the structure and direction of fiscal and investment policy by the central government acted as an equalizing force, which compensated the interior for losses and imbalances resulting from coastally-biased reforms. Second, although coastally-based policies were reversed slightly after 1985, the speed of the reversal had been much slower than that of the implementation of the equalizing policy. Moreover, a few minority areas, such as Tibet and Xinjiang, were still receiving tremendous transferred capital and other resources from the central government. Third, while the reform of fiscal and other policies were pursued, the corresponding equalizing policies were implemented to keep the "balance". For example, when capital investment reached its peaks in 1980 and 1985, almost all three regions received the same proportion of resources, which caused the absolute ratio of such resources to be much higher in the interior regions than the coastal regions.

The corollary of this "equalizing policy", together with a continuous reform policy, has been a soaring fiscal deficit that will eventually force the Chinese central government to make choices between egalitarianism and modernization. This may lead to three possible choices. First is the choice to withdraw totally from the economic reform process, which is almost impossible due to the constraints of established rules and norms, as well as the international environment. Second, the government could reduce subsidies while squeezing the resources of the coastal regions, which might undermine the relationship of the central government with both the coastal and interior regions. Third, Beijing could encourage coastally-biased reform while slowly lessening the financial burden of ties with interior regions, which is probably a better choice given the very limited resources of the central government. After Deng Xiaoping's trip to South China in early 1992, this third choice has become increasingly prominent. Moreover, strategies designed by the central government for regional economic cooperation between coastal regions and interior areas as well as the release of economic control over most interior and border areas all seem to be aimed at reducing the central government's fiscal burden while creating alternatives to help interior areas avoid lagging further behind. Nevertheless, as we have already suggested, recognition of the current inequality and creating conditions for the adequate development of a market economy are necessary steps for real equalization in the future.

Conclusion

The study of regional differences in China is primarily associated with issues such as decentralization and the cost of an imbalanced regional development policy. In a country where the distribution of resources is extremely unbalanced, China's reform requires an imbalanced development strategy. Under such conditions, decentralization is probably the better solution. The comprehensive planning of the central government has proved very inefficient and irrational in its attempt to provide direction for such large regions, which are tremendously different in size, natural conditions, and economic foundations. Decentralization should operate by allowing regional governments (provincial) more autonomy to facilitate market-oriented development. The correlated results of inequality are a necessary cost during such a process, and will eventually be reduced. However, such theoretical regional policy has, in practice, been frustrated by a policy process that always swings between stimulating growth and reining in growth to promote egalitarianism.

The choice between promoting economic growth and egalitarianism raises an interesting issue. Is this policy dilemma simply a continuation of patterns of politics and economic development from the Maoist era? The answer is no. First, as we have seen since 1978, the whole reform process has derived its dynamic from China's political leadership and Communist Party-affiliated bureaucracy, both of which have been eager to consolidate their political legitimacy since the Cultural Revolution. Second, the policy dilemma is not simply a replica of Maoist policy, because it has been closely connected to the process of reform. Finally, I assume that the further reform goes, the greater will be the impact of institutionalized factors, which would, in turn, further constrain and weaken traditional policy-making based on the preferences of some Chinese political elites. This has already occurred in terms of local resistance and central concessions to provincial governments on regional issues.

The scrutiny of patterns of regional development policy from 1949 to 1978 has demonstrated that such policy has swung like a pendulum back and forth between coastal and interior regions. These shifts have been the result of several constant concerns of the central government's economic, political, strategic, and social policies. Economically, efforts were made to overcome the problems of industrial centers in coastal China in obtaining raw materials from such regions as the northwest and the southwest. Strategically, the central government was concerned with minimizing the vulnerability of industrial centers to damage in the event of war. Politically, the central government took great care of interior areas, where many of China's political elites came from. And finally, social policy was expected to contribute to a relatively balanced standard of living around the country.

An institutional analysis of regional policy between 1980 and 1987 has found that the new dynamics of decentralization were seriously implemented. With the administrative mandate and new agenda for establishing laws and rules, relative regional autonomy was realized in many aspects, including profit retention, autonomous power to engage in foreign trade, and power to solicit investment resources from both inside and outside China. The response to decentralization varied from area to area based on special regional interests. The decentralized regional policy appeared to greatly favor the coastal areas, especially when indicators such as growth in the gross value of industrial and agricultural output, national income per capita, and so on are taken into consideration.

In analyzing national income per capita by province, a major indicator of regional difference, I have found that regional income inequality was actually reduced from 1980 to 1987 (although this finding does not necessarily support any argument that regional disparity has been reduced in all its aspects, including education, science and technology, quality of production and management, and real living standards). My analysis indicates that a "hidden hand" of the central government has contributed enormously to this process. A tremendous central government balancing effort had kept pace with the decentralized regional policy. Moreover, this almost unknown "equalizing policy" had been realized mainly through tax/revenue and investment policies, which drew less from or even subsidized the total revenues of many interior and border regions and put many times more capital investment back every year into these areas.

As a corollary to such a policy, these actions turned out to be extremely tough on efforts to keep reform going, creating enormous fiscal deficits which, if left unabated, could lead to a further decrease in China's state capacity. Such serious results of the government's regional development policy could cause, and perhaps have already forced, the central government to contribute to one aspect at the expense of another. That is, it may either withdraw the autonomous power already conferred on the provinces, or pursue a new regional development policy-- recognizing the existing inequality and reducing it only through durable effects of industrialization.

Notes

1. Zeng Chunjiu, "Thoughts on the Issues of Development in the West," *Economic Science,* No. 2 (1989), p.21; Jin Yongsheng. "National Economic Development Policy towards the West and its Effects," *Economic Science,* No. 2 (1990), p.17.

2. Ronan Paddison, *The Fragmented State, the Political Geography of Power* (Oxford:Basil Blackwell, 1983), p.28.

3. Harry Harding, *China's Second Revolution, Reform after Mao,* (Washington:The Brookings Institution, 1987), pp.80-81.

4. Ibid., pp.78-79.

5. Yu Guangyuan, *Lun Diqu Fazhan Zhanlue* (On Regional Development Strategy), (Beijing: Economic Science Press, 1988), pp.5-7.

6. Harding, pp.78-79.

7. *The Chinese Intellectual,* Autumn (1990), p.3.

8. The four modernizations are modernization of industry, agriculture,science and technology, and national defense. "The Fifth Modernization", a term first used by Chinese political activist Wei Jingshen, indicates that modernization should include political modernization and Democracy.

9. John Taylor, "The Sociology of Development: Theoretical Inadequacies," *From Modernization to Modes of Production,* (London:Macmillan Press, 1979), pp.3-41; Alejandro Portes, "On the Sociology of National Development," *American Journal of Sociology,* 1976), pp.61-74; Inkeles and Smith, "Toward a Definition of the Modern Man," *Becoming Modern* (Cambridge, Mass:Harvard University), pp.15-35.

10. David Easton, *A Framework for Political Analysis* (Englewood Cliffs, NJ: Prentice-Hall, 1955).

11. Robert Dahl, 1968; Power, *International Encyclopedia of the Social Sciences* (New York: Macmillan), Vol. 12.

12. Charles E. Lindblom, *Politics and Markets* (New York:Basic Books, 1977), pp.161-69.

13. Jeffrey G. Williamson, "Regional Inequality and the Process of National Development: A Description of the Patterns," (1965); Economic Development and Cultural Change (Chicago:The University of Chicago Press), No.13, p.4.

14. These three areas were roughly divided prior to 1949. After 1949, these three areas have been specified according to the administrative division of regions, including (1) eight coastal provinces and three municipalities: Liaoning, Hebei, Shandong, Jiangsu, Zhejiang, Fujian, Guangdong, Hainan, Beijing, Tianjin and Shanghai; (2) seven border minority areas: Inner Mongolia, Xinjiang, Qinghai, Tibet, Yunnan, Guizhou, Guangxi; (3) twelve in-between interior provinces: Shanxi, Shaanxi, Gansu, Ningxia, Sichuan, Henan, Hubei, Hunan, Anhui, Jiangxi, Heilongjiang, and Jilin.

15. Sun Jinzhi, *General Introduction to Chinese Economic Geography* (Beijing: Shangwu Press, 1983).

16. Charles Robert Roll, Jr. & Kung-Chai Yeh, "Balance in Coastal and Inland Industrial Development," *China: A Reassessment of the Economy,* Joint Economic Committee (Washington:Congress of the United States, 1975), p.82.

17. Ibid., p.82.

18. Stephan Feuchtwang, ed., *Transforming China's Economy in the Eighties: Management, Industry and Urban Economy* (London, Bolder: Westview Press, 1988), Chapter 2, p.93.

19. Bernhard Glaeser, ed., *Learning from China? Development and Environment in Third World Countries* (London, Boston:Allen & Unwin, 1987) pp.34-40; Roll & Yeh, ibid., pp.84-87; Stephan, ibid., p.94.

20. William Gormley, "Institutional Policy Analysis: A Critical Review," *Journal of Policy Analysis and Management,* 1987, Winter, p.154.

21. David Goodman, ed., *China's Regional Development* (London, New York: Routledge for Royal Institute of International Affairs, 1989), pp.21-28.

22. Victor Nee, & David Stark. ed., *Rethinking the Economic Institutions of Socialism: China and East Europe* (Stanford, Calif.:Stanford University Press, 1989) p.155.

23. Leung Chi-Keung & Joseph C.H. Chai. ed., *Development and Distribution in China* (Hongkong: Center for Asian Studies, University of Hongkong Press, 1985), p.151.

24. James March & Johan Olsen, *Rediscovering Institutions: The Organizational Base of Politics* (New York:Free Press, 1989).

25. Goodman. ed., op. cit., p.47.

26. Leung & Chai, op. cit., pp.164-165.

27. Ibid., p.166.

28. Ibid., pp.156-161.

29. Stephan Feuchtwang, ed., op. cit., pp.94-97.

30. David L. Denny, *Provincial Economic Differences Diminished in the Decade of Reform*, research paper.

31. Aguigniey. P. in Stephan Feuchtwang, ed., op. cit., pp.94-95.

32. Zeng Chunjiu, op. cit., p.21; Jin Yongshen, op. cit., p.17.

33. David L. Denny, op. cit.

34. Sum of income per capita of 27 provinces and municipalities.

35. Income percentage of each province and municipality.

36. Population percentage of each province and municipality.

37. Data available here are for twenty-seven provinces and municipalities, and do not include Beijing, Inner Mongolia, and Guangxi. All the sources thereafter are from the *Statistical Yearbook of China* (1980-1989), and the statistical yearbook of each province or municipality (1980-1989). It is worth noting that data from various statistical yearbooks of both the central and provincial governments are basically trustworthy, although some inaccuracies and inconsistencies have been found. This is true when one takes into account the fact that such statistical records are the results of the official requirements of several international organizations, such as the United Nations and World Bank in exchange for financial assistance to China.

38. This is the sum of income per capita of relevant provinces and municipalities in each year. X=indicator=sum of per capita income.

39. I had intended to use an indicator of revenue sharing by time series, but there are no such complete and/or converted data available so far except for 1985. As an alternative, however, I have used an indicator of financial revenue, for it includes rate of taxation and/or rate of profits transferred to the central government.

9

The Case of Guangdong in Central-Provincial Relations

Peter Tsan-yin Cheung

The enhancement of state capacity is a major objective of developing countries, and China is no exception. Since 1978, the Chinese state has been increasingly influenced by its extensive ties with the world political economy, as well as challenged internally by growing regional power and rivalry which have hampered the authority of the central government in Beijing.[1] Since Guangdong has been granted unprecedented special policy privileges during the reform era, it makes an interesting case study of central-provincial relations in the post-Mao period.[2] This chapter is a preliminary analysis of the changing relations between the center and Guangdong since 1978 and their implications for the capacity of the Chinese state.[3] It is organized into five parts. First, the concept of state capacity and five different dimensions of central-local relations will be discussed. This will then be followed by a brief overview of central-Guangdong relations from 1949 to 1978. The evolving relations between the center and Guangdong province since 1978 will be examined in the third section. An analysis of Guangdong's experience in understanding the changing capacity of the Chinese state will constitute the fourth part. And finally, this chapter concludes with a discussion of the prospects for the central government-Guangdong relationship in the 1990s.

Central-Local Relations and State Capacity

The measurement of state capacity is one of the major preoccupations of contemporary political science. Gabriel Almond and G. Bingham Powell, Jr. focused on extractive, regulative, distributive, symbolic, and responsive capabilities of the state.[4] Similarly, Joel Migdal suggested that state "capabilities include the capacities to *penetrate* society, *regulate* social relations, *extract* resources, and *appropriately* use resources in determined ways. Strong states," he argued, "are those with high capabilities to complete these tasks."[5] Samuel Huntington's classic study, on the other hand, highlighted adaptability, complexity, autonomy, and coherence as measures of political institutionalization, which defined the strength of the state in maintaining political order in developing societies.[6] However, such contributions focus more on the relative power of the state vis-a-vis society and external environments than on the relative powers between different governmental levels. State-society relations should, however, be separated from the internal differentiation of power within the state itself. For instance, even if a state has decentralized its power from the central to the local levels, as happened in China during the Great Leap Forward in the late 1950s, it can still be a potent force in penetrating society and mobilizing resources when it works through local governments endowed with greater powers. With the above caveat in mind, we can examine the central-local relationship in China and its impact on state capacity in five major dimensions: constitutional, administrative, political, fiscal, and policy.

Constitutional Dimension

The constitution, as the basic law of a country, is of paramount significance in understanding central-local relations.[7] For some, China's foremost constitutional problem is the ineffective implementation of constitutional provisions whenever they conflict with the dictates and expediency of the Party-State. In spite of Article 5 of the 1982 Constitution, which explicitly states the supremacy of the constitution, the Communist Party still stands as the ultimate source of authority in China. The principle of territorial distribution of power, however, has not changed since 1949 because China has remained a unitary state in which local governments are subordinate to the central government.[8] For example, the State Council can define the specific functions and powers of the local governments, nullify their decisions, impose martial law in the localities, and direct its auditing agencies to conduct inspections of financial discipline.[9] Similarly, while provincial people's congresses have the right to make local legislation, the Standing Committee of the

National People's Congress can still annul such legislation if it conflicts with national laws. There is also no clear demarcation of the scope and content of the respective legislative authority of the central and provincial congresses.

Conflicts between the centralized state envisioned in the Constitution and the increasing decentralization of economic powers to local governments have become evident in the post-Mao period. Economic reforms since 1978 have significantly enlarged the economic powers of local governments and enterprises, but such changes are neither clearly articulated nor enshrined in the Constitution.[10] While describing post-Mao China as "a federalist system without a federalist constitution" may be an exaggeration, it is evident that, during the 1980s, local governments gained much more power over budgets, pricing, capital investment, acquisition of foreign investment, foreign trade, and many other areas than ever before.[11] The Constitution hence failed to legalize and stabilize the actual economic relations between the center and the localities. The latest amendments introduced in the March 1993 First Session of the 8th National People's Congress only incorporated the concept of a socialist market economy and changed the description of "state-run enterprises" to "state-managed enterprises."[12] If the Constitution cannot articulate a clear definition and division of power for the center and the locales, it may intensify lobbying and bargaining over the terms of their relationship. In short, the Constitution still empowers the central government to intervene in local affairs as long as it sees fit, but it fails to provide a clear and authoritative power map.

Administrative Dimension

The administrative dimension of central-local relations concerns the distribution of administrative discretion between different levels of governments. The organization of administrative power is usually more subject to the political and policy orientations of a particular administration than the Constitution. The central government may, however, deem it desirable to decentralize administrative power in order to stimulate local enthusiasm and carry out policies that rely mainly upon local initiatives. Administrative decentralization in post-Mao China was compelled mainly by the imperative of reform and open policies, because local governments were considered indispensable agents in reducing the inflexibility of the rigid socialist bureaucracy and weakening the ideological strictures of the Maoist era. In particular, a wide range of administrative entities, ranging from SEZs to coastal open cities and open economic areas, were established. Hence the centralized administrative structure of the pre-reform era underwent substantial changes after 1978.

Political Dimension

The political dimension of central-local relations concerns ideological and organizational relations between different levels of party and government organs. This dimension is particularly important in socialist systems because the formal, constitutional division of power is often unclear or ignored in practice. Organizational and ideological control are major mechanisms for the center to monitor and manage the lower levels of the Party and state apparatus. Ideological control used to be a critical control mechanism in post-1949 China, but after 1978 China also underwent de-radicalization and reinterpretation of Mao Zedong Thought and Marxism-Leninism. In particular, the pragmatism of paramount leader Deng Xiaoping helped to relax the ideological strictures of the Maoist days. While some ideological campaigns were initiated in the early 1980s, they were a much less important form of control than before. As Richard Lowenthal has aptly stated, post-Mao China had entered into a post-revolutionary phase in which the idea of institutionalized revolution was abandoned.[13]

Fiscal Dimension

The fiscal dimension concerns the sharing of revenue between different levels of government. The fiscal system directly engages the interests of different governmental levels because states need resources to implement their policies. The ability to extract resources from society provides a significant indicator of state capacity.[14] Fiscal relations between the center and the provinces have changed significantly since 1978 because the localities have gained a greater share of the revenue and, at the same time, begun to shoulder more of the responsibility for expenditures.[15] Conflicts between general and particular interests are inevitable because these two levels of governments cover different jurisdictions. For instance, the central government might be more concerned with collective issues such as national security, national economic development, regional equality, population growth, and political stability. Local governments, on the other hand, might be far more concerned with local economic development and living standards. The fiscal regime is also the most intensely examined issue of central-local relations in China studies.[16]

Policy Dimension

The policy dimension concerns the distribution of power among governments in the formulation and implementation of public policy. While the nature of the policy may entail different patterns of intergovernmental interactions, the distribution of power in policy formulation and implementation is a crucial issue in central-local relations. This dimension concerns the territorial distribution of state capacity in extracting revenue and resources from society, distributing valued goods among different actors, formulating strategies and mobilizing resources for economic development, offering symbolic appeals, penetrating society, as well as regulating behavior. One of the most important policy changes after 1978 concerned, of course, the granting of "special policies, and flexible measures" to Guangdong and Fujian. Having reviewed the various dimensions of central-provincial relations, let us examine how Guangdong's relations with the center have evolved since 1949.

Relations between the Center and Guangdong, 1949-1978

The relationship between the central government and Guangdong province was rather hierarchical as a socialist system was being established in China in the 1950s. True, the central government began to decentralize more economic power to the localities during the Great Leap Forward Campaign (1958-1960) and again since the Cultural Revolution (1966-1976), but the stringent level of ideological and organizational control during the Maoist era hardly favored any meaningful deviation or flexibility in policy. The central authorities' resolute control over Guangdong since 1949 was compelled by both domestic and international forces. The primary factor seemed to be the desire of China's leadership to build a strong state, and to mobilize society and resources to achieve the objective of socialist development. Guangdong's unique sub-culture, customs, and dialects, its history as a commercial center and treaty port, its distance from the national capital, and its closeness to Hong Kong and Macao, all helped to prompt tighter central control. Whether in constitutional, administrative, political, fiscal, or policy dimensions, central authorities allowed little local autonomy.[17]

In order to build up a strong, centralized state, national policies must be effectively implemented with as little local resistance as possible. The pattern of central-provincial relations was thus shaped by the overriding task of building a socialist system. After their liquidation by the Nationalists in the 1920s, Communist guerrillas in South China had to survive for many years on their own. Hence "localism" often aroused deep suspicion among central leaders after the Communists took power in 1949.[18] For instance, because of the leniency of Guangdong's local cadres during land reform (1951-53), non-Guangdong cadres such as Tao Zhu and Zhao Ziyang ascended in the provincial hierarchy at the expense of local officials in an effort to consolidate centralized rule. Despite initial successes in establishing central control, the armed rebellion of local officials on Hainan Island and its subsequent suppression in 1958 reflected the volatility of the struggle between central and local elements in the province.[19] While the local culprits were rehabilitated in the post-Mao era, the crushing of such localism in the 1950s aptly reflected the center's desire for a strong, unified socialist state.

Aside from the paramount goal of state-building, central-provincial relations were inevitably affected by the political ambitions of China's own leaders. As Susan Shirk has observed, the "playing to the provinces" strategy was common in political competition among China's elites.[20] Guangdong's history and location made it a major arena for such political struggles. By loyally implementing central policies, Tao Zhu used the province as a stepping stone, establishing himself as Guangdong's powerful Party Secretary in the early 1950s and later becoming the First Secretary of the Central South Bureau of the Party in 1960. When Tao Zhu moved to the center in mid 1966, he helped Zhao Ziyang, one of his closest associates, become the province's Party Secretary.

After the purging of Tao and Zhao, the new elites that emerged in the wake of the Cultural Revolution followed their predecessors' attempts to use the province in their struggle for power.[21] With his associate General Huang Yongsheng as head of the Guangzhou Military Region, Lin Biao reportedly contemplated setting up another base in Guangdong as part of the contingency plan for his 1971 plot against Mao Zedong.[22] After the Lin Biao affair, Liu Xingyuan and Ding Sheng, two military officials reportedly favored by Mao, took over as Guangdong's leaders. Zhao Ziyang was able to return to work in Guangdong in 1972 and served as the provincial Party Secretary and Governor from 1974 to 1975. Yet Mao's radical policies inhibited any departures from the pursuit of egalitarianism and revolutionary ideals. When Zhao was transferred to Sichuan, his vacancy was filled by Wei Guoqing, an ally of Deng Xiaoping, who reportedly offered sanctuary to Deng when he became a target of the Maoists.[23] With the downfall of the "Gang of Four" and Deng's return to political preeminence in December 1978, Xi Zhongxun and Yang Shangkun, both allies of Deng, took over the leadership of Guangdong in 1979. As the center strove to keep the province in line, contending leaders in the center and province used it as their own power base. However, such involvement in national politics up to 1978 had hardly led to special treatment for the province because the contenders for power had put national and personal concerns above that of the province.

The competitive external environment also strongly shaped the relationship between the center and Guangdong after 1949. For instance, the lack of industrial investment in the province was prompted by China's hostile relations with the United States following the Korean War. Beijing shifted its industrial investment from the coastal provinces to the inland areas for security reasons, leaving Guangdong with only meager investment funds.[24] During the Maoist era, when the dictates of a centralized state and ideological radicalism remained prominent, significant policy variations by the localities were impossible. Yet economic policies formulated by the center had adverse implications for Guangdong. For example, the national agricultural policy which took grain production as the key priority ran against Guangdong's natural potential for agricultural diversification and inhibited its agricultural growth, especially since the late 1960s. During 1966-75, the province's economy grew only sluggishly.[25] The national policy favoring heavy industry also hardly played to Guangdong' strengths because the province lacks the necessary raw materials--nor did such an industrial policy capitalize on the province's modest foundation of light industry. The state's tight control over commerce and foreign trade further made it impossible to tap the province's past experience as a key commercial and trading center in pre-1949 China. With a rather unfavorable legacy that lasted three decades, central-provincial relations entered into a new phase only after 1978.

Relations between the Center and Guangdong Since 1978

The evolution of relations between the central government and Guangdong province in the post-Mao period can be roughly divided into five phases: (1) 1979-1984, (2) 1985-1986, (3) 1987-88, (4) 1989-1991, and (5) since 1992.[26]

Phase One (1979-1984)

An important new relationship between the center and Guangdong was inaugurated with the adoption of Central Document No. 50 in 1979, which offered special policies for Guangdong (and Fujian) on a trial basis.[27] According to this new framework for central-provincial relations, a five-year fiscal contract regime (*caizheng dabaogan*), under which the province had to remit only RMB 1.2 billion (later scaled down to RMB 1 billion) to the central government, was introduced.[28] A similarly favorable foreign exchange contract was also proposed, under which the province could retain all above-baseline foreign exchange earned from export processing, compensation trade, and joint-ventures as well as from non-trade sources.[29] A great deal of autonomy in economic policy was granted to Guangdong in such areas as formulating its own development plans, allocating resources, managing labor, and introducing price reforms.[30] Enterprises and business units under central control (except those in certain areas) would be transferred to and managed by the province.[31] Guangdong's foreign trade authority was also greatly augmented.[32] The province could decide on export processing and compensation trade projects that did not affect national balances (e.g. in funds and materials) and was allowed to set up its own investment firm to acquire foreign capital. More controversial still, four special economic zones (hereafter SEZs) were created, three of which were located in Guangdong--Shenzhen, Zhuhai, and Shantou.[33]

In the wake of bureaucratic inertia over the implementation of such unprecedented special policies, another major policy, embodied in Central Document No. 41, was issued in mid-May, 1980.[34] In this document, the radical, market-oriented reformers at the center reaffirmed their staunch support for the new special policies. Guangdong and Fujian were encouraged by this document to be more "special" in economic affairs, to alleviate obstruction from central departments, and most importantly, to act as pioneers in enlivening the reform process despite the economic readjustment that began in mid-1979.[35] Provisions regarding finance were expanded to make them even more favorable than those enjoyed by other areas, including, for instance, the power to issue stocks and bonds to absorb foreign capital, and the right to keep enterprise depreciation funds.[36] And the province would remit only RMB 1 billion to the center, rather than the amount of RMB 1.2 billion decided on in 1979. Key policies for the SEZs, such as highlighting the role of the market mechanism and setting the enterprise income tax rate at 15 percent, were also approved.

Further efforts of the reformists culminated in the promulgation of Central Document (1981) No. 27, the third major document on Guangdong and Fujian since 1979.[37] In the midst of growing disagreements between conservatives and market-oriented reformers, the 1981 document suggested that reforms in the two provinces would foster China's overall economic reforms. Reflecting the victory of the pro-reform wing of the Party, the gist of "special policies, flexible measures" was defined as "further opening to the outside," "further relaxation in domestic policies," and "further expanding the powers of the two provinces." Not only were the SEZs reaffirmed as a "significant ingredient" of the special policies, but emerging conservative critiques of the zones as concessions or colonies were promptly refuted.[38] The two provinces were told to "actively carry out reforms that would be beneficial to rectification."[39] Equally noteworthy were the favorable provisions on foreign trade and investment. The center would still control tariff revenue and keep its power over tariff reductions and exemptions, but the import of raw materials and spare parts for producing export goods in the province would be tax-exempt in order to boost exports. Guangdong's power to make decisions on its own production and construction projects that did not affect critical national balances was reaffirmed. In order to promote infrastructure construction, which was evidently inadequate in Guangdong, the province could also exempt taxes and lower profit remittances from enterprises in the needed sectors. The Guangdong Branch of the People's Bank would enjoy greater discretion in issuing loans. The center would still decide on tax laws and international taxation, yet the two provinces could levy and adjust all local taxes and decide on tax reductions.[40] These enhanced financial powers would allow Guangdong and Fujian much more flexibility and greater resources to help finance faster economic development.

These three major central documents constructed a new framework for central-provincial relations that would remain largely in force and in fact be further relaxed in the 1980s. Administratively, of course, Guangdong remained a province of China. But its newly delegated economic policy-making powers enabled it to be much more flexible in economic reform and management. This new framework differed from the economic decentralization of the Great Leap Forward and the Cultural Revolution because of the concomitant move toward market-oriented reforms and an open policy, and the regime's shift from mobilization to an emphasis on political order and economic development. The de-radicalization of Chinese politics relaxed the political atmosphere and encouraged local initiative and experimentation.

The special policies enhanced the flexibility of Guangdong's local governments in 1981, but they also brought about unintended consequences such as rampant smuggling and economic crimes, especially in the SEZs. The seriousness of central concern over these issues cumulated in a Party Secretariat meeting in late December 1980. At this meeting, Guangdong and Fujian were warned about the deterioration of social norms, the influence of Western ideology, and the need for raising foreign exchange earnings.[41] In particular, it was stated that the SEZs were only special economic zones, not special political zones. Various early warnings from the center were issued in 1980-81. Nonetheless, they did not stop the localities in Guangdong from taking advantage of their new flexibility to purchase cheaper products from neighboring areas for export or from importing consumer goods with their locally-retained foreign exchange (especially through the SEZs) and reselling them inland. Since the situation did not improve significantly, an urgent central-level meeting was convened in early 1982 to tackle the worsening economic crimes in the two provinces.[42] This central intervention resulted in several restrictions being placed on Guangdong, such as stopping the procurement of agricultural products for export from other areas, and banning the resale of imported consumer goods and the reselling of foreign exchange.[43] Thanks to the support of reformers at the center and the steadfastness of the provincial leadership,

Guangdong's special policies were allowed to continue despite these problems.

Phase Two (1985-1986)

After retrenchment in the early 1980s, the central reformers stepped up their offensive for further reform and opening. Guangdong's rapid economic growth and reform in the early 1980s provided a useful local example for reformers who wanted to deepen reform in the mid-1980s. By launching a tour of the SEZs in early 1984, Deng Xiaoping not only reconfirmed his personal support of the zones in the midst of growing conservative critiques, but also brought about the opening of the 14 coastal cities (including Guangzhou and Zhanjiang in Guangdong Province). These cities would be allowed to implement some of the special policies once monopolized by Guangdong and Fujian in order to attract foreign investment.[44] The momentum for reform gained strength with the adoption of the comprehensive reform program in October 1984.

State Council Document (1985) No. 46, issued in March 1985, extended for five years the special policies in Guangdong and Fujian. This ushered in the second phase of central-provincial relations after 1978 and substantially expanded the economic powers of the two provinces.[45] Aside from continued autonomy in planning, they were empowered to approve productive construction projects under 200 million yuan in size that were invested with their own funds or foreign capital. Similarly, they could decide on foreign-invested production projects under US$10 million that did not involve national balances and export quotas. Paralleling other open cities, they could validate all non-productive projects, regardless of investment scale. Various preferential measures promoting technical renovation were approved. Most importantly, the fiscal contract system with the same level of remittance would be continued, even though Guangdong's economy had doubled in size since 1978.

Other measures granted Guangdong much more financial power, such as the authority to establish its own financial institutions, engage in foreign exchange account business, and issue bonds overseas. The retention rates for various forms of foreign exchange income were also increased to ensure Guangdong's privileged position. The province's retention rate for export earnings was set at 30 percent, 5 percent higher than other regions. The baseline for foreign exchange earnings from export processing would be set at $20 million and all above-baseline surplus would still be retained by the province. Since export processing remained the dominant form of foreign direct investment in Guangdong, such foreign earnings were especially significant. In accordance with Zhao's suggestions, the province's foreign trade was also further augmented.[46] While this document reaffirmed the need to deal with economic crimes and capitalist ideology, these issues were mentioned only briefly in the last paragraph of the document.

In spite of the trend toward greater decentralization, several incidents almost derailed the initiative of the radical reformers. Since the fall of 1984, massive imports led to the depletion of foreign exchange reserves, while the exposure of the Hainan Island car smuggling scandal and the growing problems of the SEZs cast a shadow over further opening and reform. The Hainan scandal led to another series of central administrative restrictions over the foreign trade powers of the province.[47] Only after tough compromises and restrictions on the SEZs could a policy consensus be reached at the central level. Yet the radical reform wing of the central leadership was clearly on the defensive. In late June, even Deng Xiaoping admitted that, "The success of Shenzhen has yet to be proved" and in early July, the opening of the coastal cities was limited to only four (including Guangzhou).[48] Yet the strong backing of pro-reform leaders in the center not only helped the province survive these difficulties and prevented the reversal of open policies, but it also uplifted the morale of the reformist leaders in Guangdong and motivated them to be bolder in reform and opening.[49] Granted such unprecedented powers in economic policy, the province continued its role as a pioneer in reform and opening and achieved rapid economic growth during the mid-1980s.

Phase Three (1987-1988)

Guangdong was undoubtedly interested in getting more autonomy once it had tasted the benefits of the special policies, but only after central and provincial objectives converged over the need for further reform was it possible to undertake further decentralization of economic power to the province. In fact, the fall of Hu Yaobang from the post of General Secretary in early 1987 seriously threatened the coalition of market-oriented reformers at the center that favored Guangdong. Yet Zhao Ziyang succeeded Hu and declared the theory of the primary stage of socialism, which reaffirmed the goal of economic development and the creation of a socialist commodity economy at the 13th Party Congress in late 1987. In particular, Guangdong would play a key role in Zhao's outward-oriented, coastal development strategy. The province did not hesitate to grasp this opportunity, proposing a further relaxation of policies in mid-October, 1987.[50] With the backing of Zhao Ziyang and Deng Xiaoping at the top, as well as its impressive record in economic reform and development, the province again seemed positioned to be a reform pacesetter in the 1990s.

The 1987-88 phase of central-provincial relations extended the powers of Guangdong in the ten areas described below, making it an unprecedented test site for comprehensive reform. These changes were made possible by the 1988 central document known as State Council Correspondence 25. First, Guangdong's financial powers were greatly expanded, including, for instance, powers in extending the province's sources of credit, getting a fixed quota of credit from the People's Bank, developing financial markets, setting up stock and securities firms, speeding up the share-holding reforms of enterprises, establishing foreign exchange adjustment centers, and formulating its own plans for foreign borrowing (although the province still needed central approval for such borrowing). Aside from setting up a regional, share-holding commercial bank--the Guangdong Development Bank--the document allowed the Guangdong Branch of the People's Bank to approve the opening of other local financial institutions.

Second, while reforms in foreign trade were also proposed, these measures mainly followed the national ones. Aside from retaining the favorable 30 percent foreign exchange retention rate, the amount of direct foreign investment that could be approved by Guangdong was enlarged three times--to $30 million--for projects that did not involve export quotas and licenses or national balances. The province could also approve certain wholly-owned foreign firms, infrastructural projects, and other export-oriented projects which exported 70 percent of their products and did not use up quotas and licenses. Guangdong's foreign trade powers would also expand.[51] The power to approve processing and foreign trade transactions could even be delegated to production enterprises, especially bigger enterprises and enterprise conglomerates, so that they could directly negotiate with foreign businessmen, export their products, and--with approval from the province--set up sales and marketing units and subsidiaries abroad.

Third, the province would be granted unprecedented autonomy in price reform and management. Aside from eliminating mandatory price control targets, Guangdong could also determine when and how to introduce price reform.[52] Fourth, the contract system would be adopted as a key reform measure for enterprises. While increases in the province's total wage bill would be linked with the growth of various economic targets, enterprises would be granted authority to adjust wages provided that average wage increases did not surpass the growth of productivity and remittance of tax and profits. A social security system would also be launched in tandem with the above reforms. Fifth, the lump sum transfer fiscal regime would be modified, but the province would have to remit an annual increment of 9 percent to the center. The province could also levy new local taxes (fees) and set their rates. Sixth, important enterprise reforms such as the contracting system and various management responsibility systems would be introduced. Taking the lead in enterprise reform, Guangdong was empowered not only to propagate share-holding reforms in big and medium-sized state-owned enterprises but also to auction or lease small enterprises. Bankruptcy would even be allowed for most enterprises, except for a few major enterprises and public utilities. Seventh, reforms in education and science and technology, such as commercialization of research, were proposed and, eighth, privatization of housing and the development of real estate would be introduced. Ninth, Guangdong's autonomy in planning would continue, but with an emphasis on guidance, rather than mandatory, planning. The province could still decide on its own scale of fixed capital investment up to 200 million yuan. Finally, small steps in political reform, including democratization of the policy-making process, the creation of a civil service system, an administrative redress mechanism, as well as the expansion of consultation between the government and the people, were suggested for the first time. If fully implemented, these ten areas of expanded provincial authority would certainly make Guangdong the only province that could serve as model of comprehensive reform.

The initiation of such special treatment for Guangdong coincided with the reformists' push for further reform and opening nationwide. Soon after approval of the 1988 document, the State Council not only expanded the size of the coastal open economic area, in March 1988, but also implemented policies to further promote links with the world economy. The privileged policies that once applied to Guangdong and Fujian alone now extended to a much wider area. However, the country's rampant inflation and domestic buying spree in the summer of 1988 precipitated the adoption of an economic retrenchment program in the fall of that year. The new framework for reformed central-provincial relations was thus never fully implemented. The turmoil in the spring and summer of 1989 further introduced great uncertainties into the relations between the center and the province, as well as for the fate of reform itself.

Phase Four (1989-1991)

Central-provincial relations in the post-Mao era reached a nadir in the 1989-1991 period. Not surprisingly, Guangdong adopted a rather ambivalent attitude toward the promulgation of martial law on May 20, 1989, and the suppression of the Tiananmen event that took place on June 4.[53] The provincial leadership had little influence on such central decisions, but their repercussions would adversely affect the fortunes of the province. The crackdown on dissidents would scare away foreign businessmen and threaten reform and opening. The most long-lasting impact of the events in 1989 was the collapse of the pro-Guangdong wing in the central government. For instance, the purge of Zhao Ziyang meant that Guangdong no longer enjoyed close ties with its former patron. Various attempts to reshuffle Guangdong's leadership were made. More important were efforts to reorient national policy, slow down economic reform, and impose more restrictions on Guangdong, which not only made implementation of the 1988 document impossible but also inhibited the province from attempting a faster pace of growth and launching bolder reforms.

The ascendence of conservative leaders like Premier Li Peng and Vice Premier Yao Yilin after 1989 led to the preferential treatment of basic industries, and of large and medium-sized state-owned enterprises, rather than a focus on the coastal areas.[54] Instead of continuing in its role as a reform pacesetter and maintaining a fast growth rate, Guangdong was confronted with the unsavory task of scaling down investment, slowing economic growth rates, coping with a seriously weakened national market, and surrendering some of its economic powers to the center. The exercise of tight macroeconomic control by the central government curtailed much of Guangdong's special authority, especially over finance and investment. Another equally noteworthy challenge after 1989 was the reorientation of central attention from Guangdong and its SEZs to the development of Shanghai and the city's Pudong district.[55] In spring 1991, SEZ-style policies and privileges were further extended to 27 high technology zones, only three of which were located in Guangdong (Guangzhou, Zhongshan, and Shenzhen).[56]

Phase Five (since 1992)

The convergence of the policy objectives of influential central leaders and local officials was critical in opening a new "policy window" in Maoist as well as Dengist China. Deng Xiaoping's tour of south China in January-February 1992 was an important step in thawing central-provincial relations. After the 1989 political crisis and more than three years of economic retrenchment beginning in the fall of 1988, Deng was eager to expedite reform and opening. This task was made more urgent by his impatience with the lack of bold reform initiatives at home and the breakdown of communism worldwide in 1989-90. By deploying his strategy of "playing to the provinces," Deng made a carefully orchestrated tour of the south in order to outflank the conservatives in the center. Seeking the cooperation of local officials--especially those in Shanghai, Guangdong, and Shenzhen--in speeding up reform and economic growth, he encouraged Guangdong to catch up with the four East Asian "Little Dragons" in twenty years.[57] Quickly becoming allies of Deng,

Guangdong's officials began drumming up support for his vision. Reminiscent of the enthusiastic chorus over exerting Guangdong's strength when special policies were first promulgated in 1979-1981, provincial newspapers were soon flooded with discussions about how to achieve Deng's strategic goal. Despite the problematic promise of a fast rate of economic growth based on Deng's personal intervention rather than careful economic calculation, Governor Zhu Senlin echoed Deng's call for double digit economic growth in the 1990s. Taking advantage of this new opportunity to ask for more autonomy, Zhu requested that the central government apply an open policy to the mountainous areas in Guangdong, speed up financial reform, share the custom taxes collected by Guangdong ports for the center, and, most importantly, reactivate the implementation of the 1988 document (i.e. State Council Correspondence No. 25).[58] The special role of Guangdong in China's new modernization drive was again highlighted in the 14th National Party Congress held in October 1992, a key meeting in which Deng Xiaoping attempted to promote pro-reform cadres and articulate the goal of building a socialist market economy. In addition to leaders from Beijing, Shanghai, Tianjin and Shandong, Guangdong's incumbent Party leader Xie Fei was promoted the Politburo for the first time since 1949. Reflecting the growing representation of the provinces, a total of seven of Guangdong's Party and state officials entered the new party Central Committee in 1992.[59] The report made by General Secretary Jiang Zemin to the Congress also highlighted the role of Guangdong's reform and opening. In sum, the province would now have more direct access to the power center and would act as a pioneer in Deng's rally for building a socialist market economy.

Implications for the Capacity of the Chinese State

The enormous changes brought about by economic reforms since 1978 have contributed to the growing centrifugal tendencies at almost all levels of China's local governments.[60] To be sure, provincial leaders still have to act as "political middlemen" in the Chinese political system, balancing the demands of both the central and provincial levels.[61] Nonetheless, the reform era has witnessed the devolution of a great deal of economic power from the central to the local governments. True, central authorities can still resort to a number of control mechanisms in order to influence local governments, such as tightening macroeconomic control, reorienting national economic policy, renegotiating the sharing of resources, and, most importantly, controlling personnel appointments. Similarly, provincial authorities have devised a variety of coping strategies in order to deal with the center, such as lobbying for central support, creatively interpreting central policies, flexibly implementing central measures, further decentralizing power and resources to subprovincial levels, and voicing their disagreement with unfavorable central measures. Perhaps because of the ideological and organizational control that the center can still exercise, open confrontation and outright non-compliance by the provinces is still rare. The following is a selective analysis of how the changes in central-provincial relations and the decentralization of economic powers from the center to Guangdong province have affected the capacity of the Chinese state.

Administrative Dimension

Economic reforms in post-Mao China have had a significant impact on Guangdong's administrative structure. By the early 1990s, Guangdong consisted of a labyrinth of administrative units. In early 1993, the province had a total of 24 cities and 71 counties, but these included three SEZs, one coastal open economic area (the Pearl River Delta, with a total of 28 cities and counties), two open coastal cities (Guangzhou and Zhanjiang), one city separately listed in the central plan (*jihua danlie chengshi*: Guangzhou) as well as a host of economic and technological development zones.[62] Hainan Island was also separated from Guangdong province in 1988, becoming an independent province and a SEZ with even more special policy privileges.

The decentralization of economic power to the localities has various administrative implications. On the one hand, the leaders of some of these newly created entities have adopted a more flexible leadership style and a more simplified administrative structure in order to expedite reform and development, as exemplified by the various municipal and county governments in the Pearl River Delta.[63] On the other hand, new administrative structures, ranging from the SEZs to the management committees of various development zones, have been created to implement the preferential policies. In fact, Shenzhen's Municipal People's Congress was even granted legislative power in 1992 after years of intensive bargaining, a privileged treatment usually reserved for the provincial level. Together with six other cities like Wuhan and Dalian, Guangzhou became a city separately listed in the national plan and was granted quasi-provincial-level economic power in October 1984. The Pearl River Delta Open Economic Area and the various development zones were similarly created in the 1980s to extend preferential policies once monopolized by the SEZs over such areas as the approval of foreign investment, trade, and local capital construction. Consequently, compared with the pre-reform era, these new entities have gained increasing administrative power at the expense of the control exercised by the central ministries. In fact, the sheer volume, complexity, and loopholes of the many preferential policies granted to these entities have made it extremely difficult for the central government to coordinate and exercise effective administrative control over their implementation.

Political Dimension

Ideological and organizational matters still remained formally under central control in post-Mao China. In spite of its pursuit of economic reform since 1978, the Party has not fundamentally changed its tight organizational structure. To be sure, some reform of the organizational system has been carried out in order to adapt to changing organizational objectives. One of the most significant reforms concerned the decentralization of personnel management of the Party in 1984, in which the Central Committee and other Party Committees were given *nomenklatura* authority over only one level down the hierarchy.[64] Specifically, this meant that the center still directly controlled the appointment of key provincial posts (such as Governor, Vice-Governors, Party Secretaries and members of the Provincial Party Standing Committee), but not posts below that. The provincial and prefectural Party Committees also decentralized their nomenklatura control to prefectural as well as city and county-level Party Committees. Further, the center revitalized various mechanisms of cadre management and organizational control in the 1980s. While the central government tried to improve its administrative capacity through upgrading the qualifications of cadres and reforming the cadre system, it also revived monitory and supervisory organs. For instance, the party discipline inspection system was revived in 1978 in order to enforce party discipline and to ensure implementation of party policies.[65] In the state bureaucracy, the state Auditing Administration (*shenjishu*) and the Ministry of Supervision (*jianchabu*), both under the State Council, were revived respectively in 1983 and 1986.[66] The state Auditing Administration is responsible for supervising the observance of fiscal and financial discipline. The Ministry of Supervision is responsible for monitoring the implementation of state laws, policies and plans, as well as for investigating and dealing with official corruption and other forms of abuses of power. These organs clearly allow the central government additional mechanisms for checking the behavior of lower government units and officials, but to what extent they are effective demands a separate analysis.

Guangdong has not enjoyed any special privileges in the political, organizational, and ideological spheres since 1978. With the exception of the aforementioned 1988 document, none of the key decisions on

Guangdong's special policies included any provisions on political reform. The 1988 document referred to the need for political reform, but such reforms had already been discussed nationally since 1986. In fact, the dominant ideological line of the center has been affirmed in all of the central decisions on the province. In contrast to the decentralization of economic power, the management of cadres and the party-state establishment also remain under central control. The formulation of a cadre plan (*ganbu jihua*), special category cadre plan (*zhuanxiang ganbu jihua*), as well as the establishment of a party and state apparatus (*jigou bianzhi*) in Guangdong have to follow the State Council and the Party formulas for other parts of China.[67] True, today the provincial level participates in the making of such plans and enjoys more power in handing down the approved quotas to its lower levels, but it still has to follow the center's plans.[68] In particular, to ensure the implementation of reform and open policies, the appointment of provincial level officials remain a key control mechanism manipulated by the Center. For instance, Deng Xiaoping did not hesitate to replace Xi Zhongxun and Yang Shangkun with two other reform-minded officials, Ren Zhongyi and Liang Lingguang, as the province's top leaders in 1979 to bring about a breakthrough in reform and opening.[69] The appointment of two Guangdong natives, Lin Ruo, a veteran local cadre, and Ye Xuanping, the eldest son of the once powerful Marshal Ye Jianying, respectively as First Party Secretary and Governor in 1985, further helped advance the reform policies pioneered by Ren and Liang.

A systematic analysis of the center's organizational policy toward Guangdong and its impact on the capacity of the Chinese state is beyond the scope of this chapter, yet some tentative observations can still be made. First, while the formal organizational system still allows the center to exercise significant power over personnel appointments and organizational management, the effective exercise of such powers seems to have encountered some difficulties, as exemplified by developments after 1989. For instance, in order to weaken Guangdong's pro-reform leadership, which was also closely tied to the deposed Zhao Ziyang, conservative central leaders attempted to reshuffle the provincial leadership once the nationwide anti-corruption campaign started in the summer of 1989. Some prominent provincial officials were reportedly investigated.[70] Others, including top provincial officials in charge of foreign trade, were actually disciplined.[71] There was also a story circulated that Chen Yun's son Chen Yuan, or Li Peng's confidant Yuan Mu, the spokesmen of the State Council, would be transferred to leadership posts in the province.[72] However, Guangdong's authorities have exhibited exceptional tenacity. The retiring Provincial Party Secretary, Lin Ruo, was replaced by Xie Fei, another veteran Guangdong cadre, in January 1991. The most significant attempt at reshuffling was the effort to transfer the reformist Governor, Ye Xuanping, from the province to a central-level post. Refusing to leave Guangdong after 1989, Ye finally agreed to become a Vice Chairman of the Chinese People's Political Consultative Conference only in early March 1991, reportedly on the condition that the province could freely choose his successor.[73] The appointment of provincial insider Zhu Senlin, a former Mayor of Guangzhou, as Acting Governor of Guangdong in early May 1991 and later as Governor, seems to validate this report.[74]

Second, while the center has not decentralized much of its de jure organizational power to Guangdong, it seems quite likely that the province might have more de facto influence over such matters in the reform era. The reduction of central appointment powers to only one level down the hierarchy (i.e. the provincial level) allows the reformist provincial leadership to promote many like-minded cadres to the prefectural/ municipal and county levels. Such famous names as Li Ziliu, Mayor of Guangzhou, and Liang Guangda, Mayor of Zhuhai, are but some of the rising local stars who have established solid credentials and a reputation for launching bold reforms. The provincial official in charge of propaganda publicly defended flexible leadership styles such as the so-called "red light thesis" (*hongdenglun*), "flexibility thesis" (*biantonglun*), and "counter-measure thesis" (*duicelun*).[75] This defense is an excellent reflection of the styles of Guangdong's officials, something which is still unthinkable in most other provinces.

Third, the localities in Guangdong have resorted to their own "flexible measures" to meet their organizational needs.[76] By the end of 1990, 46,292 persons were recruited above the official establishment in party, state, and mass organization units in the province.[77] Last but not least, the province has also taken the lead in eradicating the straightjacket of official ideology. In the early 1980s, for instance, Ren Zhongyi took the lead in fighting against conservative critiques of Guangdong's special policies.[78] More recently, Guangzhou's Mayor Li Ziliu even argued that "speculation" (*touji*) and "profiteering" (*daoba*) are necessary because they are in line with the laws of prices and should be considered legitimate if they are within the boundaries of the laws.[79] In sum, while the center has not decentralized much formal organizational power to the province since 1978, central control over ideological and organizational matters still seems to have weakened over time.

Fiscal Dimension

One of the most significant changes in the central-provincial relationship concerns the fiscal dimension. The fiscal regime helped Guangdong remain one step ahead of the nation in reform, especially in the first half of the 1980s, because the province could arrange its budgetary priorities, use more revenue to support price reforms through subsidies, and spend more of its resources on local economic development. The fiscal transfer between the center and Guangdong consists of two parts: the "narrow" category and the "broad" category. The "narrow" category consists of: (1) the fixed remittance, which constitutes the bulk of this item, and (2) a host of other remittances. Central Document (1979) No. 50 established the fixed remittance, a five-year lump sum transfer regime under which the province was obliged to remit to the center only RMB 1.2 billion (later reduced to RMB 1 billion) and could keep the surplus.[80] The lump sum transfer regime remained in force from 1980 to 1985. The decline of the central government's fiscal capacity after 1980 had, however, compelled its leaders to extract more revenue for the province. Beginning in 1988, the province has to remit an additional 9 percent annual increment for a 3-year period.[81] The 1988 baseline figure was also raised to $1.413 billion yuan.[82]

The second item of the "narrow" category of remittance included (a) extra contribution (*duozuo gongxian*) after 1988, (b) specific remittance (*zhuanxiang shangjiao*), (c) remittance of two funds (the State Energy, Transportation, and Key Construction Fund and the State Budget Adjustment Fund), (d) Industrial and Commercial Tax, incorporated as central revenue since 1990, (e) remittance from enterprises reclassified as central revenue, and (f) borrowing through squeezing provincial expenditure (*yazhi jiekuan shangjiao*) after 1988.[83] During the 1980-1989 period, the total of the "narrow" category of remittances amounted to RMB 21.97 billion and registered a net of RMB 19.22 billion after deducting RMB 2.74 billion of special category subsidies from the center. In fact, the center increasingly relied upon such means to raise central income from Guangdong. Aside from imposing "involuntary" borrowing in the early 1980s, the center also borrowed extra money through the reduction of provincial expenditures in 1988 and 1989, demanded extra contributions beginning in 1988, and even reclassified a local source of revenue--the Industrial and Commercial Tax collected by the customs administration--as central revenue after 1990. In 1990, Guangdong remitted a total of over RMB 5 billion yuan within this narrow category, about 40 percent of its total revenue![84] Further, while central investment in Guangdong dwindled, various expenditures formally made by the central government have become the responsibility of the province.[85] In fact, the cumulative amount of this "narrow" category of remittance already constituted 28 percent of Guangdong's total revenue collected during the 1980-1989 period. In fact, the growth of such remittances increased 15.7 percent per annum during 1979-1990, while total provincial revenue grew only 12.27 percent.[86] In other words, even such a "narrow" category of remittance was far greater than the fixed lump sum.

The "broad" definition of remittance from Guangdong included, in addition to the "narrow" category, various sources of income that the central government acquired through the province, namely (a) tariffs collected by the customs administration, (b) income from the banking and insurance system, (c) remittances from centrally-owned enterprises in Guangdong, and finally, (d) remittances of foreign exchange earnings. These sources of income rose dramatically as a result of Guangdong's rapid economic growth, reaching respectively 53.2 percent, 28 percent, and 58.3 percent per annum during the 1979-1990 period.[87] The amount of the first three categories of remittances from Guangdong grew from RMB 499 million in 1980 to over RMB 10.45 billion, while the total foreign exchange earnings remitted during the 1979-1989 period reached about $15 billion. Further, the province has to take responsibility for selling a fixed quota of state bonds, which amounted to a total of RMB 2.45 billion in the 1981-1989 period.[88] The province also had to shoulder various expenditures that were beyond its control, including subsidies and reductions in revenue caused by national policies (such as economic retrenchment). One estimate suggests that such expenditure amounted to RMB 1.3 billion during the 1979-1990 period.[89]

As the above analysis indicates, the total revenue that the central government obtains from Guangdong has increased substantially, especially since the mid-1980s. It would be wrong to assume that the center's fiscal capacity has been depleted as a result of its special relations with the province. Nonetheless, in order to request additional funds on top of the formal fiscal regime, the center had to bring enormous pressure to bear on Guangdong (and other provinces) during such hard times as 1988-91. While Guangdong's GDP had increased more than threefold since 1979, the growing amount of remittances to the center has emerged as a major issue of contention between the center and the province. In view of the envy of other provinces and increasing central encroachment, Guangdong's leaders even publicly defend the province's record of fiscal contributions to the central government.[90] It is widely believed that Guangdong has attempted to keep the lump sum transfer regime by paying such extra remittances to the center (*huaqian maitixi*).

Did the lump sum fiscal regime strengthen the fiscal capacity of the provincial government at the expense of the center? The answer is mixed. The lump sum transfer regime has evidently been very important for the province, especially in the early 1980s, because of the autonomy it afforded and the above-lump sum revenue that Guangdong could keep. However, the actual amount that the province has to remit increased significantly over time and the province similarly established a variety of lump sum transfer contracts with subprovincial governments.[91] Consequently, the fiscal capacity of the province has been weakened. Like other provinces, the extrabudgetary funds of Guangdong also increased dramatically in the reform era, as the total of such extrabudgetary revenue almost doubled between 1986 and 1990.[92] By 1990, Guangdong's extrabudgetary revenue reached RMB 9.8 billion and its extrabudgetary expenditure amounted to RMB 9.2 billion, respectively about half of total provincial revenue and expenditure.[93] As in other provinces, the growth of income of non-profit and administrative units in Guangdong doubled between 1986 and 1990, and the funds in the hands of state-owned enterprises and their supervising organs in the province jumped 1.89 times, even higher than the increase of 1.5 times for other provinces.[94] Consequently, the changes in fiscal relations between the center and the province did not lead to an automatic increase in provincial fiscal power at the expense of the center. Rather, the province contributed an increasing sum to the center through various channels, while decentralizing many of its fiscal powers and resources to enterprises and other lower-level governments.

Policy Dimension

Several generalizations about the five phases in the decentralization of economic powers can be made. The first and foremost trend was the center's tendency to grant more power to the provincial and subprovincial governments in Guangdong since 1978. The center has delegated extensive administrative, fiscal and economic powers, which has greatly enhanced the capacity of these local governments to mobilize resources from society, promote economic development, and pursue other policy goals. The basic idea behind this new wave of decentralization after 1978 was to transfer economic power, rather than funds or resources, because the central government was either tightening its own belt during readjustment, as in 1979-81, or suffering from a growing budget deficit and declining control over investment and resources.

Second, the center also tended to recentralize already-delegated powers in economic management during times of growing social and economic difficulties. These recentralizing efforts, for instance, affected Guangdong in 1982, 1985, and 1989-91. While the general decentralization trend has persisted after 1978, tensions between the Center and the province would intensify during such hard times, as the Center arbitrarily recentralized economic power from the province. Guangdong's reformist leadership publicly voiced its differences over policies with the center during the retrenchment of 1989-91, for example. In an article published in *Qiushi*, Lin Ruo confidently defended the special policies and reminded the center that most of Guangdong's investment came from self-raised funds, not central investment.[95] In particular, one quarter of Guangdong's GDP was realized in the world market while one quarter of its national income and one third of its construction funds originated overseas by 1989.[96] Former Guangdong leaders also implicitly criticized Li Peng's retrenchment and the slow pace of reform in the 1989-91 period. For instance, in April 1991, Ren Zhongyi complained in an article in *Nanfang Ribao* that the special policies approved in 1988 "have not yet been fully implemented."[97]

Third, the basic elements of central-provincial relations have continued to be defined mainly by a number of central-level political decisions, not authoritative constitutional provisions. Each of the steps toward decentralization of power to Guangdong since 1978 coincided with the ascendancy of market-oriented reformists in the central leadership, which led to a convergence of central and provincial government objectives. Guangdong province has been performing the role of pacesetter in reform as it provides a valuable model and serves as an ally for market-oriented reformers at the central level.

Finally, this new relationship is not based on an across-the-board change in central-provincial relations, since these provisions confer special treatment for only two provinces. While Guangdong and Fujian enjoy policy privileges one step ahead of the rest of the nation in reform and opening, other provinces have been lobbying hard with the center for similar treatment and were fast catching up with the two provinces in the late 1980s. Not only has the change in relations between the center and Guangdong fueled more lobbying and bargaining between the center and other provinces, but the relationship itself was also subject to swings in leadership and policy at the apex of the Chinese political system. The lack of a constitutional framework that stabilizes and specifies the powers and responsibilities of the central and provincial governments exacerbates the tendency of Chinese leaders to "play to the provinces" in their struggle for power. Consequently, central-provincial relations are often in a state of flux caused by periodic economic and political fluctuations.

The above analysis suggested that the inherent instability and lack of institutionalization of central-provincial relations have persisted after 1978. Major efforts have been made by Deng Xiaoping to protect his reform and open policy after 1992, but the conclusion of the 14th Party Congress in the fall of 1992, and the first session of the Eighth National People's Congress in the spring of 1993 are unlikely to stabilize central-provincial relations in the run-up to the post-Deng era. With the launching of economic reforms that affect the resources and power of the central government, this relationship has clearly moved away from the more hierarchical pattern of the pre-reform era toward one characterized by intense bargaining, competition, and cooperation, between the two levels. In sum, echoing other contributions in this volume, this chapter argues that the changing relationship between the central government and Guangdong Province has increased the capacities of provincial authorities at the expense of the central government in most instances. Nonetheless, the center retained control over some levers of power (e.g. personnel appointments) and some of the provincial government's powers were dispersed to enterprises and subprovincial governments. Hence the balance of policy power between the center and the province is not simply a zero sum game.

Prospects in the 1990s

The future pattern of relations between the central government and Guangdong depends upon the interplay of domestic and external forces that are still emerging, but several factors favorable to Guangdong will clearly be relevant in the 1990s. First, Guangdong will remain a heavyweight player in Chinese politics in the post-Deng era because of its economic prowess. Having remained one step ahead in reform and opening, it has changed from a relatively backward area into a front-runner of China's economy. The province's GDP, national income, total retail sales, and exports all ranked number one in the nation in 1991.[98] Guangdong also established itself as a powerhouse of external economic activities, acquiring 50 percent of China's foreign direct investment and contributing over one third of the nation's total exports.[99] The province today has stronger bargaining power vis-a-vis the Center and will likely oppose any policies that would have adverse effects on its local economy.

Second, the entrenchment of a localized and reformist leadership in Guangdong has strengthened the province's new assertiveness in pursuing its interests. Today, most leading provincial positions are in the hands of local cadres who are either Guangdong natives or veterans who made their careers there. In 1988, about 44 percent of the Party Secretaries and Governors in China were natives of the provinces where they worked and 73 percent spent their entire career in the same province.[100] In Guangdong, however, the Party Secretary (Lin Ruo) and all three Deputy Secretaries as well as the Governor (Ye Xuanping) and one third of the Vice Governors were natives in 1988.[101] The situation has not changed much since 1988. Perhaps equally important, a staunch pro-reform leadership at the subprovincial level has emerged as well. The implementation of special policies since 1978 has further motivated provincial officials to become increasingly vocal in defending the province's vested interests. The failure of central conservatives to introduce major changes in fiscal relations with Guangdong (and other coastal areas) and the vocal dissent against their policies by the provincial leadership are clear reminders of the new assertiveness of the more affluent provinces. While the central government may still attempt to re-centralize economic power in the future, the province's new economic position has made drastic changes in this relationship more difficult. As Guangdong no longer depends upon the central government for investment and has a large stake in continuing reform and opening, its risk in defending its parochial interests has declined. With the inevitable passing of the first generation of revolutionaries, the contenders in the succession to Deng will likely appeal to important provinces like Guangdong for political support as well.

The special relations between Guangdong and Hong Kong also remain a very favorable asset for the province in the 1990s. Hong Kong investors have transformed the province, especially the Pearl River Delta, because of their role in its infrastructural development, export processing, real estate, services, and other sectors.[102] With the flourishing of export processing, Hong Kong businessmen have provided more manufacturing jobs in Guangdong (one conservative estimate claims at least 3 million) than in the colony (about 571,181).[103] With only several years left in the countdown to 1997, the province's role in China's efforts to incorporate Hong Kong and Macao and to maintain their social stability and economic prosperity will increase over time. The growing social-economic integration between Hong Kong and Guangdong has closely tied their interests together and compelled mutual cooperation and coordination on many fronts. Such special interdependence between the two areas will not be ignored by the central leadership, nor easily forgotten by the provincial authorities. After more than a decade of special policies, with the capacity of the state in exercising its many economic powers now significantly devolved to provincial authorities, Guangdong clearly possesses substantial power and resources that enable it to manage relations with the center effectively. How such provincial power will reshape China's political system is still far from clear. More certain is that the role of Guangdong, as well as that of the other rich provinces in China's political economy, will only grow as the 21st century approaches.

Notes

1. *Far Eastern Economic Review* (hereafter FEER), April 4, 1991, pp. 21-29.

2. The most comprehensive treatment of the province under reform in English is: Ezra Vogel, *One Step Ahead in China: Guangdong Under Reform* (Cambridge: Harvard University Press, 1989). Also see Toyojiro Maruya, ed. *Guangdong: "Open Door" Economic Development Strategy* (H.K.: Center of Asian Studies, the University

of Hong Kong, and Institute of Developing Economies, 1992). For a systematic and updated analysis of the Pearl River Delta, see Pak-Wai Liu, et al., *China's Economic Reform and Development Strategy of the Pearl River Delta* (Hong Kong: Nanyang Commercial Bank Ltd., 1992).

3. The "center" (zhongyang) in central-provincial relations refers to the "State Council and its commissions, ministries, and leadership small groups in Beijing as well as the Party Politburo, Secretariat, and the organs of the Central Committee." However, the term "central government," "central authorities," and "center" will be used interchangeably in this chapter. See Kenneth Lieberthal & Michel Oksenberg, *Policy Making in China* (Princeton, N.J.: Princeton University Press, 1988), p. 138. Similarly, the term "provincial government" or "provincial authorities" will be used to refer to the provincial party committee and provincial government.

4. Gabriel Almond & G. Bingham Powell, Jr. *Comparative Politics: System, Process, and Policy*. 2nd ed. (Boston: Little, Brown and Co., 1978).

5. One of the most insightful recent contributions is Joel Migdal, *Strong Societies, Weak States*, (Princeton: Princeton University Press, 1989), pp. 4-5.

6. Samuel P. Huntington, *Political Order in Changing Societies* (New Haven: Yale University Press, 1968).

7. A constitution can be defined as the "collection of written and unwritten principles and rules that identify the sources, purposes, uses, and restraints of public power." Vernon Bogdanor, ed. *The Blackwell Encyclopedia of Political Science* (Oxford: Basil Blackwell, 1991), p. 142.

8. Local governments refer to both provincial and subprovincial levels. My focus in this chapter is on the relations between the central and the provincial levels.

9. See Articles 89 and 91 of the Constitution. *Beijing Review*, No. 52, December 27, 1982, pp. 10-52.

10. I share the view of Zhao Suisheng in his "The Feeble Political Capacity of a Strong One-Party Regime--An Institutional Approach Toward the Formulation and Implementation of Economic Policy in Post-Mao Mainland China (Part Two)," *Issues and Studies* 26 (February 1990), pp. 35-74.

11. The quote is from Zhao Suisheng, op.cit., p. 58.

12. *South China Morning Post* (hereafter SCMP), March 21, 1993, p. 8.

13. Richard Lowenthal, "The Post-Revolutionary Phase in China and Russia," *Studies in Comparative Communism* 16 (Autumn 1983), pp. 191-201.

14. Migdal, op. cit., pp. 279-286.

15. Christine Wong, "Central-Local Relations in an Era of Fiscal Decline: The Paradox of Fiscal Decentralization in Post-Mao China," *China Quarterly* 128 (December 1991), pp. 701-706.

16. See the works of Audrey Donnithorne, Nicholas Lardy, Lin Zhimin, Michel Oksenberg, Susan Shirk, James Tong, Wang Shaoguang, and Christine Wong. Also see Reeitsu Kojima, "The Growing Authority of Provincial-Level Governments," *The Developing Economies 30* (December 1992), pp. 315-346.

17. This is the theme of Ezra Vogel's classic study, *Canton Under Communism*, (Cambridge: Harvard University Press, 1969).

18. Ibid., especially Chapters 3 and 5. Localism refers to demands for greater power for local cadres or resistance to central policies.

19. Vogel, *One Step*, pp. 211-216.

20. Susan Shirk, "Playing to the Provinces: Deng Xiaoping's Political Strategy of Economic Reform," *Studies in Comparative Communism 23* (Autumn/Winter 1990), pp. 227-258.

21. Ibid., p. 21.

22. Ibid.

23. David Shambaugh, *The Making of a Premier: Zhao Ziyang's Provincial Career*, (Boulder: Westview Press, 1984), Chap. 5.

24. Capital investment in the province only ranged from 2.6 percent of the national total in the 1953-57 period to 4.7 percent in the 1963-65 period. Zhongguo Tongjiju, *Zhongguo Gudingzicantouzi Tongiziliao 1950-85*, (Beijing: Zhongguo Tongji Chubanshe, 1987), p. 53.

25. The annual growth of Guangdong's Gross Output Value of Agriculture (GOVA) of 2.55 percent was slower than the national average of 4.0 percent while growth in its Gross Output Value of Industry (GOVI) of 9.7 percent also lagged behind the national average of 10.7 percent. Guangdong figures are calculated from Guangdongsheng Tongjiju, *Guangdong Tongji Nianjian* (hereafter GTN), (Guangzhou: Guangdongsheng Tongjiju 1986), p. 87. National figures are from Carl Riskin, *China's Political Economy*, (N.Y.: Oxford University Press, 1988), p. 185.

26. For a more extended analysis of the interactions between the center and Guangdong over the special policies, see my chapter in Yeung Yue-man & David Chu, eds., *Guangdong: Survey of a Province Under Rapid Change* (H.K.: The Chinese University Press, forthcoming).

27. Text of the report can be found in Guangdongshengwei, ed. *Zhongyang Dui Guangdong Gongzuo Zhishi Huibian (The Collection of Central Directives regarding Guangdong's Work, hereafter ZDGGZH) 1979-82*, pp. 20-30. The analysis in this chapter provides only a summary of the most important provisions of "special policies, flexible measures."

28. Ibid., pp. 19 and 23-24. All revenues minus the tariff and income from centrally- managed units would be defined as local revenues.

29. Only 30 percent of above-baseline earnings from export would have to be handed over to the center. Nonetheless, the province had to enter into a foreign trade contract with the central government under which its export cost rate would be fixed, and export losses above the 1978 baseline would still be mainly borne by Guangdong. This contract was terminated for a variety of reasons in 1984.

30. The province would have more freedom over price reform and price management, such as expanding the scope of locally-set prices and changing the prices of locally-produced products. Equally significant provisions for labor management were allowed so that the province would issue bonuses above the national level and abolish national control over labor targets.

31. Enterprises still under central control included railways, ports, the postal service and telecommunications, civil aviation, and banking enterprises, as well as national defense and research.

32. For instance, while the center still monopolized the trade of some profitable products and export quotas, the province was granted not only more authority

over existing branches of foreign trade companies, but also the power to form provincial foreign trade companies, and to use its own retained foreign exchange to import and manage the trade of locally produced goods.

33. One useful work on the SEZs is George Crane, *The Political Economy of Special Economic Zones in China*, (New York: M.E. Sharpe, 1990).

34. *ZDGGZH 1979-82*, op. cit., pp. 61-71.

35. Two speeches by Gu Mu on May 27 and June 12, 1981 made it amply clear that he and Zhao Ziyang wanted to grant more flexibility to the two provinces. *ZDGGZH 1979-82*, op. cit., pp. 152-160.

36. Since Guangdong would have the power to manage technical renovation projects, the center would no longer appropriate funds for such purposes.

37. Ibid., pp. 162-179.

38. In fact, the provisions regarding the SEZs constituted the major part of the document. Ibid., p. 166.

39. Ibid.

40. Exceptions included liquor, tobacco, sugar and watches.

41. The communique of the meeting was promulgated as Central Document (1981) No. 5. Ibid., pp. 128-131.

42. Ibid., pp. 245-246.

43. Ibid., pp. 308-309.

44. See Deng's comments in *ZDGGZH 1983-85*, pp. 123-127.

45. Ibid., p. 378.

46. In addition to the power to handle export of centrally-controlled products after fulfil export plans, Guangdong would receive a certain number of quotas and export licenses from the Ministry of Foreign Economic Relations and Trade (hereafter MOFERT) and could then issue them independently.

47. See Crane, op. cit., Chapter 5.

48. Ibid.

49. In fact, Guangdong and Hainan officials received rather lenient treatment for their wrongdoing.

50. The 1988 document that approved Guangdong as a comprehensive reform area went far beyond the demands in this 1987 proposal. The text is in *ZDGGZH 1986-87*, Vol. II, pp. 370-375.

51. For instance, MOFERT would give special consideration to Guangdong's exports that required export quotas or licenses. The province would still receive a fixed number of quotas and licenses and enjoy the power to distribute them independently. Further, the province would be given a quota in importing commodities restricted by the central government each year as well as the autonomy to decide the level of import within that quota.

52. With only several exceptions, the management of most prices and fees controlled by the central government would be decentralized to the province.

53. Yang Xiaofei, *Shengzhengfu De Zhizhu Xingwei--Kaifang Gaige Shiqi De Guangdong Zhengfu* (The Provincial Government's Autonomy: Guangdong Provincial Government in the Reform and Opening Era), M. Phil. Thesis, The Chinese University of Hong Kong, June 1990, pp. 53-4.

54. *FEER*, April 4, 1991, pp. 21-29. Various 1990-91 speeches and articles by Li Peng, Zou Jiahua, a newly appointed Vice Premier and the head of the State

Planning Commission, and Chen Jinhua, the new head of the State Commission for Economic System Reform, all testified to tendencies to centralize economic power at the central level.

55. *FEER*, October 9, 1990, pp. 68-69.

56. *Ming Pao*, March 19, 1991, p. 6.

57. Zhonggong Shenzhen Shiwei Xuanchuanbu, ed. *Deng Xiaoping yu Shenzhen* (Deng Xiaoping and Shenzhen), (Shenzhen: Haitian Chubanshe, 1992), pp. 6-7.

58. On the issue of financial reform, Zhu suggested that a fixed percentage of savings be allowed as credits, a fixed percentage of national income be issued as bonds, and a fixed amount of foreign exchange bonds be issued. *Nanfang Ribao* (hereafter NFRB), March 25, 1992, p. 1.

59. *Ming Pao*, October 19, 1992, p. 6.

60. See Maria Hsia Chang, "China's Future: Regionalism, Federation, or Disintegration," *Studies in Comparative Communism 25* (September 1992), pp. 211-227.

61. David S.G. Goodman, "Provinces Confronting the States?" in *China Review 1993*, eds. Kuan Hsin-chi and Maurice Brosseau, (H.K.: The Chinese University Press, 1992), pp. 3.1-3.19.

62. The following counties have been upgraded to cities in 1992 and early 1993: Nanhai, Panyu, Shunde, Taishan, and Kaiping.

63. See Vogel, *One Step*, op. cit., Chapter 7.

64. The following draws from John P. Burns, "China's Nomenklatura System," *Problems of Communism 36* (September-October 1987), pp. 36-51.

65. James Wang, *Contemporary Chinese Politics 4th ed.* (New Jersey: Prentice-Hall, 1992), pp. 86-89.

66. The following draws upon Liu Lie, et al., eds. *Zhonghua Renmin Gongheguo Guojia Jigou* (The State Structure of the People's Republic of China), (Harbin: Harbin Chubanshe, 1988), pp. 98 and 133, and Benshu Bianxiezu, *Jiancha Gongzuo Wenda* (Questions and Answers about Supervision), (Beijing: Zhishi Chubanshe, 1992).

67. Su Tinglin and Zhu Qingfang, eds. *Renshixue Daolun* (Introduction of Personal Work), (Beijing: Beijing Shifanxueyuan Chubanshe, 1992), p. 114; Su Yutang, ed., *Difang Jigou Gaige Yanjiu* (Research on Local Government Organs), (Beijing: Zhonggong Zhongyang Dangxiao Chubanshe, 1992), pp. 462-468.

68. Su Tinglin and Zhu Qingfang, eds., pp. 128-129.

69. Vogel, *One Step*, op. cit., p. 88.

70. According to Hong Kong reports, the list of cadres being investigated included many officials that achieved prominence in the reform decade, and hence, might have close ties with Zhao Ziyang. The most well-known ones included Yu Fei, Vice Governor of Guangdong, and Liang Guangda, Mayor of Zhuhai. See, *Ming Pao*, September 8, 1989, p. 7 and *Sing Tao Evening News*, November 4, 1989, p. 7.

71. These two cadres were respectively Xu Yunian and Zhang Futang, Director and Deputy Director of Guangdong's Commission of Foreign Economic Relations and Trade; *Ming Pao*, September 8 and October 8, 1989, p. 14.

72. This story was circulated in Hong Kong and Guangdong.

73. Talks of removing Ye Xuanping from Guangdong surfaced in the Hong Kong press in the fall of 1989. See *SCMP*, September 2, 1989, p. 10.

74. *World Journal*, May 11, 1991, p. 8.

75. The article was by Wang Hao, *Zhongguo Jingbao*, January 13, 1989, p. 2.

76. Su Yutung, ed., op. cit., p. 464.

77. Guojia Jigou Bianzhiweiyuanhui Bangongshi, ed. *China Government Organizations 1991* (Beijing: Renshi Chubanshe, 1992), pp. 81-82.

78. Wang Zuo, et al., op. cit., pp. 20-23.

79. *NFRB*, January 28, 1993, p. 2.

80. *ZDGGZH 1979-82*, op. cit., pp. 19 and 23-4. Except for tariffs and income from centrally-managed units, all revenues would be designated as local revenues. Using 1978 figures of foreign exchange income as a baseline, the province could keep all above-baseline incomes from assembling, processing, compensation trade, and joint-ventures, and from non-trade sources, and remit only 30 percent of above-baseline earnings from export.

81. Unless otherwise specified, the data in the following discussion draws from Wang Zou, et al., pp. 7-8 and 47-86; Lin Dengyun, "Gaige de Tupokou Ziyi: Guangdong Caizheng Gaige de Youyichangshi," *Guangdong Caizheng* (Guangdong Provincial Finance), No. 4, 1992, pp. 8-10; Shi Ri, "Guangdong Shinian Caizheng Zhichu de Shizheng Fengxi," (An Empirical Analysis on Ten-Years' Financial Autonomy in Guangdong), *Guangdong Caizheng*, No. 2, 1991, pp. 17-21; Zhou Kai, "Dui Guangdong Caizheng Shangjiao Zhuangkuang de Bianzheng Renshi," (A Dialectic Analysis on Guangdong's Financial Remittance to the Central Government), *Guangdong Caizheng*, No. 2, 1992, pp. 47-50.

82. Guowuyuan Zonghesi (Coordinating Bureau of the State Council), *Zhili Jingji Huanjing, Zhengdun Jingji Zhixu, Quanmian Shenhua Gaige* (Improving Economic Environment, Reorganizing Economic Order, and Intensifying Reform (Beijing: Dadi Chubanshe, 1989), p. 115.

83. The Industrial and Commercial Tax was shared equally between the center and Guangdong after exceeding a centrally-decided baseline in the pre-1990 period, but it turned into a source of central revenue after 1990.

84. Wang Zuo, et al, op. cit., p. 62.

85. The same applied to other localities. See Christine Wong, op. cit., pp. 701-706.

86. Wang Zuo, et al., op. cit., p. 73.

87. Ibid., p. 74.

88. Guangdong Nianjian Bianzuan Weiyuanhui, ed. *Guangdong Nianjian 1989* (hereafter GN) (Guangzhou: Guangdong Renmin Chubanshe 1989), p. 205.

89. Wang Zuo, et al., op. cit., p. 73.

90. Lin Ruo, "Gaige Kaifang yu Guangdong Jingji de Fazhan" (Reform and Opening to the Outside World), *Qiushi* (Seeking Truth), No. 18, September 16, 1989, pp. 27-32 and "Several Points of Understanding on Developing the Socialist Commodity Economy," *NFRB*, March 11, 1991, p. 3 in FBIS-CHI-91-054, March 20, 1991, p. 35.

91. Wang Zuo, et al., op. cit., pp. 62-64.

92. The actual increase was 1.89 times. General Planning Department, Ministry of Finance, *China Finance Statistics* (1950-1990) (Beijing: Science Press, 1992), p. 204.

93. Ibid., pp. 78, 157, 204, and 232.

94. Ibid., pp. 194 and 204.

95. Lin Ruo, "Gaige Kaifang yu Guangdong Jingji di Fazhan," *Qiushi*, No. 18, September 16, 1989, p. 27.

96. Ibid., p. 30.

97. *NFRB* April 3, 1991, in FBIS-CHI-91-071, April 12, 1991, pp. 54-55.

98. Guangdong's per capita GDP and national income ranked fifth in the nation. See *Guangdong Tongji Nianjian 1992* (Beijing: Zhongguo Tongji Chubanshe 1992), p. 515, and Guojia Tongjiju (State Statistical Bureau), *A Statistical Survey of China* (Beijing: Zhongguo Tongji Chubanshe, 1992), pp. 7, 12, 71 and 94.

99. These were adjusted 1991 figures. See Liu, et al., pp. 29.

100. Xiaowei Zhang, "Provincial Elite in Post-Mao China," *Asian Survey 31* (June 1991), pp. 516 and 526. Both Deputy Secretaries and Vice-Governors were included.

101. *GN 1989*, op. cit., p. 71.

102. For a discussion of the latest developments in the Delta, please see my chapter in Joseph Cheng and Maurice Brosseau, eds. *China Review 1993* (H.K.: The Chinese University Press, forthcoming).

103. *Ming Pao*, June 29, 1991, p. 34; and *Hong Kong 1993* (H.K.: Hong Kong Government Printer), p. 405.

10

Reform and Shanghai: Changing Central-Local Fiscal Relations

Lin Zhimin

The latest round of fiscal decentralization, a key part of China's economic reform since 1979, has had a dubious impact on places like Shanghai, a provincial-level municipality. For many years, Shanghai served as the economic powerhouse and cash cow of the nation. From 1959 to 1979, Shanghai contributed, on average, one-eighth of the nation's industrial output and one-sixth of all government income.[1] On the other hand, Shanghai itself had little control over its vast resources. From 1949 to 1980, Shanghai had to remit more than 86 percent of its income to the central government,[2] leaving the city stripped of funds which could have been spent on such critical local needs as housing, transportation, communications, and the environment.[3] So when decentralization started in 1979, Shanghai was as eager as any other province to benefit from it.

It turned out, however, that the path toward greater local control of fiscal resources was complicated in the Shanghai case. Unlike Guangdong, whose gains from the latest round of fiscal decentralization were overwhelming,[4] Shanghai had to see its revenue level stagnate or even decline for the better part of the 1980s before it would receive a more favorable revenue-sharing agreement with the central government in 1988. It was not until the end of the 1980s that Shanghai seemed to have found ways to significantly enhance its power in revenue mobilization and local spending.

The experience of Shanghai thus serves as a good illustration of the complexity of the latest round of fiscal decentralization in China. It also highlights the importance of local strategy in helping to convert economic reform programs to local advantages. The rest of this chapter is designed to probe Shanghai's response to the latest round of fiscal decentralization and evaluate its gains and limits. The first section will lay out the basic pattern of Shanghai-central fiscal relations prior to the current reform period. Section two will discuss how these patterns were broken and to what extent this could be attributed to Shanghai's own strategy. The third section will evaluate the changes in Shanghai's fiscal relations with the center in the context of the overhaul of China's fiscal management system.

Shanghai under the Old Fiscal Management System

Shanghai's pre-reform fiscal relations with the center symbolized the kind of relationship that tilted to central control but in a subtle way. The city was rich in revenue but poor in cash. There was a local budget but the city itself had little say in local spending. Despite its standing as a major municipal government, Shanghai had little rule-making power, and little flexibility in implementing these rules.

Revenue-Rich but Cash-Poor

Shanghai had been the nation's most important commercial center well before the 1949 revolution. However, as late as 1957, Shanghai's revenue base remained small. The total local revenue in that year was 462 million yuan, or only 1.49 percent of the nation's total.[5] In 1958, the center transferred jurisdiction over a large number of state-owned enterprises (SOEs) to Shanghai (480 out of 536 centrally-administered SOEs were located in Shanghai) as part of the Great Leap Forward movement.[6] As a result, Shanghai's revenue shot up to 8.51 billion, or 17.47 percent of the nation's total. That ratio has remained at essentially the same level ever since.

In addition, the center gave Shanghai special treatment that guaranteed the city a much higher revenue growth rate than that of most provinces. This special treatment focused particularly on SOEs, since their income constituted the bulk of Shanghai's income. For years, Shanghai's SOEs enjoyed a higher profit margin than their counterparts elsewhere, for they received a steady supply of low-priced raw materials and enjoyed guaranteed shares of the domestic market and high prices for the goods they produced. All these benefits helped Shanghai achieve an annual revenue growth rate more than 10 percentage points higher than the national average.[7]

In return, Shanghai was able to produce more revenue than any of the provinces. However, once these revenues were generated, it was the center and not the city that decided how they should be distributed. Shanghai not only had to remit to the center nine cents on every dollar it earned, but it was reminded time and again that the reason Shanghai was rich in revenues was thanks to the "contributions" made by the center and other localities.[8]

Local Expenditures but Central Decisions

A second aspect of Shanghai's pre-reform fiscal relations with the center was overwhelming central control over Shanghai's local expenditures. To be sure, Shanghai's local expenditures, if measured per capita, were among the highest in the nation.[9] In 1981, for example, Shanghai's per capita local expenditure was 141 yuan, ranking fifth in the nation. The problem, however, was that Shanghai had little control over how the money was divided and spent. One good indicator of this was

TABLE 10.1: Shanghai Expenditures (1950-1983)*

Categories of Spending	Percentage of Total Expenditures
Capital Construction**	39.88
Enterprise Renovation	6.40
Science and Technology	7.37
Enterprise Circulation Funds	6.48
Agriculture	3.04
City Renovation	3.85
Culture, Education and Health	17.17
Social Welfare	1.32
Administration	5.97
Others	8.52

* 1983 is used as the cut-off point because, while the latest round of fiscal decentralization started in 1980, it did not affect Shanghai significantly until 1984.
** This figure covers all capital construction expenditures including those of centrally-administered SOEs located in Shanghai.

Source: Chen Minzi, "Wuanshan Shanghaishi Difang Caizheng de Yanjiu", in *Shanghai Jingji Fazhan Zhanlue Yanjiu* (Study of Shanghai's Economic Development Strategy), (Shanghai: Renmin Chubanshe, 1985), p.243.

the fact that the distribution of local spending money did not necessarily reflect the priorities of the city. TABLE 10.1 shows the breakdown of Shanghai's total expenditures from 1950 to 1983.

Almost half of Shanghai's expenditures were on industrial projects. Many of these projects reflected the needs of central planners rather than those of city officials, who would have preferred more spending on such items as city renovation and education that would benefit its citizens more directly.

Nor did Shanghai have much control over how the money would be spent once it was divided. For example, in the largest spending category--capital construction investments--most spending decisions were made directly by the relevant central ministries. From 1953 to 1978, Shanghai spent a total of 18.37 billion yuan in that category. But 13.53 billion yuan or 72.9 percent of this amount was funded by central ministries.[10] Other spending categories such as funding for research in science and technology were in fact grants from the central government, only earmarked as local expenditures.

Little Power in Rule-Making and Implementation

By any standard, Shanghai served as an important link in the chain of command in China's fiscal management system, commanding an economy larger than that of many third world countries. However, for the most part, Shanghai had virtually no rule-making power in fiscal management. The city's annual budget was strictly subject to the consolidated state budget. Indeed, Shanghai's own budgets served as no more than an accounting device, mainly for the purpose of maintaining the unity of the national fiscal management system.[11]

Nor did Shanghai have flexibility in revenue collection. Tax categories and rates were decided by the center. The only discretionary funds the city had were the few surcharges allowed by the center (reduced to only one--a surcharge on the industrial and commercial tax--after 1962). The amount was marginal--from 1958 to 1965, it amounted to only 1.7 percent of Shanghai's total income.[12] Shanghai could also appropriate unused reserve funds (3 percent of local expenditures) for its own projects and collect limited user fees on public services. But none of these was big enough to allow Shanghai sufficient room in discretionary spending.

Shanghai also had little say in dealing with lower levels of government and SOEs.[13] Policies in this regard were handed down by the center and implemented universally. In other words, following the way in which the center yielded its power over the provinces, the city was supposed to collect almost all the profits made by SOEs and pay for almost all their expenses.[14]

A Two-Way Relationship and Its Impact

In short, pre-reform fiscal relations between Shanghai and the center were a two-way street. Shanghai produced a large amount of local income due to a large extent to central policies. The center took in most of the revenues generated in Shanghai. It then rewarded the city with numerous favors. Some of the favors were critical to the city's well-being. During the Cultural Revolution, for example, Shanghai managed to avoid the financial chaos that other provinces suffered. Part of the reason was a central decision to protect Shanghai, so that the "contributions" it made would not be disrupted. Under a campaign called *Quanguo Bao Shanghai* (the whole nation protects Shanghai), Shanghai received steady supplies of scarce materials not always available to other provinces. As a result, Shanghai's economy grew more than 11 percent a year during the whole period of the Cultural Revolution![15]

Taken as a whole, the fiscal relations between Shanghai and the center were not always detrimental to Shanghai, even though the city was sometimes bitter about its lack of control and discretionary funds. On the other hand, such relations came at a hefty cost. They contributed to the chronic underfunding of such items as city renovation, leaving many parts of the city's infrastructure in poor repair. They made SOEs in Shanghai more dependent on central planning than their counterparts, and thus more vulnerable to any changes in the existing system. Moreover, because the existing arrangements served Shanghai reasonably well, the city was caught off-guard when fiscal decentralization began in 1979.

Shanghai's Experience under the Recent Fiscal Decentralization

In 1979, the center decided to spearhead its economic reforms with an extensive program to decentralize fiscal management. Part of the program dealt directly with central-provincial fiscal relations.[16] Under the plan, provinces were entitled to some fixed local income plus certain adjustable income. Once the sharing ratios over these adjustable incomes were decided, provinces could retain any increment they could produce and use it for local purposes. In return, provinces were to be responsible for the majority of spending responsibilities. This new regime, known as "eating in separate kitchens" signaled a major shift in central-provincial fiscal relations.

The changes affected Shanghai as they did other provinces. Shanghai's response can be divided into three phases. From 1979 to 1983, Shanghai missed the opportunity, as did some other provincial-level units, to take full advantage of the new regime of sharing packages. By the end of this period, the city's revenues plummeted, which in turn forced the center to give Shanghai a new revenue sharing regime in 1984. From 1985 to 1988, the city began to come to terms with the changed environment. It managed to retain more revenues for local projects, but it was also confronted with new problems. Meanwhile, the overall revenue situation in Shanghai remained bleak. The center was once again forced to assign a new revenue sharing regime to Shanghai in 1988. Since then, Shanghai's efforts have moved beyond the traditional bargaining over revenue sharing. It has looked for non-conventional ways to enhance its incomes, adjusted spending priorities, and gradually but steadily asserted itself as the true authority in managing its local fiscal matters.

Missed Opportunity, 1979-1983

When the latest round of fiscal decentralization was launched in 1979, Shanghai reacted the way it did before--it waited for the center to apply a similar policy package to all provinces, including the provincial-level municipality of Shanghai. However, the 1980 decision on decentralizing fiscal management took a more parochial approach--it assigned different revenue-sharing regimes to different provinces, ranging from lump-sum contracts in places like Guangdong to multiple-years' fixed sharing ratios for others. Shanghai (along with the municipalities of Beijing and Tianjin), on the other hand, was deliberately left out of the initial round of changes.

Instead, Shanghai was asked to continue the revenue-sharing arrangement it had been under since 1976. Under that arrangement, Shanghai's share of local incomes was a mere 13 percent. While the city was given an additional 150 million yuan a year in central transfers and was entitled to 30 percent of revenues collected beyond the planned targets, the arrangement was seen as very restrictive and unfavorable to Shanghai overall.[17]

Partly to placate Shanghai, the center agreed to give the city some additional funds--200 million yuan in 1980 and 400 million in 1981.[18] But by then, Shanghai's revenue level had already reached a plateau. It could thus no longer count on rapid increases in local revenues to significantly enhance the city's balance sheet.

There were several reasons why Shanghai missed the initial opportunity. The sheer size of Shanghai's revenues made the center less willing to let this cash cow go free. In 1978, Shanghai, Beijing, and Tianjin combined contributed 25.89 billion yuan, or 23.1 percent of total government revenue, with Shanghai alone contributing 16.92 billion, or 15 percent.[19]

TABLE 10.2: Local Spending as a Percentage of Income in Beijing, Tianjin, and Shanghai

	1978	1979	1980	1981	1982	1983*
Beijing	40.39	42.00	28.99	30.22	35.56	49.22
Tianjin	36.97	40.41	35.83	35.92	55.23	52.89
Shanghai	15.37	15.67	10.77	10.93	12.31	14.32

* The percentages are larger than the agreed-upon sharing ratios since local spending here includes central transfers.

Source: *Quanguo Gesheng, Zhiziqu, Zhixiashi, Lishi Tongji Zhiliao Huibian* (Historical Statistics Data of All Provinces, Autonomous Regions, and Municipalities), (Beijing: Chinese Statistical Publishing House, 1991), pp.85, 117, and 336.

Given the uncertainty associated with the ongoing reform and fiscal decentralization program, the center could hardly risk a major fluctuation in income from places like Shanghai. Shanghai was also hurt by a leadership vacuum. Many provinces such as Sichuan, Jiangsu, and Guangdong, which played key roles in the 1980 decision, had access to the central leadership at the time when the decision was made. Shanghai, by contrast, was still paying a price for its close association with the radical faction during the Cultural Revolution--three of the members of the "Gang of Four" came from Shanghai. To make things worse, the post-Gang of Four leadership team sent to Shanghai, led by Su Zhenghua (a general), Ni Zhifu (an official from Beijing) and Peng Cong (the former party boss of Shanghai's neighbor, Jiangsu) had closer ties with Mao's immediate successor, Hua Guofeng, than with the rising reformist group led by Deng Xiaoping.[20] This group was replaced around 1979.[21] Their successors: Chen Guodong, Hu Lijiao, and Wang Daohan, were of marginal national stature--only Chen held the rank of member of the central committee of the Chinese Communist Party at the time of the appointments. As a result, there was not a strong and consistent voice for the city at the central level when key decisions were made.

Shanghai's own inaction was also to blame. Still nostalgic for the good old days, officials from Shanghai reportedly did not take the challenge seriously before the 1980 decision. Nor did they press hard for concessions from the center after the decision.[22] By contrast, Beijing and Tianjin, while also denied access to the new revenue-sharing regimes, worked hard to at least obtain better revenue-sharing ratios. TABLE 10.2 shows the different results each city achieved in this regard.

For Shanghai, the costs of missing the initial round of fiscal decentralization were doubled by the fact that the ongoing reform started to cut into the profit margins of Shanghai's traditionally highly profitable SOEs. Using *zhijing lishuili* (profit and tax ratios) as a parameter,[23] the fall in profit margins in Shanghai was startling. In 1980, the ratio was 75.4 percent for all SOEs in Shanghai, way above the national average of 24.1 percent. By 1984, however, that ratio fell to 63.0 percent while the national average remained at 23.2 percent.[24]

The fall in the profit margin of SOEs was particularly damaging to Shanghai's government incomes, since 91.7 percent of the city's total industrial output came from SOEs as opposed to the national average of 77.6 percent.[25] This meant that while Shanghai's industrial output continued to grow at 4.3 percent a year from 1980 to 1984, the profits and taxes contributed by Shanghai's SOEs actually fell by 4.8 percent.

As a result, Shanghai's overall revenues began to fall in 1982. Total local income was 17.47 billion yuan in 1980 but fell to 15.64 billion by 1983. The next year, total income edged up a little but remained far below the 1980 level.[26]

Searching for Change, 1984-1988

This fiscal predicament prompted Shanghai to search for solutions. Under the reforms, provinces had a number of ways to enhance control over their fiscal resources. According to Christine Wong, these options included: (1) negotiating with the center for a larger local share of revenues; (2) encouraging the growth of the local economy to boost revenues; or (3) reaching outside the budget process to tap other possible sources of income such as extra-budgetary funds.[27]

For Shanghai, however, the choices were more limited. Shanghai's industries were already among the most efficient in the nation. It was thus difficult to expect rapid growth without a major infusion of new investment.[28] From 1979 to 1983, the national average growth in industrial output was 7.63 percent. In Shanghai, the rate was a little more than half of that.

Nor was Shanghai able to tap alternative sources of income as quickly and successfully as some other provinces. Shanghai did not enjoy the special policies given to places like Guangdong which allowed them to offer better deals to attract foreign investment. Shanghai's economy was also too dependent on SOEs, which employed 79.54 percent of the city's urban work force and accounted for 91.18 percent of its industrial output. While other provinces such as Jiangsu boosted incomes from the non-SOEs sectors from 42.3 percent in 1980 to 55.12 percent in 1984 in terms of local revenues, Shanghai managed to lift the ratio to only 18.4 percent in the same year.[29]

Shanghai therefore concentrated its efforts on seeking a better revenue-sharing agreement with the center. The results, however, were mixed.

Beginning in 1983, Shanghai adopted a two-pronged strategy to press for a more favorable revenue-sharing arrangement. On the one hand, the city practiced the tactic of "crying wolf." In article after article, Shanghai began to publicize its precarious fiscal position in local media by using such phrases as *caizheng huapo* (fiscal slide). On the other hand, Shanghai began to draw up ambitious revitalization plans to justify its call for more money.

That strategy worked to some extent. The center was forced to pay more attention to Shanghai's problems. In August 1983, Hu Yaobang, then Party General Secretary, toured Shanghai. He called for reviving Shanghai's leading role in the nation's economic development. Zhao Ziyang, then Premier, held a similar view. Shortly after Zhao's visit in late 1983, he sent an investigative team to Shanghai to help determine what the city needed in order to revitalize its local economy.

Meantime, under a new leadership team led by Rui Xingwen and Jiang Zemin, Shanghai wasted no time in arguing for a new revenue-sharing regime.[30] In a report sent to the center in December 1983, entitled *Guanyu Shanghai Jingji Fazhan Zhanlue de Huibao Tigang* (A Report on Shanghai's Economic Development Strategy),[31] the municipality outlined what it would do for the remainder of the 1980s. The city promised to revitalize its role as the nation's center for international trade, finance, and commerce by opening up more widely and upgrading its industries, concentrating on high-tech sectors. The catch, however, was that in order for Shanghai to achieve these goals, the center was asked to give the city more control over its resources. As the report put it, in addition to Shanghai's own efforts, "It is necessary for various central ministries concerned to offer some help, including delegating power, assigning special policies, and providing needed funds (to Shanghai)."[32]

In February 1984, the State Council formally approved Shanghai's plan. Prior to that, the Ministry of Finance also approved a new revenue-sharing regime for the city, known as *Heding Jishu, Zhonge Fenchen* (verifying base lines and sharing the total). Under the new regime, Shanghai was to receive 1.5 billion yuan spending money a year on top of its actual budget outlay in 1983 of 2.2 billion yuan. The new arrangement was to boost Shanghai's actual revenue retention ratio to 23.54 percent. Moreover, the deal was to be good for six years.[33]

The new revenue-sharing arrangement gave Shanghai a needed shot in the arm. In 1985, Shanghai's expenditures rose more than 52 percent, to an unprecedented 4.61 billion yuan. In particular, the funds used on city renovation increased by 74.5 percent.[34] The new money made it possible for the city to start a series of local projects it had long planned but lacked the cash to pay for.

But the 1984 revenue-sharing regime was not a panacea for all the fiscal problems Shanghai was facing. To be sure, the amount of remittance the city paid to the center each year fell steadily as a result of the new regime, as shown in TABLE 10.3.

TABLE 10.3: Shanghai's Revenue Sharing, 1983-1988 (Billion Yuan)

	Remittance to the center	GDP(Percent of change)	Local Revenue	Local Spending
1983	--	35.2	15.6	2.2
1984	13.69	39.1 (+11.1)	16.4 (+ 5.1)	3.0 (+36.4)
1985	13.53	46.7 (+19.4)	18.4 (+12.2)	4.6 (+53.3)
1986	14.41*	49.1 (+ 5.1)	17.9 (- 2.7)	5.9 (+28.3)
1987	11.99	54.5 (+11.0)	16.9 (- 4.6)	5.4 (- 8.5)
1988	10.50	64.8 (+18.9)	16.2 (- 4.2)	6.6 (+22.3)

* Planned target, actual figure not available.

Sources: Remittances are from Shanghai's yearly budget reports. All other figures are from *Lishi Tongji Ziliao Huibian*, pp.311, 335, and 336.

TABLE 10.4: Central Government Subsidies to Shanghai, 1985-1988 (Billion Yuan)

Year	Total Fiscal Subsidies*	As Percent of Local Expenditures
1985	0.673	14.6
1986	0.768	13.0
1987	1.190	22.1
1988	2.457	37.3

* This includes all subsidies borne by local budgets, but does not include grants-in-kind from the central government. In particular, it includes subsidies on staple and non-staple food, consumer goods, public services and raw materials used by producers of these goods. Since the subsidies of the last category are also counted as enterprise losses, they are not reported in Shanghai's yearly budget under the category of price subsidies, which covers only the first three categories.

Source: *Shanghai Caishui* (Shanghai Finance and Tax), No.7, 1990, p.26.

The additional money retained meant it was possible for Shanghai to spend more. Not surprisingly, overall local spending went up sharply. However, as seen in the same table, the overall revenue picture was far from bright. Since 1986, despite the decent GDP growth rate, Shanghai experienced another round of fiscal decline, which meant there was less additional money available to the city than there would have been had overall revenue grown the way it used to.

The profit margins of Shanghai's SOEs continued to decline precipitously. From 1983 to 1988, the average *zhijing lishuili* fell from 65.65 percent to 31.98 percent.[35] More and more SOEs began to lose money in their operations. The increase in the total losses of SOEs in Shanghai was alarming. In 1987, the total loss was 586 million yuan. In 1988, the loss jumped by 65 percent to reach 1.48 billion yuan.[36]

What made Shanghai particularly unhappy was that the decline of profits at SOEs was by no means even. From 1984 to 1988, the revenue contributed by Shanghai's own SOEs fell sharply. By contrast, the amount of revenues generated by centrally-administered SOEs located in Shanghai more than doubled, from 4.79 to 10.01 billion yuan.[37] The reason was simple: most of Shanghai's own SOEs were outdated and poorly equipped. They were also charged higher tax rates than their counterparts.[38]

The ongoing economic reform also diverted more and more funds from the city's budget. The effort to allow SOEs to retain a portion of their profits meant less money for the city's coffers. In 1985 alone, SOEs in Shanghai retained a total of 2.25 billion yuan of their profits, a 53 percent increase over 1984.[39] While not all the money would have become part of Shanghai's budgetary income should the change not have occurred, it reduced the revenue base on which the city's incomes depended.

Another diversion came in the form of new spending obligations, or the simple transfer of profit from one locality to another. Since the beginning of reforms, the center often issued new policies such as a required cut in taxes paid by non-SOEs, letting provinces pick up the tab. Similarly, the increase in the prices of materials still controlled by the center, such as coal, took away profits that would otherwise go to Shanghai's SOEs. It was estimated that these reform-related policies cost Shanghai about 1 billion yuan in 1986 and another 1.1 billion in 1987.[40]

Shanghai's problem was not confined to revenues. On the expenditures side, problems were also on the rise. Beginning in 1984, the total amount of local expenditures went up sharply. However, a large portion of the increase was due to the fact that government subsidies almost quadrupled, as shown in TABLE 10.4.

To be sure, many of the subsidies were in essence welfare expenditures, since many were distributed on the basis of need, and almost all aimed at offsetting the adverse effects of economic reform on city residents, such as inflation. In many other countries, such expenses are normal government expenditures. What worried Shanghai most, however, was the speed of increase and the growing demand for such subsidies.

The growth of fiscal subsidies outstripped the growth of revenues by a large margin. Given the current rate of increase, it was estimated that even during the period when Shanghai's industrial growth reached 6 percent a year, the added revenues could hardly cover the expansion of subsidies.[41] More importantly, the demand for subsidies was not likely to fall anytime soon unless there were major policy changes. For example, the economic reform meant more volatility in the supply of raw materials. In order to play safe, Shanghai had to stockpile more and more items such as pork, which in turn caused more losses among meat processing factories. By the same token, many of Shanghai's public services such as bus transportation used to be rather profitable. However, reflecting mounting costs as a result of the reforms, one by one these services began to lose money and remained operational only because of large and continued subsidies.

On balance, the 1984 revenue-sharing agreement put Shanghai in a better position in terms of financing important local projects. The city, in turn, used the opportunity to boost its spending significantly. However, by 1987, with stagnant incomes and an increasing diversion of local money to such items as subsidies, the initial benefits of the 1984 regime were exhausted. After local revenues declined for a second consecutive year, Shanghai once again pressed the center for more changes. In a report sent to the center in late 1987, Shanghai formally requested that a series of new policies be implemented to allow the city to become more market-oriented and more focused on the international economy. Of these policies, the city particularly singled out a new revenue-sharing regime that would give Shanghai some true control over its resources.

New Revenue Sharing Scheme and Aftermath (1988-)

In February 1988, the State Council issued Document No.27 (1988), which answered Shanghai's request.[42] Shanghai was allowed to practice a new fiscal contract system starting in 1988. The new regime was similar to the one that Guangdong had received nearly a decade earlier. Under it, Shanghai would remit a lump sum of 10.5 billion yuan a year to the center from 1988 to 1990, and was entitled to retain all additional income. For 1991 and 1992, Shanghai would remit the same amount, and would share 50 percent of any revenues collected over the 16.5 billion yuan base figure.[43]

The package finally put Shanghai on the same footing as Guangdong. In 1987, Shanghai remitted nearly 12 billion yuan to the center. Under the new regime, Shanghai expected to retain an additional 1.4 billion yuan in 1988. Moreover, Shanghai was given a wide range of new authority, including redefined fiscal relations with lower levels of governments. However, the actual benefits associated with the 1988 package turned out to be much smaller than they originally appeared.

The amount of remittance Shanghai had to make each year was still very large. By comparison, Guangdong, even though its total income had reached 10.08 billion yuan in 1988, had to remit to the center a mere 1.54 billion yuan, or 15.3 percent.[44] Given the fact that Shanghai by now had great difficulty in maintaining its current income level, the new lump-sum contract arrangement was actually seen by some officials in Shanghai as more beneficial to the center than to the city, since it allowed the center to lock in a large portion of Shanghai's hard-won revenues. One Shanghai official bluntly suggested that far from getting a windfall from the 1988 arrangement, the city actually *chikuile* (got a rotten deal).[45]

TABLE 10.5 Shanghai Revenue, 1987-1992 (Billion Yuan)

Year	Total Revenue	Budgetary Income	Non-Budgetary Income	ETKPFs*	Self-generated Income**
1987	16.89	16.51	0.38		0.38
1988	16.16	15.36	0.81	0.39	0.42
1989	16.69	15.87	0.82	0.43	0.39
1990	17.00	16.27	0.73	0.30	0.43
1991	17.52	16.51	1.01	0.33	0.68
1992	18.56	17.56	1.00	0.26	0.74

* Energy and Transportation Key Project Funds. This tax was imposed in 1983. Starting in 1988, 30 percent of what a province collected would go directly to local budgetary income. In 1991, the provincial share was raised to 50 percent.
** These include various user-fees the city charged and a number of newly installed items such as land-use fees.

Sources: *Shanghai Tongji Nianjian, 1992*, pp.53-4. The 1992 figures are from *Jiefang Ribao* (Liberation Daily), February 27, 1993.

Furthermore, the 1988 agreement did not rule out the possibility that the center could ask for additional "contributions" from Shanghai should they became necessary. After a nationwide economic retrenchment policy was adopted in late 1988, and especially after the 1989 Tiananmen incident, the center began to take a series of measures aimed at strengthening central control over fiscal resources. For example, Shanghai, like many other provinces, was asked to remit to the center an additional 400 million yuan in 1990 and 570 million a year thereafter.[46]

Fortunately, by now Shanghai had finally realized that it could not walk out of its fiscal predicament by relying solely on a better revenue-sharing deal. In order to revitalize the local economy, Shanghai had to look for ways to be more creative and less confined by the existing fiscal system. It also realized that it had to move fast if it did not want to be left further behind by more prosperous places such as Guangdong or even Jiangsu. As a result, the last few years have seen Shanghai making some real progress in this regard. In particular, Shanghai managed to expand its sources of income, reset its spending priorities, and establish a new fiscal relationship with its subordinates.

Expansion of Income Sources

Since 1988, Shanghai's budgetary income showed little increase, with the exception of 1992 when the high economic growth rate (over 14.8 percent) pushed the revenue level up significantly. On the other hand, non-budgetary incomes, especially the funds collected by the city itself, grew considerably, as shown in TABLE 10.5.

Of the budgetary income, the revenue from SOEs continued to decline, with losses from 1988 to 1992 reaching 1.48, 2.82, 2.87, 2.53, and 2.48 billion yuan respectively.[47] On the other hand, other sources of income went up sharply. Fixed local income ranging from real estate taxes to the newly installed stamp tax went up from less then 500 million in 1987 to over 1.27 billion yuan in 1989.[48]

But the most significant advance Shanghai made was the mobilization of funds that were not included in previous categories of local income, whether budgetary or non-budgetary. First, Shanghai was able to attract more foreign investment and utilize more foreign credits. From 1980 to 1987, Shanghai received a total of US$ 1.18 billion of such funds, of which more than 65 percent came from foreign governments or multinational institutions such as the World Bank. From 1988 to 1991, Shanghai received more than US$4.42 billion in such funds.[49] The infusion of these funds helped to boost Shanghai's economic growth. In 1990, 60 percent of the increase in total industrial output and 40 percent of the increase in total exports came from overseas-funded enterprises.[50] The proliferation of overseas-funded businesses, in turn, offered Shanghai a major and increasing source of income. In 1987, Shanghai collected no more than 193 million yuan in taxes from overseas-funded businesses. In 1990, it collected more than 620 million yuan from the same sector.[51]

Moreover, in 1986, the center approved Shanghai's request to borrow funds directly from the international market.[52] In response, Shanghai set up a special fund to distribute the money generated through this channel. The city provided credits to businesses or projects which used such funds. In return, the portion of taxes remitted by these businesses to the city would be used to repay the loans which were then used to finance still more projects. Using such a device, Shanghai was able to snowball the funds it received from international creditors.[53]

Second, Shanghai was able to utilize resources that were either marginal or not available to the city just a few years earlier. For example, Shanghai issued construction bonds, leased pockets of land, and utilized extra-budgetary funds (EBFs) to help finance the growing cost of city renovations,[54] as shown in TABLE 10.6.

Clearly, Shanghai was able to increase overall spending on the city's infrastructure with more and more financing coming from non-budgetary sources. Indeed, even with funds still appropriated from the budget, Shanghai tried to use these more like loans than credits. In 1988, using the 1.4 billion yuan of additional funds available to the city under new fiscal contract, Shanghai established a separate funding company. This company then distributed the funds to various projects with interest. In this way, Shanghai hoped to undertake more construction projects than it otherwise could.

TABLE 10.6 Shanghai Infrastructure Expenditure, 1987-1992 (Billion Yuan)

Year	Total Expenditure on City Renovation & Construction	Percentage from Budgetary Appropriations
1987	22.32	56.41
1988	26.05	n/a
1989	22.32	n/a
1990	27.67	57.40
1991	38.65	33.42
1992	38.83*	31.83*

* Planned figures.
Sources: Yearly Shanghai Budget Reports.

Because of the use of non-budgetary sources of income, Shanghai was able to generate enough funds to start some costly new infrastructure projects. These include two bridges across the Huangpu River that separates east and west Shanghai, the city's first subway line, and several environmental improvement projects.

Resetting Spending Priorities

In addition to efforts to generate more resources within and outside the budgetary process, Shanghai was also interested in rearranging its spending priorities. These rearrangements had several key elements. First, Shanghai was determined to increase spending on education, scientific research, and cultural items, even though it had many other pressing needs. From 1987 to 1992, such spending went up more than 90 percent, higher than the 75.6 percent increase in total expenditures.[55]

Second, the city tried to curb the rapid increase of fiscal subsidies by setting an overall limit on such expenditures. In 1990, Shanghai pledged to cut government subsidies by 200 million yuan, and managed to do that. By 1992, total subsidies were actually lower than in 1989 by about 12 percent.

Shanghai also introduced a number of reform measures aimed at not only reducing such subsidies but eventually phasing them out. For example, the largest item of fiscal subsidies was staple foods, especially rice and cooking oil. The price of rice supplied by the central government was 0.4 yuan per kilogram in 1985. Since then, the portion supplied by the center declined. Shanghai had to rely more and more on rice imported from other provinces at the market price. In 1990, a kilogram of rice imported from another province cost 1.4 to 1.5 yuan. As a result, in less then five years, Shanghai's subsidies on food items went up five times and counted for 85 percent of total fiscal subsidies. To bring this under control, Shanghai adopted several measures. It allowed residents to turn in unused rice coupons for a small reward (5 kilograms of rice coupons for 0.5 kilograms of cooking oil, for example) so that the actual amount of rice consumed could be reduced. Since 1991, Shanghai went even further. It began a phased process to eliminate rice coupons. Instead, local residents received several yuan a month from the city in subsidies. The goal was two-fold. By shifting from covert subsidies to direct subsidies, the city hoped its residents would be more appreciative of the efforts the city made. Second, since the subsidies-per-capita were fixed, Shanghai hoped to keep the cost at a stable and relatively low level. It was estimated that these changes alone saved the city more than 500 million yuan in subsidies.

But the main thrust of the rearrangement of local spending priorities was the clear decision to rapidly increase investment in infrastructure. Shanghai justified such a strategy by arguing that these investments were preconditions for Shanghai's revival. Indeed, as one official put it, while there was a need to increase spending on almost everything, investment in the city's infrastructure could in fact lower such needs as the city became more attractive to investors, both domestic and international.

There was a political side to the strategy as well. In order to please local residents, Shanghai officials promised to complete ten projects each year that touched upon their urgent concerns. China's 1989 turmoil brought additional pressure on the city to do more to diffuse public discontent. Not surprisingly, some of the major increases in local expenditures from 1987 to 1992 were items that were most visible to local residents, such as spending on city renovation, which jumped 78.7 percent.

Redefining City-Local Fiscal Relations

The 1988 revenue-sharing regime also gave Shanghai broad power to determine its fiscal relations with lower levels of government. Shanghai lagged behind most other provinces in this regard for years. In part this was because Shanghai's overall revenue sharing agreement with the center left it little incentive to sub-contract with districts and counties under the city's jurisdiction.

Since 1988, using its newly-gained power to freely decide its relations with lower levels of government, Shanghai moved quickly to redefine such relations. While the actual provisions accorded to different localities varied, the overall plan was to allow them to retain a fixed portion of revenues collected above a base figure so that they, too, would have a stake in revenue collection. Shanghai also gave its districts and counties full authority to distribute local funds so that the money could be used more efficiently. As a result, the revenues generated by the districts and counties grew more than 11 percent in 1988,[56] 16 percent in 1989,[57] and reached 450 million yuan in 1990.[58]

The new city-local fiscal arrangements were an important part of Shanghai's overall strategy to gain more fiscal control. The additional fiscal efforts by the districts and counties increased Shanghai's overall revenue base. Even better, the city was able to use some of the surplus in local budgets to cover its overall deficit. In 1990, for example, Shanghai's budget deficit was 170 million yuan. Without the contribution made by local governments, the actual deficit would have been more than 250 million yuan.[59]

Boost from the Pudong Project

Shanghai's efforts to expand local authority were reinforced by the central government's decision to develop the Pudong District in early 1990. Billed as the core of the new wave of China's open door policy, the project brought Shanghai an additional 6.5 billion yuan of funds from the center to help build infrastructure in the eastern part of the city over a five-year time span. It also brought Shanghai the authority to implement several special policies it had long hoped for, such as the authority to issue stocks to overseas investors and the decision to allow branches of foreign banks to open in the Shanghai area. All these changes have helped fuel a construction spending spree in Shanghai. In February 1993, the city announced that it would spend a total of 8.8 billion yuan on key construction projects, including 3.4 billion on city renovation alone. If implemented, this would almost double the city's total expenditure in 1995, not including projects exclusively in the Pudong area!

Evaluations and Conclusions

In his 1989 book, *One Step Ahead in China, Guangdong under Reform,* Ezra Vogel wrote:

> The 1980s may well be seen as a turning point in socialist history, when leaders in many countries acknowledged that the socialist system had not achieved the economic progress they had sought. At a time when some were beginning to draw on lessons from the capitalist world to overcome their economic stagnation, Guangdong's leaders enabled their province to take full advantage of its special opportunity to walk a step ahead.[60]

Compared to Guangdong, this paper shows that, for many years, Shanghai was clearly left one step behind. The center, while embracing reform, was not willing to give up its control of key areas such as Shanghai. On the other hand, as a "late-comer", the ability to gain local control became a major test for Shanghai. As discussed above, it took several years for Shanghai to learn the process, and to develop a sound local strategy to make the necessary changes happen.

The Shanghai strategy had several important aspects. First, it was not confrontational. Indeed, the reason Shanghai was able to slowly but gradually obtain more concessions from the center was the fact that the city was able to convince the center that to do so was in the best interests of both Shanghai and the center.

Second, it became clear that as far as gaining local control over fiscal resources was concerned, it was no longer sufficient to confine the thrust of local strategy to a better revenue-sharing agreement with the center. It was the ability to gain access to new opportunities and the policy discretion to turn such opportunities to local advantage (not necessarily the specific amount of central transfers) that would make the difference between gaining concessions and gaining control. Shanghai was finally able to do the latter, and therefore gradually became much more in control of its vast fiscal resources than at any previous time.

Finally, Shanghai's experience also shows that even under the best of circumstances, provincial efforts to gain greater control are not a linear process. Individual actions by provinces are constrained by actions of the center and actions of other provinces. Changes in one area are accompanied by changes in other areas. But the general trend is clear. After more than a decade of changes, even such a stronghold of central planning and central control as Shanghai has finally managed to establish its own identity, gained control over a sufficiently large amount of resources, and learned to convert such resources to concrete local gains. All these changes in Shanghai and other localities helped pave the way for the rise of the provinces as critical actors, not only in local affairs but in China's national affairs as well.

Notes

1. Calculation based on *Quanguo Gesheng, Zizhiqu, Zhixiashi, Lishi Tongji Zhiliao Huibian* (Historical Statistics Data of All Provinces, Autonomous Regions, and Municipalities, Beijing: Zhongguo Tongji Chubanshe, 1991).

2. Chen Minzi, "Wuanshan Shanghaishi Difang Caizheng de Yanjiu", in *Shanghai Jingji Fazhan Zhanlue Yanjiu* (Study of Shanghai's Economic Development Strategy, Shanghai: Renmin Chubanshe, 1985), p. 243.

3. According to one estimate, Shanghai had a deficit in spending on city renovation of about 30 billion yuan from 1940 to 1979. See Xu Reqing, "Wuoguo Chenshi Caizheng Fazhan de Tantao" (An inquiry into the development of city finance in our country). *Shanghai Shehui Kexue Xueshu Jikan*, No.1, 1990.

4. Ezra Vogel, *One Step Ahead in China, Guangdong under Reform* (Cambridge, MA: Harvard University Press, 1989). Toyojiro Maruya, "The Development of the Guangdong Economy and Its Ties with Beijing", in *China Newsletter*, No. 96 (1992), pp. 2-10. I also benefited from Peter Cheung's chapter in this book.

5. Shanghai's revenue and expenditure figures are from *Shanghai Tongji Nianjian, 1992* (Shanghai's Statistical Yearbook, 1992, Beijing: Zhongguo Tongji Chubanshe, 1992) unless otherwise noted.

6. For a detailed account of the transfer, see *Shanghai Shehui Zhuyi Jingji Jianshe Fazhan Jianshi*, 1949-1985 (A brief History of Shanghai's Socialist Economic Construction and Development, 1949-1985, Shanghai: Renmin Chubanshe, 1990), pp. 430-32.

7. From 1953 to 1978, the revenue growth rate nationwide was 7.2 percent. In Shanghai, the rate was 17.5 percent. See *Quanguo Gesheng, Zizhiqu, Zhixiashi, Lishi Tongji Zhiliao Huibian*, op.cit., p. 51.

8. Interestingly enough, Shanghai's official publications seemed to have accepted this line of argument as well. For an example, see *Shanghai Shehui Zhuyi Jingji Jianshe Fazhan Jianshi*, 1949-1985, op.cit., p. 432.

9. *Zhongguo Caizheng Tongji* (Chinese Financial Statistics), 1950-1985, p.93.

10. *Shanghai Jianshe 1949-1985* (Shanghai's Construction, 1949-1985), Shanghai: Kexue Jishu Wenxian Chubanshe, 1989), p.973.

11. This view was expressed by a Shanghai official during an interview with the author in the summer of 1987.

12. *Shanghai Jingji* (1949-1982) (Shanghai's Economy, 1949-1982, Shanghai: Renmin Chubanshe, 1984), p.885. There are two versions of the book. This study uses the internally circulated version, which has more data on Shanghai's budgets.

13. There were 10 city districts and 10 urban counties at the time the current reform started. The numbers changed to 12 districts and 9 counties in 1992.

14. There were some variations in the city's fiscal relations with the 12 counties.

15. Political considerations played a role too. Zhang Chunqiao (a member of the so-called "Gang of Four" who rose to power from Shanghai) wanted Shanghai's economy to grow at a decent rate so that he could take credit for it, since he was also in charge of Shanghai during the heyday of the Cultural Revolution. See *Shanghai Shehui Zhuyi Jingji Jianshe Fazhan Jianshi*, 1949-1985, op.cit., p. 475.

16. For a translation of this document, see *Chinese Economic Studies*, Fall 1990, pp. 40-46.

17. *Shanghai Jingji Tizhi Gaige Shinian* (The 10 Years of Economic System Reform in Shanghai, Shanghai: Renmin Chubanshe, 1990), pp. 113-14.

18. *Shanghai Jingji* (1949-1982) (Internally circulated version), p. 892.

19. Figures from *Lishi Tongji Zhiliao Huibian*, op.cit.

20. There are, of course, different accounts of this in some official publications. See *Jiefangjun Jianglingzhuan* (Biographies of Generals of the People's Liberation Army, Beijing: Jiagangjun Chubanshe, 1988), pp. 305-6.

21. Su and Ni were recalled to Beijing in mid-1979 while Peng left in early 1980.

22. I am grateful to Zhang Aimei for her comments on this point.

23. Total tax and profits as a percentage of all funds (net value of all fixed assets plus average year-end remaining circulation funds) in SOEs.

24. *Lishi Tongji Zhiliao Huibian*, op.cit., p. 19 and p. 328.

25. Ibid., p. 15 and p. 323.

26. *Shanghai Tongji Nianjian*, 1992, op.cit., p. 53.

27. Christine P. W. Wong, "Central-local relations in an era of fiscal decline: the paradox of fiscal decentralization in post-Mao China", (unpublished paper) 1991.

28. According to one estimate, for rural enterprises to maintain production, they need to have at least an annual growth rate of 8 percent. Many state-run enterprises can still survive even if their growth rate is substantially lower than

this since the state will ultimately pick up the losses. Still, the pressure for the local economy to grow for the sake of survival is substantial. Shanghai: *Jiefang Ribao*, "We must maintain a certain rate of growth", March 4, 1990.

29. *Lishi Tongji Ziliao Huibian*, op.cit., p. 355 and p. 323.

30. Based on author's interview conducted in Seattle in summer 1989 with a Shanghai official who was close to the new team.

31. The main part of the report can be found in *Shanghai Jingji, 1983-1985* (Shanghai's Economy, 1983-1985), (Shanghai: Renmin Chubanshe, 1986), pp. 25-34.

32. Ibid.

33. *Shanghai Jingji, 1983-1985*, op. cit., p. 830.

34. Ibid., p. 831.

35. *Lishi Tongji Ziliao Huibian*, op.cit., p. 328.

36. *Jiefang Ribao* (Liberation Daily), April 27, 1989. Note that under Chinese budgetary practice, the budgetary subsidy to cover the losses of SOEs was not listed as a government expenditure. It simply offset income. As a result, both the figures for local incomes and expenditures were smaller than the actual.

37. *Shanghai Jingji Tizhi Gaige Shinian*, op.cit., p. 415. These SOEs include some of the newest and best equipped factories in Shanghai such as the Baoshan Steel Mill and the Jinshan Petroleum Chemical Factory.

38. In 1985, for example, the average income adjustment tax charged to SOEs in Shanghai was the highest in the nation--27.91 percent. It was reduced to 15 percent by 1988 but the higher tax rates left Shanghai SOEs less capable of financing renovations to existing facilities. See *Shanghai Jingji Tizhi Gaige Shinian*, op.cit., p. 33.

39. *Jiefang Ribao*, April 29, 1986.

40. "Shanghai's budget report", *Jiefang Ribao*, op.cit., April 27, 1987.

41. *Shanghai Caishui* (Shanghai's Finance and Tax), No. 7, 1990, p. 26.

42. *Shanghai Jingji Nianjian 1989* (Shanghai Economic Yearbook 1989), (Shanghai: Shanglian Shudian, 1989), p. 477. Note similar regimes were extended to 12 other provinces and cities. It was ironic that this time Shanghai took the lead since the rest did not receive the same deal until July 1988. For more on this, see, *1988 Nian Caizheng Guizhang Zhidu Xuanbian* (Selected Financial Rules and Regulations, 1988), (Beijing: Zhongguo Caizheng Chubanshe, 1989), pp. 104-08.

43. Details see *Shanghai Jingji Tizhi Gaige Shinian*, op. cit., p. 114.

44. Maruya (1992), op. cit., p. 8.

45. *Sheke Xingxi Jiaoliu* (Shanghai, Social Science Information Exchange), No.44, 1989, p. 5.

46. This additional contribution to the center was originally ordered to offset the huge budget deficit of 1990, which totaled 16.9 billion yuan. However, the contribution has been made semipermanent since then.

47. Figures are from Shanghai's yearly budget reports.

48. *Shanghai Jingji Nianjian, 1990*, op. cit., p. 458.

49. The 1992 figures were not included here because they were so large that they easily topped any previous record. Figures from, *Shanghai Tongji Nianjian, 1992*, op. cit., p. 357.

50. *Renmin Ribao* (People's Daily), July 23, 1991.

51. *Shanghai Jingji Nianjian, 1990*, op. cit., p. 462.

52. *Shanghai Jingji Tizhi Gaige Shinian*, op.cit.

53. *Shanghai Caishui, No. 9, 1991*, pp. 17-18.

54. While most extra-budgetary funds were still controlled by SOEs or government agencies, Shanghai required them to deposit such funds at a special account in city-controlled banks. The city could then use the net balance to issue credits to various projects with interest. This method, known as *caizheng xingdao* (fiscal credit), has become more and more popular in recent years.

55. Calculation based on *Shanghai Tongji Nianjian, 1992*, op. cit., p. 54.

56. *Shanghai Jingji Nianjian, 1989*, op. cit., p. 478.

57. Ibid., *1990*, p. 451.

58. Ibid., *1991*, p. 493.

59. Ibid., *1991*, p. 493.

60. Ezra Vogel (1989), op. cit., p. 449.

About the Contributors

Editors

Jia Hao, a research fellow from the Shanghai Institute for International Studies and a Ph.D. candidate in political science at the George Washington University, is currently President of the Washington Center for China Studies, Inc.

Lin Zhimin, from Fudan University (China), earned a Ph.D. in political science at University of Washington and is currently an assistant professor at Valparaiso University.

Authors

Chen Feng, from Fudan University, earned a Ph.D. in political science at Syracuse University and is currently an assistant professor at the State University of New York, Oswego.

Peter Tsan-yin Cheung, from Hongkong Chinese University, earned a Ph.D. in political science at University of Washington and is currently a lecturer at Hongkong University.

Gong Ting, from Fudan University, earned a Ph.D. in political science at Syracuse University and is currently an assistant professor at Ramapo College of New Jersey.

Huo Shitao, from Fudan University, is currently a Ph.D. candidate in political science at the University of Wisconsin, Madison.

Luo Xiaopeng, a research fellow from the Center for Rural Development and Research in China, is currently a Ph.D. candidate at University of Minnesota.

Xiao Geng, from the University of Science and Technology of China, earned a Ph.D. in economics at the University of California, Los Angeles and is currently a lecturer at Hongkong University.

Wang Mingxia, from Fudan University, is a Ph.D. candidate at the State University of New York, Albany and currently works as a fiscal policy analyst at the New York State Division of the Budget.

Wang Shaoguang, from Beijing University, earned a Ph.D. in political science at Cornell University and is currently an assistant professor at Yale University.

Zhang Amei, a research fellow from the Institute for Economic System Reform under the State Council of China, is currently a Ph.D. candidate in political science at Columbia University.

Zhao Suisheng, from Beijing University, earned a Ph.D. in political science at the University of California, San Diego and is currently an assistant professor at Colby College in Maine.

Zou Gang, from Chinese People's University, is currently a Ph.D. candidate and research associate at the Center of International Business Education and Research of the University of Southern California.

Index